Praise for Deep Medicine for Trauma

This book is a balm for anyone carrying unseen or unhealed wounds. With wisdom, story, and compassion, Jane Hiatt offers a radical reframe: you are not what happened to you, and you are not broken. Through the gentle yet powerful practices of hypnotherapy and imagery, these five treatments illuminate a path back to wholeness. I found myself both comforted and awakened as I read, reminded that beneath every scar lives a brilliance waiting to be revealed. This is deep medicine, lovingly written, for a world aching for light.

> Rachel Macy Stafford,
> *New York Times* bestselling author
> speaker
> certified special education teacher

Deep Medicine for Trauma is a rare and powerful offering written with clarity, courage, and heart. It invites readers into a deeper kind of healing, one that reaches beyond the surface and awakens what's been waiting within. A truly transformative read.

> Keila Shaheen,
> bestselling author of
> *The Shadow Work Journal*

Deep Medicine for Trauma lives up to its name—offering a multidimensional exploration of healing that goes far beyond symptom relief. It is a sacred and smart invitation to heal from the inside out. With poetic power and clinical depth, it blends story, hypnotherapy, and radical self-trust to reach the subconscious—where inherited wounds and internalized beliefs quietly live—and return us to the garden within. A true guide for those ready to shine their lovelight fully.

As a neuroscience-based coach and Infinite Possibilities trainer, I found each chapter to be a compelling call to expand what we believe is possible in trauma recovery and emotional integration. From inherited trauma to developmental wounds, from subconscious healing to spiritual reclamation, this book doesn't just offer insight—it facilitates transformation.

For anyone seeking healing that touches the nervous system, the energy field, and the soul—*Deep Medicine for Trauma* is wise, beautiful, and deeply needed.

Rev. Tamera Schmidt,
founder of Enlightened Coach
certified neuro-transformation coach
Infinite Possibilities trainer

Deep Medicine is a universe of its own. It acknowledges the challenges and troubles of being human—the experiences that dimmed our love-light, buried our magnificence, and left story potions festering in the pits of our existence. Through the vessel of hypnotherapy, this book encourages us to recognize the stored beliefs and narratives that keep us stuck, unhealed, and unhappy. With a decade of experience counseling women in public service, I recognize in these treatments what has so often been missing: a way to understand our trauma stored in the subconscious, and to discover that by retelling our story, we create a new reality—one that is vibrant, whole, and embodies love-light.

Genesis Ilada,
founder of Bliss Chains
creative legacy artist
sacred photographer

As someone who spends time with victims of trauma every day in my work, I was delighted to find myself immersed in Jane Hiatt's magical and inspiring book *Deep Medicine for Trauma*. Her compelling use of story to clearly illustrate previously unappreciated truths makes this book a must-read for laypeople and professionals alike. Highly recommend.

Jane Guyn, PhD,
intimacy coach
certified hypnotist

Jane Hiatt has written a wonderful book, so expansive and rich that it is medicine itself. The fearlessness and trust on every page speak of a lifetime's experience of the healing and transformation that can only happen when we go deep.

The five "deep treatments" Jane Hiatt explores are a framework not only for healing, but for living in challenging times. For all of us on planet Earth in the 21st century, nothing is more important than what this book tells us about the capacity of life to heal, transform, and regenerate—that it is unlimited, wide-ranging, and deep, no matter what we have faced, no matter what we fear, no matter the obstacles before us. This message is an ancient one, but *Deep Medicine* offers it to us in a way that is fresh and authentic, with new tools and approaches for meeting life with vibrance and joy. This book is a powerful resource for tapping new levels of resilience and grace. I can't recommend it highly enough.

Marcia Wade,
Star Sister Astrology

DEEP
MEDICINE
for TRAUMA

5 Powerful Treatments for
Healing That Experts Have Overlooked

JANE HIATT

ISBN: 979-8-9932093-0-2 (Trade Paperback)
ISBN: 979-8-9932093-1-9 (eBook)

Publisher's Cataloging-in-Publication
(Provided by Cassidy Cataloguing Services, Inc.)
Names: Hiatt, Jane, author.
Title: Deep medicine for trauma : 5 powerful treatments for healing that experts
    have overlooked / Jane Hiatt.
Description: [Bend, Oregon] : Sparklighter Publishing, [2025]
Identifiers: ISBN: 9798993209302 (trade paperback) | 9798993209319 (ebook)
Subjects: LCSH: Hypnotism--Therapeutic use. | Psychic trauma--Alternative
    treatment. | Prenatal influences--Psychological aspects. | Conflict of generations-
    -Psychological aspects. | Reincarnation--Psychological aspects. | BISAC:
    BODY, MIND & SPIRIT / Healing / Energy. | PSYCHOLOGY / Hypnotism.
    | BODY, MIND & SPIRIT / Healing / General.
Classification: LCC: RC495 .H53 2025 | DDC: 615.8512--dc23

Dedication

I dedicate this book with gratitude to all of my clients, over all the years. Whether you recognize your story here or not, your courage and willingness to heal, and the honor you paid me by choosing me to accompany you on your journey, are the reasons this book can even exist. May this book help you remember just how far you've come and the brilliant love-light you truly are.

Table of Contents

Five Overlooked Treatments For Healing

You, the one seeking deep medicine, who do you imagine yourself to be? I believe you are precious, just as you are. You are a powerful, unique expression of creation, sparkling with love, possibility, and purpose. Do you know that? Or do you find yourself responding, "Whoa! I wouldn't go that far." Most of us feel less than all that. Maybe in our dreams, we suspect we are more. Or we've read books that tell us we are wondrous beings, and we want to believe that, but it seems like such a stretch when we look in the mirror or think about our lives, traumas, and mistakes. Most of us, truthfully, have been infected with a belief in lack, feeling we are missing something essential and so are not quite candidates for love and the fullness life promises. We believe we are unsafe, unworthy, and unlovable at our core because there is something wrong with us. This is a lie—yet we have fallen for it, and it plays on repeat in our heads.

This book is deep medicine to bring you back to health. Imagine the great mother of life is leaning over you and whispering, "Wake up. Let me tell you a story. It's time to remember who you are." This is the first treatment, helping you remember the truth about your identity. This treatment is essential because the world is calling for you now in your fullness. None of us has time to dally with playing small. We need to unleash our love-light. Love-light is what I call that innate energy of creation, everywhere present, continually bringing consciousness into form.

The lie that we are lacking gets its start with trauma. Like the story of Eve and Adam eating the apple and thereby opening the portal to suffering, we imbibe beliefs when we are traumatized at an early age, and they affect us as if we had swallowed an insidious potion. This potion spreads through our consciousness and changes how we perceive reality. As a result, we get stuck in specific ways, and our best efforts fail to get us back to the garden where life feels good and we know how perfect, beloved, and brilliant we really are.

In this book, I'll be sharing five treatments that employ hypnotherapy, a healing modality that brings the powerful antidote of stories to the subconscious mind where the poisonous beliefs live. When tendered with love and imagination, hypnotherapy awakens an ancient knowing and can take your consciousness back to the garden. Once back, your love-light can shine fully.

This book is not a scientific, clinical explanation of trauma. It's a book of stories to wake you up and restore you to the possibilities quivering in your soul. I'm sharing these stories to give you hope and a window into what is possible when you know who you really are and what you are truly worth.

We have been hooked on stories since humans gathered around fires listening to tales of danger, valor, and victory. They speak to us in ways that seep deeply into our minds and hearts. As I tell you these stories, I hope something will shift in you, and just by reading, you will start to expel the lies you may have swallowed. Ultimately, my hope is that reading this book helps you to look in the mirror and begin to see your own brilliance and value shining bravely back at you. Then let yourself shine on a world desperate for your light.

Five Deep Medicine Treatments

How could the experts in the trauma field have missed as powerful a treatment as hypnotherapy? There are many good treatments for trauma being used in the field, but in none of the books I've researched has hypnotherapy even been mentioned. Yet it's incredibly powerful and could be the right approach for you. As we journey through this book of deep medicine, I will share a protocol for transforming trauma by creating an antidote for the energetic residue it has left in your body and mind and making space for your love-light to shine without hindrance. I'll elaborate with both explanations and stories about each of the five treatments based on hypnotherapy as the conducting vehicle. Here is a brief list of the five treatments, which I'll delve into more fully in this introduction:

1. Embracing Yourself

   Recognize who you are and what you are. You are a brilliant expression of love-light. No matter what trauma you have experienced or what people have told you, you are not what happened to you. You are not what you have believed or the choices you've made. This treatment entails shifting your identity from egoic measurements like personality, experiences, accomplishments, and failures to a more cosmic understanding of yourself.

2. Using Language of the Deep

   Learn to use the language of the subconscious mind. As you shift from logic to imagery, emotion, and story, you will find that you are getting through to the part of you that is actually controlling your feelings, beliefs, and behavior. You will forgo giving yourself reasoned, motivational encouragement or angry beration. Instead, you will speak in a way the traumatized self can hear.

3. Uncovering Your Story Potions

Discover the potions you have swallowed. Story potions are the poisonous beliefs you have adopted as a result of the trauma you have experienced. You have to remember what happened, the feelings you buried, and how that trauma affected you.

4. Going Beyond the Physical

Reach beyond the third dimension for information. In the third dimension—i.e., the material world—lie circumstances and the "facts" of what happened. Trying to adjust these is not possible. They already happened. However, powerful remedies for trauma exist within the realms of cellular and generational memory, the collective consciousness, the imagination, the supernatural, and the spiritual. By opening your mind to non-physical dimensions of reality, you can receive the deep medicine you need to transform trauma into light.

5. Steeping the Imagery

The doctor prescribes medicine and tells you to take it faithfully. The same is true for deep medicine. Only by steeping your consciousness regularly in the imagery and stories you receive in hypnotherapy will these powerful antidotes have a lasting effect.

Now that you have a cursory understanding of the five treatments, let's explore them a little more fully.

The First Treatment—Embracing Yourself

You don't see the foundation of a house, but it has to be there. Deep medicine requires a foundation of knowing that each of us is a spiritual being. We are pure light and love and that gives us our value and power. Because we get caught in the allure of material reality and our human expressions, we think of ourselves as bodies, personalities, and experiences, and we fall prey to low self-esteem.

We may accept in theory that we are spiritual beings but still be so out of touch with that truth that our lives don't reflect it. We seem to have lost the thread connecting us to that supernatural reality. Believing is not enough. We need to experience it. This is foundational but doesn't usually happen first, so a hypnotherapist holds space for that remembrance. Meanwhile, the deep-medicine healing process usually involves treatment two (Using Language of the Deep) and treatment three (Uncovering Your Story Potions) first. It's a bit like having a facial. The dead skin has to be exfoliated before the glowing light of the face can be seen.

The first treatment—Embracing Yourself—is an ecstatic experience. We glimpse the love-light and realize it's not separate from us. Sometimes that happens in a first session, and other times it requires more preparation. Nora was a young woman who was very depressed when she came to see me and told me how much she loathed herself. In her session, she went to a cave-like area with a waterfall. Everything was pretty dark. But behind the waterfall, she discovered iridescent flowers. They were beautiful. When she imagined a stream of light coming through, she admitted that she liked the dark better because the flowers shone more brightly. She remained in the dark with the flowers while I reminded her that they represented the truth of her being. Afterward, Nora was very quiet. Her recriminating mind had shut up, at least for the time being, and she had experienced the whole-i-ness that the first treatment brings about. She left with her "prescription" for the fifth treatment, Steeping the Imagery, to practice simply thinking about those iridescent flowers without any demands of them.

The first treatment of embracing ourselves allows us to move from the idea of being stuck or broken because of what happened. We realize that we are not our traumatic experiences. Not our appearance, our personality, our knowledge, or our achievements. We are so much more—a fullness of life expressing. With this awareness, we open ourselves to an unlimited, flowing stream of possibility. As we change our idea of who we are, we become candidates for life at its highest vibration.

The Second Treatment—Using Language of the Deep

If you are stuck in a cycle of struggle despite everything you've tried, you may be speaking the wrong language. When we give ourselves pep talks trying to inspire change, use reasoning, dangle rewards, or threaten punishments, we don't create real change. Our subconscious minds run the show, and all that motivational chatter gets ignored. This is because the subconscious mind speaks with emotionally rich pictures. If you're not using that deep language, your subconscious is not understanding the message. You won't change your mind, and you'll keep doing exactly what you've been doing. The second treatment involves speaking the native language of the subconscious—imagery, story, and emotion.

You also need to be talking to the aspect of you that's tucked away in that subconscious mind: younger, forgotten, and possibly riddled with trauma. Adult-you may not remember the traumatic events or may think what happened early on was not such a big deal, but younger-you may feel differently. You need to get curious. Ask what happened. Inquire about how that younger self felt—and feels—about what happened. You need to offer the deep medicine of a new story to that hidden, little one. And you need to do it with loving compassion and tenderness. Scolding will not help. You can offer guidance through a new story, but only after you've gained rapport and that littler self is ready to hear a story.

In this book, I'm going to speak to you in imagery and story because I want to get through to your subconscious as you read. I've been a hypnotherapist for over thirty years, so this is my language of trade. I have worked with thousands of people who struggle with anxiety, depression, relationships, and addictions and found that, underneath it all, they bear the marks of trauma. Because of something really hard that happened when they were young, they formed limiting beliefs about themselves and their prospects. I call those beliefs story potions to convey their absolute toxicity. People believe they aren't safe, don't matter, and are unlovable and unworthy. How can anyone succeed with that kind of energetic residue gunking up their flow? As a result of those trauma-based beliefs, deep down, and sometimes on the surface, people are mad, sad, and scared. And stuck. Do you relate?

We humans seem to learn better from stories of other people. I'll be giving you tips for how to communicate with your subconscious by illustrating and sharing stories from my own life and my clients' sessions. When we don't think we are being targeted as having a problem, we don't get defensive and can listen to the other person's story. We end up identifying with them and are open to receiving the same healing. Only as we do this healing does our love-light start to shine in all its brilliance.

Do You Need Deep Medicine?

If you are in pain, you need the medicine. You may dismiss the idea that you had trauma. I've had countless people show up in my office telling me they had a happy childhood. Then, a few sessions in, they admit they had an alcoholic father, tell how they always waited hours for a forgetful mother to pick them up from school, or describe how hard they worked to be perfect. When we live with difficult conditions, we come to see those as ordinary, and we develop coping skills. We can even imagine everyone else lives that way. We tell ourselves that it's no big deal, we've forgiven that parent, and we're fine. But there's still that matter of pain. There are certainly levels of trauma. It's a spectrum, really. I like Gabor Mate's definition: "An event is traumatizing or retraumatizing only if it renders one diminished, which is to say psychically or physically more limited than before in a way that persists."

You may not think you have been traumatized. So much depends on how old you were when the trauma happened and what support structure was available, as well as the internal resources your soul brought to this incarnation. You might explore trauma if you struggle with relationships, finances, addictions, promiscuity, betrayal, anxiety, or depression, or you lack self-confidence or the ability to follow through on promises to yourself. If you had what therapists call adverse childhood experiences, something like being abused, neglected, or adopted—or losing a parent to death, divorce, or prison—you may well have trauma from that showing up somewhere in your life. This is not an exhaustive list. Trauma is widespread and under-acknowledged. Beyond personal family trauma, societal trauma may be affecting you if you are part of a group that is being targeted, discriminated against, or lacking power.

It's true that some people have lived through incomprehensible levels of abuse or neglect. Hopefully you didn't experience that level personally. But that doesn't mean that the hurts that made you feel like something was wrong with you don't count or that you're not a candidate for deep medicine. Regardless of the level of trauma in your childhood, you are not what happened to you. You deserve all the beauties life has to offer. You are a precious light in this world.

There is one other aspect of trauma—what we witness. Given the globalization of our world through technology, we are seeing the trauma of people and animals, forests and oceans, villages and countries, all over the world. Because of mirror neurons, whatever we see, our minds process as happening to us. That's why bullies suffer from the damage they do to others. So really, there is probably nobody out there, outside of perhaps mystics on top of the mountain, who is free of trauma. Whatever your experience with trauma, may this medicine serve to free your light to shine more brightly.

Content Warning

If you're reading this book, you probably have some unhealed trauma. It's important to know that trauma can be evoked just by reading or listening to stories of trauma. In case that happens to you at some point, I want to be sure you have some tools to help you.

When we are upset, we don't always have mental awareness of what's happening, but we can train ourselves to pay attention to our physical sensations. Rapid breathing, perspiration, pounding chest, or increased heart rate are all symptoms of trauma. If that should happen to you, here are a few simple physical things you can do to soothe yourself.

1. Focus on your breathing. Count from one to four as you breathe in. Count from one to six as you breathe out. This works best if the breath is getting into your belly, not just your chest. The longer exhale starts to engage your parasympathetic system and helps you to relax.
2. Rub your hand gently on the inside of your opposite wrist.
3. Tap repeatedly on the place where your thumb and wrist meet or along the collarbone.
4. Drink something—water or a warm drink. Just holding the warm drink in your hand can also be helpful.
5. Rock back and forth.
6. Cry. If you notice your facial muscles working overtime to hold the tears in, you'll actually feel better if you let them flow. If you've stopped simply crying and are aware that you're thinking about your crying, you've probably moved past pure emotion and would benefit from focusing on your breathing.

Be willing to read at a pace that works for you or skip around. You are the one who knows best what you can handle. No badges will be awarded for ignoring your instincts and emotions.

The Third Treatment—Uncovering Your Story Potions

When traumatized, we tell ourselves tales, trying to make sense of what happened to us. These stories are tied to both traumatic events and toxic relationships. The strong emotions these experiences spark give the stories their destructive power. We can think of those narratives like potions that penetrate our subconscious minds and affect how we see the world and behave in response. Our consciousness and the resulting behavior shape our opportunities. The world we perceive narrows because of our traumas and the story potions connected to them. The third treatment is to identify not only what happened to us but to recognize the story potions we swallowed as a result. As we connect these potions to our trauma, we can see them for the lies they are.

Let's get into how this deep medicine works. Because trauma is lodged in the subconscious, we need to use the language of the subconscious to create an antidote for whatever story potions we have imbibed. Hypnotherapy is an intuitive process that uses this language to expose the story potions contaminating our consciousness and to create an antidote. We do this by telling a more compelling tale, drawing on the powers of imagination and love. Perhaps you wonder if altering a story makes it less true. The answer is no. A story potion is an illusory brew, so it's not true in the first place. In other words, it's a negative spin concocted by your mind, but it's not truth. In creating an antidote, we are adjusting the story to align with the eternal truth about us: we are shimmering love in form.

I'll give you some examples of what I mean by story potions. See if any of these false accusations match beliefs you hold.

- There's something wrong with you.
- You'll never amount to anything.

- You have nothing worth saying.
- You don't have what it takes.
- You ruined someone's life (usually a family member's life).
- You made your father mad.
- You are a bad boy/girl.
- You're different.
- You don't belong.
- You are so stupid.
- It's all your fault.
- You'll never be safe.

Please hear this. No matter how long you may have held such a belief, it is not true. No matter who professes it as truth, or how much evidence you have amassed to prove it to yourself, it is completely false.

You are made of the same energy that swirls through and creates the entire cosmos—pure love-light. Your essence crackles and sparkles with life, imagination, wisdom, strength, and creative power. You have come to earth with a purpose and the means to discover and express it. You are not expendable. We need you.

You may think you know for sure who you are, but trust me, you don't. None of us do. Even the cosmos that astronomers have studied with such passion has only yielded 4 percent of itself to their measuring gaze. The rest, dark matter, is alive but unmeasured, invisible, and unknown. It is full of mystery and possibility. Just like you. Like all of us, you are made of the elements floating in that cosmos. You are not your trauma or what you made it mean. Do not limit your identity to the 4 percent you have experienced, wrongly judged, and found wanting. You are pure mystery—a still undiscovered field of delights, ready to unfold with new spark and sizzle. Even if this is hard to believe, it is your reality. The liberating journey of hypnotherapy can help you to realize this for yourself.

Trauma leaves a crippling and layered legacy on body, mind, heart, and soul. It travels across bloodlines and lifetimes. Our world is riddled with trauma. The National Survey of Children's Health found that almost 50 percent of children in the US have had at least one extremely traumatic experience. According to the US Centers for Disease Control and Prevention, 60 percent of adults reported at least one traumatic childhood experience, and at least 25 percent had three or more. These traumas are either a single event or an ongoing struggle where our safety, security, trust, or sense of self is threatened or violated. These organizations believe the numbers are under-reported. And that doesn't take the rest of the world into account. Clearly, there is a tremendous amount of trauma going on.

Even our planet earth has been damaged by traumatized humans and the systems we have created. If we are ever going to create peace on earth and a world that works for all of us, we need to begin within, healing our own hearts. As long as trauma dictates individual actions, our world will be a troubled place.

Our lives are fraught with circumstances that plague and puzzle us, defying our desires and best efforts. Seeing no way out, or exhausted from trying to find solutions, we are flooded with emotions that take a toll on our bodies. The primary emotion is fear or its derivatives. Because of trauma, we see the faces of fear all around us. We fight with those we love and with people we've never met who are different from us. We run away from conflict, avoid responsibility, and medicate our fear with substances. We freeze, paralyzed by the enormity of violence and drama before us. We fawn over powerful people, hoping to curry favor and protection. But there is another way. Trauma does not have to be a life sentence.

According to Dr. Bruce Perry, who co-authored the book *What Happened to You?* with Oprah Winfrey, "the word trauma is used very casually these days. For most people, it means a really bad event or experience, usually one that 'sticks,' that you don't forget and that can have an enduring impact on you."

He goes on to say that the key to defining an experience as traumatic is knowing how the individual is experiencing the event. Depending on what happened to us as we grew up, and how the neural networks of our brains were affected, we can have different experiences of the same event. The age at which something happens to us also matters. The younger we are, the more damaging an experience will be. Perry and Winfrey's excellent book will really help you to understand the brain science of trauma.

Although trauma is usually associated with serious harm, I have seen damage done by seemingly offhand remarks. Clay, a man in his forties, recalled in hypnotherapy how excited he'd been in second grade when he got to use a microscope. When he'd examined pond water and saw an amoeba, he proclaimed he wanted to be a scientist. His mother told him to forget about it. He'd never be a scientist with those grades. He put away the microscope and proceeded with a lifetime of poor grades that matched her expectations. More importantly, he lost his passion and ability to go after a dream. The "not good enough" story potion had made its way into his system.

Story potions start by affecting your core beliefs. Because you swallow them at such an impressionable time in your life, they remain lurking in your consciousness like a parasite, hidden and harmful. You can begin to heal when you identify the story potion and trace it back to the time when you first swallowed it. As you allow yourself to remember and feel the emotions that were too dangerous at the time of the traumatic experience, the story potion begins to dissolve into the nothingness from which it came. Then you can receive a new story, one that brings you freedom and life.

You will read powerful alchemical stories where a person's willingness to love the part that swallowed the potion is mixed with unique images that emerge from within, from the soul's pharmacy. These images may seem fantastical, or at least oddball, but because they are designed by the person's subconscious, they have tremendous power for that individual.

For example, a woman found her voice and learned to set boundaries by walking through a wall. A man resolved a relationship that was in limbo by returning to a life in the Civil War. A woman learned self-acceptance by finding a rusty chamber pot. As the book goes on, you'll read these stories and many more.

If you are tired of feeling like you don't have what it takes to create the life you long for, like you are inferior in some way, or like love, health, or success are just not on your life's menu, I hope you will join me in this adventure of possibility. Indulge your imagination and, by hearing the stories of others' transformation, consider that you may be able to change your life in ways that will amaze and delight you and benefit others. Just because you swallowed a story potion or two doesn't mean you are condemned to the potions' limiting effects. Remember who you are, powerful cosmic love. You can love yourself back to your original whole-i-ness by telling a better story.

The Fourth Treatment—Going Beyond the Physical

This is the pivotal deep-medicine treatment. Sometimes this treatment reaches into cellular or ancestral memory to find a hidden trauma and the potion that goes with it. Other times, we've unearthed the toxic potion but now need an element from beyond the material plane—such as the collective consciousness, the multiverse, or the spiritual realm—in order to create a healing story. Either way, there are so many more healing resources we can draw on when we are willing to reach beyond what we can experience with our senses and travel to an inner reality of consciousness.

Cellular memory is still material, in a sense, because our cells form our bodies. Because we can't experience our cells with our five senses, we don't usually think about asking them what they know. Yet all of our memories are held in our cells. This is why hypnotherapy is able to access memories from before a person's episodic memory begins. Episodic memories are those we can see in our mind's eye. We can recall the details of when and where they happened and travel back to the memory. Pleasant or traumatic, we remember them. This kind of memory doesn't start to develop until a child is three or four. That's why it's highly unusual for someone to remember what happened when they were an infant, much less while being born or in the womb. Yet, in hypnotherapy such memories are common because they are held in the cells. If trauma occurred during those formative years, we can pay it a healing visit.

The collective consciousness is another dimension where stories vibrate. Experiences that have happened to someone, somewhere, sometime are still alive and we can tap into them. When it comes to past-life experiences, I wonder if we are pulling from something personal to our soul or if we are mining healing stories from the collective. Some teachings say that we are living multiple lives at once because time and space are illusions. I don't know the answer, but I absolutely know that, whether it's from the collective consciousness, actual memories, or parallel lives, there exists a rich library of stories and images that we can use for our personal healing.

If you can believe that we are expressions of "All That Is," the creative force everywhere present, unbridled light, then we share consciousness with everything. Indigenous traditions tap the wisdom of the rocks, the waters, the animals, and the trees. You'll find stories in this book where such healing connections are evident.

Tales abound of messengers and helpers who materialize from the unseen spiritual realms. A wolf finds and nurses to health the abandoned twins Romulus and Remus, who later founded the city of Rome. A dove appears out of the heavens and lands on Jesus after his baptism to affirm his anointing. White Buffalo Calf Woman appears to the Lakota in a time of famine, providing them with buffalo and teaching them sacred rites. The Rainbow Serpent guides the aboriginal Australian people to water. An angel gives the verses of the Koran to Mohammed. It's important to know that there is help if we turn to the heavens. To create a healing story, we will often require the intervention of a being from outside the physical realm. In this book you will find stories where spirit animals, angels, and even Harriet Tubman step in to assist.

You may wonder whether this is real or imaginary help. I believe it is real but not material. This is the key to understanding the fourth treatment. Many dimensions exist beyond what we can perceive with our senses. Imagination is our secret power that allows us entry to these other very real, non-material realms. Think of them as an inner world because we turn within, to our own spiritual awareness, to access them. When we are young children, imagining normally comes easily. Then we reach a stage where we are developing logic, and we demand that things make sense. That may be developmentally appropriate, but if we want to heal trauma, we have to come back around to the mystery that pulses in the realm of imagination.

For now, I really just want to assure you that there is help for you in moving past trauma, help that is beyond your wildest dreams. Whether it comes from the spiritual realm of imagination, the memory of your cells, the collective consciousness, or out there beyond the stars we can see, you have access to so much more than what you think is realistic. Remember who you are: pure cosmic light. You have no boundaries. You are in all those dimensions at once and so you can access them for healing.

The Fifth Treatment—Steeping the Imagery

Tea that hasn't been steeped is just mildly flavored water. But if you give it time, the flavor of the tea seeps into the water and transforms it into a satisfying beverage. Healing images work in a similar way. If you encounter a powerful story or image during hypnotherapy, it will make quite an impression in the moment. If you're like most people I've worked with, you'll be feeling quiet, full of awe, maybe vibrating a bit. Then you go back to your life. The challenges and busyness and shiny objects grab your attention. Unless you practice thinking about your image or story—in other words, letting it steep—you risk forgetting you ever had such a healing experience.

Practicing daily to hold your image or story in your mind and heart, even multiple times, doesn't take long at all, but it creates a mental habit. Since the healing image is soothing or empowering or creates new possibilities, your whole nervous system begins aligning. This takes time, but the more you practice, the more ingrained the new story or image-reality will become.

The most powerful experience of steeping I had was when my oldest daughter was eighteen. We had sent her off to live on her own because she wasn't willing to follow our house rules around using pot. She moved across the mountain to a college town but wasn't interested in taking classes. Though she had a job, she was depressed and continuing to smoke pot wasn't helping her mood. She would call up crying, and I felt so helpless. I knew she had to do this on her own. I started to imagine placing my daughter in a golden hand of light. That image would fill me with peace for about five minutes. Then I'd have to repeat. And repeat.

I let that image continue to steep for at least six weeks, and then something that seemed miraculous happened. A gap-year program appeared in my field of consciousness. It was a brand-new program (before gap years were so popular) being advertised in a newsletter that I subscribed to. The features of this program seemed to have my daughter's name written all over them. It was perfect for her, and I excitedly called her up to tell her about it. She thought it sounded interesting, but nine months was more commitment than she was ready for. I said, "Maybe another time," and let it go. The image, evidently, needed more steeping. Ultimately, my husband persuaded her to do the program, and it completely turned her life around. That's a powerful example of how steeping can change reality, and not just for you, but for the people whose lives are affected by your state of mind.

Tales of Veils

Trauma is a mechanism that veils our magnificence. Fictional and historical stories remind us how this works; they paint pictures of forgetting who we are and finally coming home to ourselves. The first treatment involves remembering and embracing who we are, and stories help us do that because they involve the second treatment, using the deep language of the subconscious. The hidden, traumatized aspects of your consciousness are listening eagerly, curled up beside you on the pillows of your heart.

Before I go further, let's talk about stories. In childhood, most of us loved listening to them, as long as someone safe read to us. In adulthood, the word stories may be used like excuses, to describe lies we tell ourselves. This can help us to confront our excuses or can be used to shame us. I use story potions to represent lies we've come to believe. Those lies do lead us to actions that don't serve us, and we do need to face them. That's the third treatment. But this needs to be done kindly. At the point you were poisoned by the story potions, you were not in control. You were a child. In adulthood you get to reclaim your power by challenging these lies. Instead of giving into shame, do your best to step into your power and remind yourself who you are.

The word *story* has a wider application, evoking ancient wisdom, magic, and innocence. Throughout this book, you will come across many tales. Some may be familiar, some not. There may be stories that have negative connotations for you, for personal reasons or cultural reasons. For example, many fairy tales have been presented in a way that implies a woman needs to be rescued by a prince. But because stories live in an archetypal, metaphysical realm, they may be interpreted in different ways. The princess and the prince represent our feminine and masculine aspects as well as our innate royalty—our worth.

Sleeping Beauty, a familiar childhood story, tells of a royal child who is born blessed with every good and necessary quality, beloved and shining with light. The name given to this child is Aurora, which means the dawn of light. This child begins to grow in beauty and grace until curiosity leads to encounters with the force of illusion, disguised as a crone with a spinning wheel. When the young soul reaches out to touch the wheel, the crone's spell overpowers their consciousness. Aurora falls asleep for a hundred fairy tale years. Aurora's world seems to sleep, too. Everything is under the veil of illusion. But finally, a time comes when the spell can be broken. Love, personified as a prince, moves through the tangled briars, a forest of negative beliefs, and delivers a powerful kiss, which awakens Aurora and the world.

A more modern story has a similar message. In 1957, monks in Thailand were moving a large stone statue of the Buddha. In the process, the hardened mud exterior was nicked, showing a flash of gold underneath. They got to work chipping away at the covering until the entire statue was revealed, glittering with gold. Through research, they discovered that centuries ago, the Golden Buddha had been intentionally caked with thick mud to prevent Burmese marauders from finding this treasure. The monks were slaughtered, and the secret of the treasure was buried with them. Their muddy veil, placed out of fear, was later perceived as the statue's reality. That's what happens to us.

Trauma scares and scars us badly enough that we bury it. We especially hide the emotions we felt at the time from our conscious awareness. The trouble is that, under that pain, we also stash our brilliant, vulnerable selves for safekeeping. Then we forget that brilliance even exists. Because we've forgotten, our options seem limited. But they aren't. Regardless of how much trauma we've had, our light lives. We can cut away the briars of false beliefs, lift the veil, scrape away the mud, and reveal our golden beauty for all the world to see.

Besides being a hypnotherapist, I'm a Unity minister. I have studied consciousness and spirituality and seen apparent miracles when people are able to change their beliefs and access their innate spiritual power. The key to making the change is understanding the layers of consciousness and learning to move between them.

We pay most attention to our thinking. We call it the conscious mind, like it's the only mind there is, because it's the only one we think is active and speaking. However, the subconscious mind is packed with all our memories and the beliefs we formed based on our experiences, especially the traumatic ones. This subconscious mind is the part that directs all our actions, protecting us by limiting our possibilities, until we lift the veil. In the story of *The Wizard of Oz*, the wizard represents the subconscious, giving all the commands, seeming all powerful, and keeping out of sight. When we lift the veil of illusion as the little dog Toto did, we realize we've been following the dictates of a frightened part of our mind. We need to take charge by learning to speak to this mind and reprogram its thinking.

The most powerful way to claim our power is by accessing our superconscious mind. This is the aspect of us that never fell under the spell, the self that has been there right along, a direct connection to the original love-light of creation. Hypnotherapy is a reliable path between these realms of consciousness, allowing us to override trauma's stories and liberate our true selves. With the superconscious, we are bringing the fourth treatment into play because we move beyond the physical dimension that our conscious minds are focused on.

Whether you experienced great trauma in your life or you care about someone who did, I encourage you to read or listen with an open mind and heart. Our world is crying out for the metaphorical kiss of love and recognition and the hundred fairy-tale years may be coming to an end. Operating from your superconsciousness, you can be part of the wake-up team.

Just For the Men

Gentlemen, you are at a disadvantage when it comes to emotional healing and getting free of trauma. At least in Western culture, most men have been socialized to distance themselves from their emotions. Except for anger. But you have tender feelings, too, and they may be bottled up along with those pesky potions that make you feel like you have to try so hard to get what you really want.

Because of this socialization handicap, you may think a book like this is not for you. Yet nearly half the stories in this book are of men who have benefited from exploring their frustrations in life and learning to antidote the story potions that have seeped into the foundations of their consciousness.

You'll read of men such as a national expert on immigration whose health was impacted by injustice, a vet who was still at war in his mind and with his family, and the grandson of gangsters with his own anger management issues.

These are just a few of the men's stories you'll read. Maybe you will recognize yourself in some of the struggles reported. Or maybe you'll understand the story potions that an important person in your life is struggling with. More importantly, maybe you will find a clue that will bring you greater hope, peace of mind, and the freedom to be your best self. You, too, deserve love's wake-up kiss.

CHAPTER I

The Power Of Hypnotherapy

When there's a five-alarm fire, use all the resources available. Trauma in our world is a five-alarm fire. Hypnotherapy is one of those resources and it's powerful, but nobody's talking about it. Somatic therapy and psychedelics are just two of the impactful and popular options, but they aren't right for everyone. Throughout this book, I'll be demonstrating how hypnotherapy can dissolve the illusion of trauma-based story potions. It accesses buried memories or trauma as well as hidden resources and makes a far bigger impact than just talking does. It addresses the mind, body, heart, and soul.

The stories that follow are based on examples with clients or stories of my own life. My hope is that as you read them, you will be encouraged that you, or the people you love, have a path to freedom from trauma. Just knowing the path exists is transformational. For the most part, this is not DIY terrain. A key part of trauma involves feeling that you're on your own with nobody to turn to for help. Peter Levine, author and pioneer of the somatic experience, says, "Trauma is not only what has happened to us; rather, it is what we hold inside in the absence of an empathetic, fully present witness." In the healing process, you want someone you trust who has the heart to accompany you and the skill to guide you. Let's explore more about hypnotherapy and how we can call in that special wake-up kiss, the love your soul has for you.

These first stories involve a simple trauma, with lasting effects. Whether a person's trauma is simple or complex, it matters and limits them and is deserving of an antidote.

Dr. Pete walked into my office and slumped into the chair. I knew him by reputation. He was a successful naturopath in town. I'm not sure what I was expecting, but this man, who seemed to be in his early forties, looked weary. The kind of exhaustion that doesn't come from a hard day's work but from a soul-sucking experience. I wondered what had happened to him and when.

"I hope you can help me," he said softly, a plea that suggested I might be his last chance. "I had surgery nine months ago and had an allergic reaction to the anesthesia," he told me with a clinical tone. "I've been nauseous ever since. I've tried everything. I'm a naturopathic doctor, you know, so I do mean everything. Nothing has helped. What do you think? Can you help me?"

I never guarantee that a physical symptom can be cured, and yet, over the years, I've seen some remarkable physical results. "There's a good chance I can," I told him, and we began the hypnotherapy process. I wanted to see if a story potion was causing the trouble.

In the hypnotic state, Dr. Pete began reliving his fifth birthday party.

> *There are lots of balloons and cupcakes. I like chocolate icing, so that's what Mommy made me. My friends are here. Uh-oh.*

Dr. Pete's face paled, and he caught his breath.

"What's going on?" I asked.

> *Mike is here. He is bigger than me. He's mean, but he has a present for me.*

I asked Dr. Pete to focus on what he was noticing in his body.

I feel scared. I'm not breathing right. Mike is handing me the present, and I open it. It's markers. I love markers.

Suddenly, Dr. Pete jumped as if he'd been punched in the stomach.

"Tell me what happened."

Mike is making fun of me. He says the markers are so I can connect all my ugly freckles together. I'm confused. I'm ugly? I didn't know my freckles were ugly. I didn't know I was ugly.

Dr. Pete started to cry.

Even though the child Pete knew Mike as a mean boy, he was also a bigger boy, so little Pete had given Mike the authority of knowing what was true. Essentially, he had pricked his finger on the crone's spinning wheel. He had swallowed a lie. There was something wrong with his appearance. He was ugly.

After the session, Dr. Pete looked vulnerable and astonished.

That surgery I had nine months ago? It was plastic surgery to reshape my nose because I thought there was something wrong with how it looked.

Dr. Pete now understood it wasn't anesthesia that made him nauseous but a story potion. His belief that there was something wrong with his looks was making him sick.

He proceeded to talk to that five-year-old and give him positive messages about his appearance and his freckles, delivering in the process a healing kiss. He continued by assuring the little one that his looks were not what made him lovable. He also had to forgive his forty-two-year-old self for judging himself so harshly that he felt he needed surgery, reassure him he deserved love just because he exists, and communicate directly to both his child self and his adult self how much he loves them.

Within a few weeks, as he integrated this subconscious awareness into his actions, the nausea began to dissipate. He also had to face how many choices and life experiences had issued from this one incident and the story potion of "not good enough." But he was on a fast track to dissolving the potion, because once it is seen for what it is, it loses its power and the illusion is broken.

Ray was another freckled child, a wavy strawberry blond with a penchant for fashion that was fun and just a little different. When Ray came to see me, we never suspected that his childhood appearance would be relevant.

Ray told me that he'd found a job he wanted and just needed to write the cover letter. He said he was planning to do it right after our session. However, two weeks ago, he'd seen another perfect job that was snapped up before he got around to applying. I thought he would have learned his lesson and sent his resume immediately, but it had already been two days since he had seen the listing. I knew he was procrastinating, which he'd acknowledged was a lifelong issue, and had a hunch this habit was based on a story potion, and we needed to expose it to the light.

In hypnotherapy, Ray discovered that he'd had a series of messages in childhood about how his appearance was wrong. He recalled his father taking him to a barber to buzz his long locks when he was three, and a memory of kids taunting him for wearing jeans that they thought looked like "girls' jeans" when he was twelve.

Ray discovered in this session that his habit of procrastinating was a smokescreen to keep people from finding out that he was different, weird, and unlovable. His appearance was proof that something was wrong with him, and he supersized that illusion with his extra weight and by creating a chaotic environment. He procrastinated about cleaning out his messy car, organizing his cluttered home, changing his eating habits, or going to the gym. Those were all things he intended to do. Someday. And after that he'd be able to find a life partner and a good job. What Ray actually needed was to realize that he was hiding his brilliance and understand why.

Once the story about being different and therefore unacceptable had come to the surface, I asked Ray to imagine a warm, golden light filling his body, melting away all the messages of being somehow wrong. I also suggested that in every cell of his body wildflowers were blooming from the warmth of the light. He was colorful and wondrous to behold. After the session, he told me: "The light was so intense. It was like I'd lost consciousness."

Two weeks later, when I saw Ray next, he'd written a cover letter for that job he really wanted and sent it in. He'd cleaned out his car and made extensive headway on fixing up his house. He'd been to the gym every day and was making much healthier eating choices. He was creating a vision board that included the kind of clothes he saw himself in as he released the extra hundred pounds he was lugging around.

It may be hard to imagine that getting in touch with a freckle-faced, red-headed boy with a flair for fashion could uncork a flow of determined activity to let his brilliance shine, but that's exactly what happened.

Are you bottling up your magnificence? If so, ask yourself why and start wondering what happened way back when to make that seem like a safe option. Hidden within you is an illusion that has the weight and tenacity of belief but is a lie. Beyond that lie is a field of wildflowers where you can lay yourself down in your wondrousness and dream your life into form.

How Does This Work?

Now that you've gotten a tiny glimpse into the power of hypnotherapy, it's time to explain it, since that's the medium for delivering the five treatments.

Images are the best way that humans can understand the mysteries of the mind. I'm going to describe the mind using two metaphors—a library and a garden. I hope one of them will resonate for you.

We can think of the subconscious like a high-tech international library. All the impressions and experiences of a lifetime, and the beliefs we formed based upon them, are recorded there—in the stacks or in the cloud. This is where we keep our trauma. Because our skin doesn't mark the end of our awareness, we can also access impressions and experiences from beyond our physical domain.

Very much like we can retrieve information from all over the world through the literal internet, so can our subconscious minds access information from many sources. We can obtain information from the past but also from the future. Albert Einstein said, "People like us, who believe in physics, know that the distinction between past, present, and future is only a stubbornly persistent illusion. Time, in other words, is an illusion."

We can tune into past lives, parallel lives, and ancestral memories. We can envision possible future scenarios as already existing, allowing them to pull us forward. Memory is imaginal, cellular, and holographic. Each cell carries blueprints of the whole system, infused with consciousness that keeps expanding from the moment of conception.

For some of you, this next part may seem astonishing, but it's logical if you can accept the idea that cells have consciousness. Every one of us began as an egg in our mother's body. All of her eggs, including the one that became you, were already present in her ovaries when she was born. So her experiences, up until the point when you were born, were recorded in that egg cell and all the cells that multiplied to form your body. The same is true for her and her mother. And so on down the line. As a result, you can remember her experiences and ancestral memories as if they were yours, and you won't necessarily realize they're not. This doesn't just apply to the memories your mother had before your conception. Throughout her pregnancy with you, she was feeling plenty of emotions, and they weren't all necessarily positive. Those feelings and the beliefs they instilled are all recorded in your cells. If you were carried by a surrogate, you have an extra person's energy influencing your cells.

This is why you can feel emotions that make no sense to you. You can be carrying your mother's trauma as fear, grief, or rage. In our metaphoric library, imagine borrowing virtual reality headsets where all the experiences seem real. As you tune into your cellular consciousness, it's hard to distinguish what your emotion is and what might be someone else's. Your mother's emotions and beliefs have been part of you on the cellular level from day one. They seem like yours, but they're not. But here's the good news. As you differentiate, you can release all that pain from your energy field and start having more space for positive energy. Hypnotherapy can help you do that.

It's a little different with your father's energy. Sperm cells begin forming at puberty and continue throughout a man's life. So the sperm that started you out carried a cellular, holographic imprint of your father's consciousness and experience at the time it formed. While you were in utero, your father's energy (or the absence of it), as well as your mother's reactions to that presence or absence, was making an impression on the growing you. If your father was someone offering protection to your mother and developing you, then you have a psychic reservoir of safety. On the other hand, if your father was violent and dangerous, you got the message that the world is not a safe place even before you were born. If your father was missing, simply checked out, or a sperm donor who never interacted with your mother, there is a hole in your energy pattern where love and safekeeping belong.

If you have siblings who didn't share a womb with you, you've probably noticed that you seem to have different parents. This is because your parents' consciousness continued to morph through their lives, so it was different for each child's gestational experience as well as their upbringing. Sibling variations are more complex than just the genetic mash-up.

So far, I've been referencing the material recorded in your subconscious mind. You'd be stuck with that if it weren't for the superconscious, which allows you to completely overhaul that inner subconscious library.

The superconscious mind is a realm of unchanging, infinite potential. It vibrates as love, wisdom, life, and creative power. Some people would call this God. It doesn't matter what you label it. What's important is to realize you can tap into this infinite field and align with love and wisdom and possibility. Using your imagination, you can experience these powers as the reality they are for you. You can activate a guidance system that will steer you beautifully through your life. You can experience greater vitality and know and feel that you are cradled in a field of benevolence. If we continue with the library metaphor, this is like being able to import the latest, most important books from anywhere on the planet—and maybe beyond.

A different way to understand our minds is by using the metaphor of a garden. Hypnotherapy helps you tend the garden of your mind. Think of your subconscious mind as soil. Whatever experiences you had that were difficult and left a "bad impression" in your consciousness function like weeds. They keep growing and can choke out healthy life. In hypnotherapy, you have the opportunity to pull them out. As you expose them to the light of awareness, they start to dry out and wither. Then you get to plant something new. You make a conscious decision about what you will plant. This is the part where your rational mind has a role. Pick good seeds.

You can find seeds anywhere. Some of them are from the collective unconscious that Carl Jung described, and they aren't necessarily good seeds. For example, the ideas that my tribe is better than your tribe or your tribe is dangerous to me are part of our collective, but not idea seeds we want to propagate if we want to create a harmonious garden of life.

The best source of seeds is the superconscious. By getting quiet and tuning into this energy through meditation, seed ideas show up. We can plant them in our subconscious and continue to tend them by paying loving attention to them. You can recognize seed ideas when you read or hear them because you'll feel their resonance.

"You are part of my identity. I cannot understand me outside the context of you." This paraphrase of the African philosophy called *ubuntu* is an example of a superconscious seed that would be healthier than the competitive, territorial tribal seed.

The idea that we are born an original blessing is a superconscious seed that can replace the weed of original sin spread by some Christian sects.

"If you realize that you have enough, you are truly rich." This superconscious seed found in the Tao Te Ching is better than the capitalistic "too much is never enough" meme that suggests we are lacking and will never be or have enough.

If you have had traumatic experiences that led you to conclude falsely that you were unloved, unworthy, and unlovable, it is critical that you do some weeding and then fill your garden with the beautiful seeds of your higher nature. As you do so, you will find the dazzling flowers of the superconscious, raising your vibration and creating a garden of peace and love—a metaphorical Garden of Eden consciousness where innocence and harmony and delight are rampant. If you're up for that, keep reading.

Will Hypnotherapy Work for Me?

"What about me? Can I be hypnotized?" That's usually the first question when the topic of hypnotherapy arises. The short answer is "Most likely." Here's the long answer.

Some people are easily hypnotized. They don't need a complicated induction. With them, it can be nearly as simple as saying, "Okay, go inside now." Most of us, however, need a bit more coaxing. Over the years I have encountered many people who are sure they will not be able to be hypnotized. Of the thousands of people I've worked with, I've only had a small handful I could not hypnotize. Here are some techniques I've learned to help people get into that deep space where healing shifts can happen.

First, you must be able to trust the person who is guiding you. You don't have to believe that you can be hypnotized, but it's helpful to leave a corner of your mind open to the possibility. However, if you don't have a good feeling about the hypnotherapist, save yourself some time and money and find someone else to work with. A hypnotherapist is guiding you into territory that is sacred and tender and often traumatic. Choose your guide carefully. It's not just about credentials. It's about energy. You can either feel your body tensing up or relaxing. Let that be your criterion for trusting.

It's important to understand that not everyone has the same channel for experiencing the inner world. Many people are visual. The scenes and symbols we see with the eyes of our imagination can vary from sparse and blurry to high-definition theater of the mind. But some people are not wired for the visual channel—or they get to that inner world through an alternate channel. You may just hear words or get a taste or a smell, a texture, or an emotion. I've had clients describe a flower scent, the song of birds, or the taste of soup from the school cafeteria as their first noticing when they go within.

My personal way into my subconscious came through the kinesthetic channel, and I've marveled at how many people this has helped. Here's how it works. Move your hands as if you were a blind person navigating this inner terrain, and you may be surprised at the impressions that come to you. I discovered this during a group visualization. The leader suggested that we were traveling into outer space, and there was a door in front of us. She had been talking for a while before she got around to mentioning this portal, and I was experiencing nothing but frustration. When she told us to notice the door, I followed an impulse to lift my hands and trace its shape. My hands intuitively made a triangle, so I went with it, and suddenly I was able to enter the visualization through my triangular door.

I'm sure you've had the experience of using your kinesthetic channel. Have you ever been trying to remember someone's name and you start making circles with your hands, as if that could shake loose the memory? Often it works, right? Call it talking with your hands, hypnosis braille, or kinesthetic power; if you apply it in hypnotherapy, you may be amazed at the impressions that start to flow.

My third suggestion also involves trust. But this time, you are not trusting an outer guide but your own intuition. If you are working with a guide, you will benefit more by sharing whatever you are experiencing with that person. It's so frustrating for me to find out at the end of the session that a client experienced something way back at the beginning that they didn't share—a headache, a symbol, or maybe a memory. Had they spoken up, we could have mined that for the richness it contained. When people don't speak up, it's often because they don't trust what is happening. They tell themselves, "It's just my imagination." There is no "just" to imagination. Einstein said, "Imagination is more important than knowledge," and I believe he was correct. Don't get hung up on whether something you're imagining is factual. The realm we enter in hypnotherapy is not a literal space. It's consciousness and it's so much larger and more powerful than the space we walk through in the physical world. Trust lights the lamp that illumines your way through the darkness of unexplored mind terrain.

One of my favorite exercises with clients that helps make access to the inner world a little easier is to start out by helping them relax their body deeply. Once they are floating in serenity, I ask them to complete this sentence: "Right now I feel as relaxed as a…." Their task is to go with the first thought and trust it. Many will come up with symbols that I've heard repeatedly—a cloud, a feather, or ocean water. Others receive more uncommon symbols—maybe the smell of lavender, the color blue, an opening flower, chocolate melting in the mouth, the feel of satin, the sound of the river, or a sleeping child. Some symbols are quite unique—an elephant or a beanbag. My own image is raindrops running slowly down the windowpane of a glass door. One woman thought of a photo of herself as a child with a butterfly sitting on her head.

Especially when the symbol is unusual, the person may argue about it, but inevitably it's perfect for them because of the associations it holds in their subconscious. Whatever image you get, no matter what channel it comes through, if you trust yourself and practice using it, you can get to the point where you relax very quickly and deeply, simply by focusing on that image. It works like a key to open the door of relaxation. This powerful key is just one gift of trusting yourself.

My final technique is in some way also a form of trust, but it's particular. Call it the "rule of two." Sometimes, clients don't go very deep on their first try. A part of them is so curious about the process that they are analyzing and taking mental notes rather than simply relaxing and experiencing. Others may be so fearful of letting go and trusting that they keep the brakes on all the way. The "rule of two" is that since you've discovered how hypnotherapy works and that you will come back unharmed, try it again.

I hope this explanation convinces you to delve into the inner world and begin to explore the story potions you've swallowed and the kiss that you need for full living. If you aren't persuaded yet, please read the stories in this book and allow yourself to wonder whether you might experience the same powerful transformations should you dare to try hypnotherapy for yourself. Let yourself imagine opening to love and allowing it to lead you to a whole new world that is perfect for you.

Trust Your Voice

The Oracle of Delphi was a rock star of the ancient world, a renowned voice of truth. People traveled from all over Greece and held their ears close to the rocks to hear her prophecies, which came from an underground source. Each of us has such an oracle within.

I talked about the importance of trusting the hypnotherapist you choose. It's equally important that the hypnotherapist access and trust their intuitive guidance, a source I call the voice, their personal oracle. This is the secret of my success. I listen and I trust what comes to me. This is bigger than hypnotherapy.

A voice of deep, reliable wisdom and inspiration resides within each of us. We must pay attention and follow its promptings. The more we trust, the clearer that voice becomes. While I haven't always listened in life, for reasons I don't understand, I've done it from the very start with hypnotherapy. My start was quite unusual. I'll tell you how it happened for me.

I did not start out wanting to be a hypnotherapist. The voice led me along a circuitous path to get there. I began listening to the voice through my writing. In the late eighties, I attended a workshop with Lucia Capacchione, who pioneered writing with the nondominant hand. At that point in my life, I couldn't visualize, so I wasn't able to follow Lucia's suggestions. But when she told us to draw a picture of what we'd imagined using our nondominant hand, the kinesthetic experience of drawing allowed me to access a powerful impression of myself as a dancing stick-figure bee, lifting another bee in the air. I wrote the words: "I want to dance, to heal with dance, to set free to fly with dance the crying children within."

I was immediately in tears because that voice had the power of truth. It knew me on a deeper level than I knew myself. After that workshop, nondominant writing became my daily practice for five years, and I still use it sometimes.

Following the direction of the voice through that exercise, I started taking transformational dance classes. I was not a likely candidate to become a dance therapist since I'd never taken a single dance class and, to this day, I have no talent for learning dance steps. Luckily, transformational dance classes are not about steps but rather about listening to the body.

After several years of dancing in groups and leading groups, I decided to create my own class. In this class, I led students in vigorous, emotionally charged dancing, followed by a visualization, and then art and writing with the nondominant hand. Chalk it up to an impulsive personality or pure grace that I didn't pause and ask myself why I thought I could lead a visualization if I couldn't follow one. Thankfully, I didn't question the voice. What happened as a result was remarkable. I just opened my mouth and created a story. I know now that the voice was leading the way. I just said whatever came to my mind without second-guessing.

The students reacted powerfully to these visualizations. After a few weeks, one student asked me to work with him privately. Too naïve to know this was not a wise idea, I agreed. Once again, the voice took over and created an impactful, interactive healing session. The client regressed to a scene from his childhood when he'd done something he was terribly ashamed of that was deeply buried in his subconscious mind. By freeing that memory, he released the shame he'd hidden with it. We did several sessions together and that was the beginning of my hypnotherapy practice, which continues to grow more powerful with time.

In the beginning, I would sit back in awe after a session. But I was never quite sure if I'd be able to do it again. I didn't completely understand yet that the voice was both leading and reliable. In time, I did, and from that point on, I've just trusted.

To be clear, I am not "knocked out" during this process and neither are my clients. I don't follow a script, and I am even reluctant to guide a client to a particular place such as the scene of a known trauma. My approach is to set the compass of the session for a general intention such as "Let's get to the bottom of this." Then we head off into the metaphorical weeds of the subconscious and see where we end up. As we go along, I say whatever pops into my head. I instruct my clients to do the same. Depending on what they say, the story takes a turn. Sometimes they say what is happening and sometimes their body takes the lead in expressing.

We are co-creating the journey every step of the way. The images and insights may come from me or from the client, but either way the voice that is speaking is bigger than either of us. I may be more of a guiding force, introducing new ideas, or I may be more of a witness as something is unfolding for the client. I understand now that the voice is an energy of love and wisdom that connects me and the client and guides us wherever we need to go. I've never been let down. Today I understand that I am a channel of divine healing, following this voice. The deep medicine I describe is possible because it doesn't issue from the ego level.

The voice I channel is expansive and knows more than either the client or I about what is needed. Once I worked with a vet who was still trying to heal from all the violence he'd experienced in Iraq. It was compounded by his romantic relationship blowing up when he got home. He didn't know how he could ever feel whole again. In hypnotherapy, I felt guided to mention the eruption of Mount St. Helens and how, despite the destruction, new life was growing there now. Even though I had been aware of that explosion for years, I'd never used that metaphor before. Subsequently, with tears streaming down his cheeks, he told me that he sat on his grandma's porch and watched the volcano blow when he was a little boy. It was so real for him that he could begin to imagine healing from his own life's eruption.

This wise voice can be trusted even when it says oddball things, so we need to trust the strange ideas that pop to mind. Sometimes those impressions are just the corner of a tapestry of memories that will be profound when you have the whole picture, so you must start in the corner with an image that doesn't yet make sense.

For example, Megan was a successful professional in the banking world who felt stuck and dissatisfied. She had an inkling that she wanted a career change, but something was blocking her. In hypnotherapy, she saw herself moving into an empty house. Well, it was almost empty. There was a single dumbbell in the living room. She picked it up, puzzled. It was not her dumbbell.

I was very curious where this was going and surprised when she revealed that the dumbbell didn't belong to her. It represented ideas that she had swallowed about what kind of work would give her value. She recalled an incident as a young child where she had been blissfully painting pictures and announced confidently that she would be an artist when she grew up. Her father, a repressed artist himself, began scolding her and told her painting was only for little children and she needed to get a serious job that made a lot of money. After that, she lost her joy in painting. All this awareness from a single dumbbell.

I have seen this over and over. I know the voice is trustworthy and that we all have access to it. The voice will be there for you as it has been for me, growing stronger the more you listen.

Now that you understand the hypnotherapy process, we'll move into chapters that explain how trauma happens and how it can be healed, demonstrated with client stories.

CHAPTER 2

Developmental Trauma

The first way people are traumatized is simply by growing up. We start as infants dependent on caregivers, who vary widely in their ability to nurture without harm.

As babies, we grow physically while learning on multiple levels. We learn we are safe in the world through the container of the family. We also learn that we are loved and worthy. Unless we don't. Back in 1943, psychologist Abraham Maslow articulated a hierarchy of needs that all humans have. The first level is survival. While trauma at that level is serious and real, it's usually also fatal, so those who don't survive are not reading this book. It's the next three levels where lifelong trauma occurs. Level two is about safety, level three is about love and belonging, and level four involves a sense of worth. If you are aware that you had trauma, it probably happened during these developmental years. Maybe you know you experienced trauma in your youth, but you may not realize it's the reason you are suffering. You're probably more aware of anxiety, depression, relationship struggles, or unhealthy patterns that keep you from realizing your goals and dreams. Whatever symptom you are noticing, the general pattern is that your soul feels diminished, and your options seem limited.

Safety

We humans are more alike than we realize, and often not in a comfortable way. As I reviewed my files, preparing to write this book, I noticed that one story potion stood out: "unsafe." The traumas that instigated this potion varied, as well as the way the residual misery was being expressed in the present, but the clients all shared the illusion of continuing to be unsafe. Those who were unsafe as children got scarred on a very deep level. Because safety is the most basic need after survival, being convinced that safety is missing has a profound effect on a person's life. Sometimes the feelings are triggered by certain situations and other times the person lives in a state of hypervigilance and anxiety that feels omnipresent, uncontrollable, and debilitating. One client described it as walking on landmines. Getting to the root of what is causing anxiety is something that hypnotherapy is well suited for.

Sometimes that anxiety stems from trying to hide from a big truth. One very anxious woman was on the verge of moving out of state to be with a man she didn't trust. However, she was hiding that truth from herself. The anxiety was an ally, like the warning light on the car dash, trying to alert her that something was wrong. When she got quiet in hypnotherapy, she was able to face the truth.

Sometimes a person is aware of how their anxiety began, but that's not what matters. For example, the pandemic prompted many people to experience anxiety. Understanding the pandemic-related factors and the beliefs that prompted anxious feelings was just not helpful enough because it did nothing to quell the anxiety. The needed antidote was to be able to access a state of calm and resourcefulness.

Love and Belonging

Moving up Maslow's hierarchy of needs, the next set of human requirements is love and belonging. In an ideal world, a child is born into welcoming family arms and is showered with love throughout their life. Unfortunately, in this far-from-ideal world, trauma occurs when love is not given at all, is given unreliably or conditionally, is overshadowed by violence, or is contaminated by molestation. This leads to story potions like "I'm not lovable" and "There's something wrong with me." The very first story I shared about Dr. Pete is an example of that story potion.

In a trauma-ridden childhood, the child is scarred by the absence of compassion and loving touch. Homes where abuse or neglect is prominent are breeding grounds for trauma. The "unlovable" and "unworthy" story potions lead to behaviors like people-pleasing, isolation, aggressive behavior, addiction, promiscuity, and inability to commit. Dr. Pete treated his body violently, attempting to change the appearance that he thought made him defective and unlovable.

Self-Esteem

Even though a sense of esteem is level four, in the world of trauma, it's hard to separate it from level three. If I reason, through a trauma lens, that I am not lovable, I am likely to also decide I'm not worthy of love—or anything else life has to offer.

Practically speaking, in a healthy family, love is poured on the infant, and that outpouring never stops. As the child begins to toddle around, the family cheering squad is letting this little one know they are accomplishing wonders. The child is encouraged to take on age-appropriate challenges and is accompanied compassionately when they fail. Self-confidence grows and with it a sense of deserving.

On a personal level, as I watch my three daughters and their partners parent my grandchildren, I see such examples of healthy, loving environments. These children also have the advantage of caring grandparents and friend-families to enrich their lives and support their parents.

Watching this love flow while reading through my files and reflecting on all the trauma my clients suffered as children saddens me.

In the stories that follow, you'll see developmental trauma at work and perhaps get insight into your own suffering and the soul-shrinking story potions that caused it. Most importantly, you'll get concrete examples of how people can heal, using the treatments hypnotherapy entails. Safety, love, belonging, and self-worth are on your life's menu.

First, Pitch the Tent

"Open sesame" was the magic phrase that opened Ali Baba's cave of wonders. You have your own entryway and hypnotherapy can help you find it by using the second treatment, Using Language of the Deep. To open the subconscious mind, we have to start not with magic words but with images that evoke safety and open the door. People are unsure what they will find in their hidden inner chambers, and so they tend to drag their metaphoric feet. However, if I take them somewhere beautiful, where they feel safe enough to pitch a tent and enjoy the scenery, then eagerness and curiosity replace their fear and misgivings. A beach, a lovely campground, a mountain retreat—any location that meets the criteria of beauty, peace, and safety will do. This location then becomes a base camp. They return again and again, as in treatment five, Steeping the Imagery, to the safety the environment offers. Soon they are willing to uncurl those white knuckles and slip inside their personal cave of wonders.

Charlotte was a client who definitely needed a base camp. She procrastinated about even setting an appointment with me. She waffled between knowing she needed to face the trauma in her past and being terrified to look at it. When I suggested she just have an experience of the inner world and absolutely not revisit the trauma on the first day, she jumped at that option.

In her session, I painted a picture of her three little girls digging a deep hole in the sand. I told her they wanted her to go down the staircase they had built in the hole because they had a surprise for her. When she got inside, there was a room festooned with party decorations and a delicious-looking cake. The children were giggling and happy to show her their surprise. Charlotte felt relieved and delighted and cherished—all good feelings to associate with the inner world. I also brought in a wise woman who was kind and gentle and took Charlotte's hands in her own warm hands. Charlotte felt the protective energy, which she had never enjoyed in her life. At the end of our session, this is what she told me.

> *I feel like I went to another world. I feel so calm. I am trusting my intuition more lately, but I haven't had much faith in it before this. But I trust the wise woman. I believe she will guide me. I liked the feeling of her leading me, holding me by the hand. I didn't have to go first. Nobody has ever done that for me. I feel safe.*

We didn't do anything else that day, but Charlotte had found her base camp, her "Open sesame." The next day I received a text from her.

> *I wanted to say a huge thank you to you. You were truly amazing yesterday, taking me to that beautiful scene. It made my heart so much lighter. It was very emotional, but in a good way, and such a positive experience—much more than I expected. The level of trust I felt from seeing and sensing the wise woman has left me speechless. Holding my hand, ready to lead the way. It was all very deep and moving. I know Spirit presented it all with your help. It was such a gift. I will definitely be rescheduling.*

Many of the stories that follow involve clients riddled with anxiety or scared about something. In every situation, we had to start with some version of pitching a tent. Often, the tent is pitched in a tree, or the door to the base camp is found in the roots of a tree. (That's why the cover image for this book is a tree.) In the next story, a tree was the portal to safety.

Just Climb a Tree

Texas trees beckon you to climb them. They called Cole back to a time before anxiety got its hooks in him. Cole was an empathic man in his late forties. On the surface, he seemed successful and confident, but secretly, he had been plagued lately by unpleasant dreams of death and destruction. The dreams were exacerbating, or maybe stemming from, his anxiety about keeping his children safe. They were teens now, and he couldn't keep them by his side the way he had when they were little. If they weren't by his side, he didn't know how to protect them. The pandemic was contributing to his anxiety, but he really couldn't pinpoint when it had begun.

Cole's session began in a meadow with tall grass. He was aware of the sound of wind and the birds and the smell of the dirt. The sky was a deep blue and there were trees all around him, especially live oak trees, the kind that were prevalent in Texas, where he'd grown up. "These are the kind of trees you want to climb," Cole said. Notice how he was already feeling comfortable and safe in this meadow.

I encouraged him to choose a tree and climb it.

This one is easy. I'm in a perch, in the crux between two branches.

"Cole, affirm this aloud," I instructed.. "'This is a safe place for me.'"

As he felt into that affirmation and sense of safety, Cole slipped inside the tree. He imagined a chamber that was warm, quiet, and safe.

It's a little creaky when the wind blows the branches, but it's sturdy.

"Go deeper, down into the tree."

He tunneled down to where there was an old door with a brass handle.

It's a little loose. It makes a rasping sound when I turn it.

"Once you are through the door, see if you can find your anxiety."

It's a dark room in an old house. I know it's in there. There's a dusty old carpet and creaky floors. The carpet smells. I can't see anything.

"Imagine you're wearing infrared glasses so you can see."

It's a dog! It's anxious or afraid—maybe angry. It's growling. I'm anxious. I don't want him to bite me. I'm afraid to move.

Because he seemed paralyzed, I had Cole imagine stepping out of the scene and observing it from the outside. Your imagination will allow you to make any shift that leads to safety.

I'm ten years old. The dog is a Dalmatian.

"Do you know the dog?"

It belongs to the headmaster at my school. It bit me in the headmaster's front yard. I was running during gym class. He ran after me and bit me. A kid with a cast on his arm used it to try to beat the dog off me. There was nothing I could do about it. I just had to let it bite me. There was nothing I could do.

Whether this was an actual memory, which I believe it was, or a metaphor for his anxiety, makes no difference. At the root of his anxiety was helplessness to avoid danger—a risk that he projected now upon his children. Helplessness was the story potion we needed to remedy.

I suggested Cole imagine that his future self warned his younger self to keep dog treats in his gym shorts pockets. That gave young Cole a sense of calm and security. He could replay the scene but alter it, imagining that he tossed the treats and got the dog off his trail. This is how he described the safety he now felt.

> *I feel sturdy like the branches of a tree, like giant knots of the tree keeping everything together, planted. I feel solid as if the tree is wrapped around me like a suit of armor. I like that.*

With that feeling of safety for himself, Cole was able to transfer the feeling to his kids and imagine them heading off into the world, resourceful and resilient.

At the outset of the session, Cole told me he had been in therapy for depression off and on since he was a teen. He fully expected this session on anxiety to be the first one of many. He was surprised and pleased to discover that one session completely shifted the anxiety. Maybe this is because Cole's trauma, while hidden, wasn't ongoing. It was a single incident, and it happened when he was ten. The age of a traumatic experience is key. The younger the person is, the more long-standing the effects. Also, this experience didn't carry the shame and betrayal that comes along with trauma that happens in a family setting. It wasn't personal. It was still a trauma at the time, and it was causing him trouble now, but the nature of this difficult experience meant it was easier to put to rest.

The next story involves a chronic trauma and it's one that many of you may share on some level.

Test Anxiety

Have you ever felt stupid in school? Jia, in her late twenties, was struggling with test anxiety and overwhelm as she prepared to get into nursing school. To achieve her goal, she had to prove herself by passing the entrance exams and she was sure she would fail them. Tests had never been easy for her.

Jia had grown up in a family that only spoke Chinese and moved back and forth from the US to China multiple times while she was in elementary school. As a result, she mostly didn't understand what was being said in school and she felt stupid. It was clear Jia had a story potion of "not good enough because I'm stupid" but reasoning didn't help her. We had to connect with the little girl who had swallowed the potion and held the conviction about her ability.

This may not seem like a trauma to you. While there is no physical abuse in this story, only ridicule, allow yourself to imagine how it might be for you to grow up feeling stupid. The blows are to one's self-confidence rather than to the body. And the person on the receiving end is helpless to ward off those thought traumas. In the past or the present.

We went back to Jia's first experience of feeling overwhelmed in school. She was very aware of feeling scared and that her legs felt numb and tingly. Her whole body stiffened with tension. Her mind fluttered. She didn't know what to do. She felt very young but was unsure of her age. I asked her to run her hand through her hair. It was short, so this was before her mother had moved her to China. She was about five years old.

Jia tuned into sounds and was aware of a lot of kids playing.

> *I'm just standing there. I don't know what they're saying. I'm ignoring them. I'm afraid to play with them because I don't know how to talk to them.*

Then Jia started describing the time after her family returned from China, when she was around eight. She was back at school in New Mexico. The kids were mean. Even the teachers were mean.

I didn't know how to spell my last name in English, and the teacher made fun of me in front of everyone.

I encouraged adult Jia to tell off the teacher. She said the teacher didn't care so we imagined the principal coming in and marching the teacher out. We talked to little Jia and encouraged her. Jia noticed that all the tingling and numbness had disappeared.

With some new messaging, Jia was able to start taking in the idea that she was brilliant. By middle school, she was getting top grades in all her classes and was fluent in both English and Mandarin. Back in the early elementary years, besides dealing with the trauma of her parents' divorce, the lead-up to that event, and the instability of the travel back and forth to China, Jia had been learning a second language through an immersion process. Neither she nor the children in her school understood that, and there was no tender refuge for her at the time.

Luckily, the subconscious is not bound by time or factual events. Her child self was very open to positive assurances now. Moving forward, convinced of her own brilliance, Jia was able to move beyond her traumatic start, pass all her tests, and get into nursing school. Today, Jia is a successful nurse with an excellent career that she loves.

As you read this, you may not have struggled with mastering two languages at once, and yet still have felt stupid going through school. This has certainly been true for kids with neurodivergent brains and learning differences. It's also often true for kids with an older, smarter sibling. Whatever your story, if you've swallowed the "I'm stupid" story potion, my hope is that Jia's story will give you hope. Stupid is a perception. You can still uncover your own form of brilliance.

The next story involves safety and anxiety, but the root cause goes much deeper.

New Tools

A tool can be a lifesaver—but only if you have the right one. Bennett loved tools and had a large collection, but he was missing a critical one. Trauma leaves a devastating and deep imprint. Its illusion clouds our thinking so completely that we can't see anything but danger when we get triggered. Bennett didn't have a tool to clear trauma's illusion.

At 75, Bennett was a successful builder with many rental homes that provided a comfortable income. He had just completed building a new house and intended to use the sale proceeds to fund his grand-son's education. However, completion of the house happened in tan-dem with one of the wild downward fluctuations of the economy and instead of having a price war with offers way above the asking price, he accepted an offer below what he had hoped to get. Meanwhile, his condo in the Florida Keys had suffered water damage caused by the upstairs owner. Bennett was wrestling with the insurance company to pay for the repairs. The reality is that he was still fine financially, but he'd lived through two recessions, which had both hit suddenly, and he felt like another one was imminent. That worried him. The veil of illusion was making him feel desperately unsafe.

Bennett came to see me when his wife suggested he might be having a nervous breakdown. He was angry all the time and felt out of control. His hands had started shaking and occasionally he was in tears—a rare state for him. He was taking half a Valium daily to stay calm and didn't like relying on that. Bennett had seen me in the past with great success, so he came hoping I could help him.

We began with deep relaxation. Once Bennett was completely relaxed, the image of a turtle came to him. I spent time giving him messages affirming, "You are the turtle; you are peace; you are riding the waves of the economy and life with ease." This ocean oasis allowed him to go within.

Guiding him deeper, I suggested that as I counted from ten to zero, he would sink deeper and deeper to the bottom of the sea. At the bottom, he would find a sunken ship, filled with the skeletons of memories that were affecting his current state of mind.

I see the ship and the skeletons. The closer that I get, the more memories.

"Please focus on them in detail and share what you're experiencing."

I am in the kitchen in our house on Cape Cod. Mom and Dad are crying. They say, "We lost your brother." I didn't know he was sick. My brother was two years old. I was five.

After that we moved to Maryland and Dad started drinking. Mom was fearful. They were both mean. I was the oldest and got most of the abuse. When we moved to California and Mom had another baby, she seemed to get better, but Dad kept drinking and getting worse.

Because Bennett had been so young when his little brother died, he had no emotional memory of the experience. It was just a factual detail of his childhood. But the younger a child is when trauma happens, the stronger the story potion's effect because it affects the brain more radically. The emotional toll of his parents' responses to their son's death was stored in Bennett's mind as a condition of not being safe. His mother was fearful and sad, and his father was angry. Neither one of them was present with Bennett. Children pick up on emotional energy and draw their own conclusions. But because he was so little when this happened, adult Bennett was not aware of the significance of the experience.

As the session continued, this memory didn't seem to be as painful for him as the grisly memory that followed, but I believe it arose first because it was his foundation of insecurity. When the next incident happened, it was layered over this early experience.

Bennett was quiet for a bit as he moved to this subsequent terrible memory.

> *I got drafted and was headed to Vietnam, but before I went I was going fishing with a buddy. It was night and we were on the L.A. freeway headed to the ocean when we got hit by a drunk driver. My buddy was decapitated in the accident. I was alive but there was blood everywhere. When the ambulance came, they put us both in the back. I spent many weeks in the hospital.*

> *When my father took me home from the hospital, I was doing okay until it got dark, and I saw all the headlights. I panicked. My panic got worse by the day. I was so scared. I didn't know what was happening. I had an emotional breakdown and couldn't leave the house. I spent most of the insurance money I got on a psychiatrist, but they didn't know about PTSD back then, so it didn't really help.*

> *Eventually, I bought a truck, but I could only drive a mile. I put a camper on it and would drive to the hospital parking lot and sleep there. It was the only place I felt safe. I started looking in the papers for a job I'd be able to handle.*

> *I found an ad for working in Yosemite. My brother-in-law drove me up there and that's where I finally found peace. There was so much natural beauty. The pain eventually ebbed, and I became more mobile. After two years I left and moved to Oregon. I couldn't be around all that L.A. concrete and traffic anymore.*

Bennett told me that although that degree of desperation had largely diminished over the years, it was exactly what he was feeling now. He was triggered in the present circumstances and had been reliving his past trauma without realizing it. I asked Bennett to dwell on the beauty he found in Yosemite. Although the trauma had been buried in his past and been reactivated by current circumstances, the medicine he needed was hidden there, too.

During our session, Bennett spent time in the Yosemite of his inner world, remembering the waterfalls, the river, the sheer cliffs, the granite rocks, the most beautiful big ponderosas, and the mirror pond that reflected Half Dome. I asked Bennett to imagine looking in the mirror pond and seeing his old buddy coming up to him. I suggested that he was happy and laughing about how good the fishing was in the cosmos. I asked Bennett to imagine sitting with his buddy on an asteroid with lines of light cast into the cosmos. These images offered the deep medicine that Bennett needed.

When he came out of the hypnotic state, Bennett said he realized he had never walked away from that accident. Although he thought he was over it, he had buried it deep inside. I told this builder that he now had three new tools he could use. He could imagine himself as the turtle riding the waves, he could wander through Yosemite in his mind, and he could go fishing with his buddy in the cosmos.

I like tools. Before coming here, I didn't have any tools that could help.

Love's kiss doesn't have to look like a scene out of Disney. Practical tools forged in love are also a great way to break a spell. But tools are only good if you use them. That's why practice is important. Steeping the Imagery, treatment five, keeps you enjoying the relief you find in hypnotherapy.

In the next story, a hypnotherapist faces the origin of her sugar addiction. She discovers that it involves so much more than a sweet tooth. Trauma laced through her childhood and continuing into her adulthood is responsible. You might think she could have healed on her own, since she was a professional. She couldn't because trauma work is not DIY. No matter how skilled a person is, they still need a protective, accompanying presence to navigate the inner world with safety.

Dust in the Wind

Did you ever think your stuffed animals might kill you? Simone's feeling of being unsafe went that far. She wasn't sure she had a right to be alive. While Bennett felt unsafe financially, Jia was afraid of tests, and Cole was freaking out about his kids, Simone was using food and drugs to stay safe. But the existential right to simply exist was a deeper level of angst.

Simone was a hypnotherapist herself and had helped many clients. She was very aware of her emotions and her history, yet the skills that were so helpful with her clients didn't seem to work for her. She came to me hoping to deal with her habit of getting stoned and eating sugar as the highlight of her day. Simone was very uncomfortable with downtime. "If time passes slowly, it's like I question my existence," she stated. So, to distract and comfort herself, she would eat sugar if she had time on her hands.

Simone was beautiful and voluptuous. However, her narcissistic mother still criticized her weight and expressed shock that an attractive man would want to date Simone. Her father, who had been her primary parent after divorcing Simone's mother when she was five, was constantly suggesting she go on a diet. Her ex-husband, who had been stingy with affection, had also been very controlling of her weight. When they got stoned together on the weekend, she got to enjoy snuggling and eating sweets with him. Sugar and pot felt like love. She hadn't received a lot of nurturing or nourishment, but now she pretended she could provide both by giving herself a steady supply of sugar and pot. This was one layer of the illusion she was operating under.

Simone was aware that, as a teen, she had often gone to bed hungry, because her mother told her that would help her lose weight. Although she had teetered on the edge of anorexia, Simone was very good looking and drew plenty of male attention, which pleased her mother. In true narcissist fashion, her mother appropriated the attention as proof that she had produced a beautiful girl.

Simone's father had been physically abusive.

> *I never thought he would kill me, but I remember being afraid of being obliterated.*

She wondered if maybe all kids were afraid of that. (They're not.) Her older brother, who was very large, had bullied her, too. One time she ran to her mother after he hit her.

> *"If I didn't see it, it didn't happen," my mother said.*

That's when Simone knew for sure that she was on her own. So she had no one to turn to when her then-husband became abusive, raping her and threatening to kill her. Simone told me she had often had suicidal thoughts after that, although she had not attempted suicide.

I'm not sure why I was curious, but I asked Simone about her birth.

> *I was a diaphragm baby. It's not that I wasn't wanted at all, but they were hoping for a bigger gap between me and my older brother. I didn't feel welcome in utero. I came out in twenty minutes, shocking the doctor as I practically shot out of that womb. I've been told that after my birth I couldn't stop shaking for a very long time.*

Simone seemed very extroverted and skilled at drawing attention to herself, though I suspected the authentic Simone was much softer and quieter. It was as if she was demanding that the world notice her.

We spoke of story potions, and she was aware that "unlovable" was one of her big ones, but underneath that, a more insidious one involved an uncertainty over whether she even existed—or deserved to. The words that stood out to me as Simone spoke were *"empty," "oblivion," "unsafe,"* and *"alone."*

I spent significant time helping Simone relax deeply and then led her to a Mother Tree that would envelop her as her safe entryway. As she went deeper into the earth, I asked her to find a wise one who was there to help her.

> *It's a giant angel. He's about ten feet tall with huge wings. He's crouched down, showing me my inner child.*
>
> *He tells me, "This is what you need to see."*
>
> *As he says that, I'm aware that the child is clenching every body part. Her knuckle is in her mouth and she's biting down hard so no sound will escape. She's afraid to open any orifice. I remember I couldn't ever poop easily back then. She's terrified.*

As Simone recounted this, she became aware that the back of her head and her lower back had become extremely tight. She told me that she had frequent migraines as an adult. She realized now that these tight areas were her inner child still expressing terror.

> *She's always prepared for physical pain. I had no idea she was such a ball of fear. I remember I used to arrange my stuffed animals in perfect order so they wouldn't kill me while I slept.*

Simone was crying and telling me the child was upset that Simone had been ignoring her. She was starting to incriminate herself for not caring for the child sooner. I suggested she begin to talk with the child, allowing trust to build slowly.

> *I didn't remember it was that bad. I'm so sorry. It wasn't okay—even if there was nobody to save you. But I'm stronger now. I'm here. I won't let anyone hurt you.*

Simone explained to me that reaching out for food was a way to tether herself.

The child feels like she could blow away and if she didn't exist, nobody would notice. She doesn't feel solid and real like a person.

Simone also told me that smoking weed helped her to relax her constant vigil for the bad things that were sure to happen.

I asked Simone to take another step and tell the child she would take her away from that home. She let the child pack whatever she wanted to bring with her. They headed off in Simone's car and I told Simone to look in the rear-view mirror and see the house crumbling into oblivion. She was satisfied to see that.

Once they were in her home, I had Simone imagine helping the little girl get settled and imagine the fun things they would do together, the tutus and sparkly shoes, and most of all the safe feeling. I told her to look out the window and see all the angels that ringed the perimeter of the yard, keeping her and her child-self safe. Simone released a big sigh when she saw them. Then the big angel took Simone and the child up high, traveling through time and space, experiencing that they were protected through all time and space now. This is treatment four—going beyond the physical.

After, Simone told me that she was surprised at what she had discovered. We talked about why she hadn't been able to do this for herself. I told her (and I'm repeating this for you, too) that deep trauma excavation shouldn't be done on your own and usually can't be. We will unconsciously put the brakes on before we get into the difficult places. Also, when the original wounding occurred, most people were on their own with little or no support and protection. If we attempt DIY trauma work, we re-create the acute pain of being all on our own.

We all need someone to hold a safe container for us so we can do this challenging work.

Not surprisingly, Simone had not fully appreciated the significance of what she was doing for her clients. She went home feeling lighter and freer, and very tired. Now that she had unearthed the origin of the story potion underlying her sugar and drug habits, Simone could strengthen the antidote by practicing in the imaginal realm being present for her inner child and building trust. No longer was she simply dust in the wind. Now the child was tethered to grown Simone and that would make all the difference.

The next story also begins with terrible trauma from childhood, this time with later traumas stacked on top like a sinister tower of rocks left on life's trail.

The Strange Medicinal Value of Leaping Fish

"Blind" justice is independent of personal traumas, right? Maybe not. This story is about a woman whose "unsafe" story potion extended from childhood all the way to the courtroom. When you hear this part of the story, you may be skeptical, but consider this. In a quantum world, we have learned that our expectations shape our results. Is it too far-fetched to imagine that, in the random way that judges are assigned, subconscious expectations could determine the luck of the draw? Again, the fourth treatment suggests that we can count on information from non-physical dimensions. Maybe what we call luck is the operating program from a different field of being.

As a toddler, Gail had been molested by an elderly neighbor. She told her big sister what happened, but her sister didn't believe her. "You're lying and that's bad," her sister said. Gail married a violent man and that created additional trauma. When she ended up in divorce court with him, she told the truth about what he had done, and he lied. She drew a magistrate who believed her husband and then ordered her to pay a sum of money that was totally beyond her financial ability. Traumatic strike number three. Gail wanted to be free of this pattern. The "unsafe" and "on my own" story potions were wreaking havoc with her life.

In hypnotherapy, Gail began imagining very literally, only able to see her own feet. Then she became aware of a key on a rock and a fish in a body of water, which had all somehow materialized. Although she didn't understand why they were there, this mysterious apparition was her turning point.

When we are afraid, we will cling to the shores of what we know, avoiding the wild waves of our imagination. But as we go deeper into the unconscious mind, those waves roll over the shore of predictability and take us someplace where healing can happen. Gail realized through this process that she had ditched her imagination and her dreams back in childhood when the molestation happened. Her discarded imagination was the medicine she needed to heal.

I asked Gail to imagine that the small child she was now could safely ride on this fish. The fish, of course, was a magic fish. Together they rode, leaping up and down joyfully in the water, then careening over boulders. I asked her to experiment with the size of the boulders and notice there was no size that she couldn't ride over.

As she got comfortable riding the fish, I had Gail imagine the court-ordered payment plastered to a boulder. She was able to hop right over it. Then we got to the hard part. Her childhood molester was plastered to one of the boulders. She jumped over him but not without feeling emotions. I affirmed that he was behind her but then he was back, disguised as her ex-husband. Again, she leapt. Then she had to leap over her unbelieving sister only to have her reappear as the judge. Another jump. Then the fish placed Gail on a different boulder and transformed into a mighty warrior. He gathered the three boulders that represented her abusers, her unbelievers, and the judgment and piled them atop one another. He then smashed them with his mighty hand into tiny pieces.

The warrior scooped her up and poured light into her body and her mind. At this point I gave her many affirmations that she was free and powerful. I also told her that she was the mighty warrior fish. After all, this character existed inside her imagination.

People want to stick with reasonable ideas, but reason is not sufficiently healing. Reason is a function of the prefrontal cortex, and that's not where trauma is stored or resolved. Because trauma resides in the unconscious mind, we need to set loose images that originate in our imagination into the unconscious. That's treatment two, Using Language of the Deep. Once we have such an image, then it's important to play it repeatedly, accompanied by powerful affirmations, so that it becomes our new reality. That's treatment five, Steeping the Imagery. In this case, Gail could say something like, "I am a mighty warrior fish. I leap over obstacles. Nobody can pull me down or stand in my way. I am joyful and free. People believe me because I stand in truth." With this process we retrain our brains and our bodies to adopt new supportive beliefs and let go of patterns that no longer serve us.

Woodland Sanctuary

It is important for us all to realize that qualities like safety are not localized outside us. We source them from within. However, if we have been dominated and abused, the traumatic story potions of "unsafe" and "trapped" control our experiences. This was true for Gail, and in this next story it was true for Jill.

If you're a fairy child, you must stay near the woods. Or so Jill unconsciously believed. Jill was a pixie-like woman with a penchant for vintage hippie clothing. She lived in a beautiful cottage at the edge of national forest land. She loved to hike in the woods and photograph the wildlife and trees she found there. Living near the woods wasn't just Jill's preference. It felt mandatory.

Jill had been raised by an alcoholic, abusive father and she felt like Cinderella. Her father gave her many chores, which she was never able to do to his satisfaction, so he would yell or beat her. Unconsciously still trying to earn his approval and love, she married two abusive husbands in a row. Now in her sixties, she was married for a third time. This husband was very introverted and mild. She knew he would never beat her, or even rage at her. Still, Jill experienced intense anxiety on a regular basis and was unable to relax into sleep at night. On her hypnotherapy journey, she set out to find the part of her that was so frightened.

I suggested she look in a big oval mirror, with gilt edges, foggy with clouds. As she stated her intention to find her scared self, the clouds parted, creating a doorway into a landscape. As she stepped through in her imagination, she recognized the backyard from the house she lived in as a young child.

> *There's my backyard, with the woods and the flowers. It's beautiful. I'm four or five and there's the garden, the backyard, the driveway, and the swing set. It's just me here. It's sunny and there are yellow flowers. I'm walking around. It feels like summer or spring. I remember really liking the woods where I could be alone and happy without my father. I tried to climb a tree but couldn't do it. I tried but got scared when I got too high. I wanted to climb the tree to the top so I could show my father I could do it. I was ashamed of being scared.*

> *My father's wood pile is there. It was loud when he chopped wood. I liked to watch him stack the wood. I loved the flowers, but only if he wasn't looking. I picked the pink lady's slipper if he wasn't looking. I liked being in the woods. I pretended I could swing through the trees.*

I suggested Jill amplify this woodsy wonderland by imagining she could see the animal spirits and fairies that were present in her sanctuary. She wove her way between imagination and memory, her voice filled with wonder and delight.

> *I'm like Tinker Bell, making the flowers bloom as I walk by. There are beautiful wild violets all through the woods. They're my favorite. Over by the tree, there's a big old dead tree trunk. I used to go almost inside of it. A little gnome wants me to play hide-and-seek with him. There are monkeys, too, in the trees. I feel protected there. I knew the woods. There was a pond. I'd bring a mason jar and get tadpoles— sometimes a frog or turtles. It was murky but I didn't care.*

I made a series of suggestions to Jill that these woods now existed inside of her. The woods were a strong emotional memory of safety and freedom that had the liminal power to transcend time and counteract her painful memories and potions. They were her antidote and they had to be inside her.

When she came out of hypnotherapy, Jill had an astonishing revelation. She realized that the worst treatment from her father had begun when she reached adolescence. When she turned thirteen, the woods had burned to the ground. The family was afraid their house would burn, too. From that time on, she had no safe quarter. As if in a fairy tale, she began a period of exile from the safe home in the woods and had to wander through a perilous world.

As an adult, Jill was fanatical about ensuring there was a wooded area near her home, though she'd never made the connection of why that was so important. Now Jill needed to end her exile from safety that had begun at thirteen when her special woods had burned down and stake a permanent claim on safety by consciously inhabiting her inner forest.

As Jill practiced consciously living in both the inner and outer woods, she gradually felt safer and began to sleep restfully and make other life changes that felt harmonious with the playfulness and freedom of her inner wooded sanctuary. If you have an image that conjures peace and safety, practice imagining it as emanating from within you rather than being something you need to find outside of yourself. Peace is an inside force.

In the next story, Peter has to find safety outside first and then bring it into his inner reality. He does so in a most unusual and duplicatable way. As you read what he imagines, you may find yourself wondering how to do the same for yourself.

The Rope into the Unknown

How do you climb a rope that isn't tethered to anything? For an anxious young man who believed he was worthless and unsafe, that rope led to peace with himself and his journey.

Peter was in his early twenties. His father had died when he was a young boy, and his mother went over the edge mentally, filling him with story potions of worthlessness. "You're nothing without me," she'd tell him routinely. "You'll never go anywhere or be able to function on your own."

Fulfilling her toxic words, Peter had struggled. He'd been on drugs, been homeless, and suffered from extreme anxiety. His thoughts tormented him. His mother's sister had taken Peter under her wing and asked me to work with him to help him find inner peace, stability, and motivation. I worked with him for several years, doing plenty of counseling as well as hypnotherapy, making slow, mostly steady progress, with many breakthroughs. Ultimately, his story had a very happy ending. But, along the way, one session stands out for me.

Peter arrived in the inner world, ushered by angels, on a quest to find something he hadn't seen before that he needed to face to be free. He appeared to be in a cave. Darkness was all around him. The ground was sandy, and he was barefoot. A thick rope hung in front of him, large enough that his hand couldn't reach around it. He began to shimmy up the rope.

When I asked him where the rope was leading him, Peter described a ledge. We considered the possibility that this was the destination, or that perhaps it held a clue. With discussion, he revealed that he was on the ledge because he started to think that the rope might not be leading anywhere. In other words, he was settling for security even though staying on the ledge of a cave had little to offer.

Peter made the decision to get back on the rope and head into the unknown. We are always heading into this mysterious realm, but we buy into the illusion that we know what we are doing and where we are going, rather than feel the loss of control that comes with facing the unknown.

When we let ourselves face that, we wonder what the abyss may hold. Is it friendly? What will happen to me? Will I survive? That last one is a core question. The answer is no. None of us will survive in our current form. Our life journeys are about transformation, and only by releasing what we have and what we know can we become and have something greater.

Having made the decision to trust the angel's guidance and get back on the rope, Peter noticed that the climb seemed easier and somehow the darkness seemed lighter. He continued climbing but still didn't find a destination. I speculated with him that perhaps the destination was a state of being—ease, light, and trust. He considered that possibility.

I asked Peter what he imagined was holding him up since the rope he was clinging to didn't seem to be tethered to anything or going anywhere.

> *It must be God, but it's not like there is a person standing there. It's more like an energy fabric.*

This was a profound shift for Peter. The energy fabric held him like a cocoon of love and grace. He stayed in it, simply being, without evaluating or doing anything.

After a while, I encouraged Peter to imagine that this divine fabric could rearrange his mind, transforming it from a wild and dangerous jungle to a garden flourishing with flowers and vegetables.

Peter pictured negative thought weeds being pulled from his mind as easily as weeds are pulled from the ground in the spring. Then he imagined new positive mind seeds being planted.

- You deserve good things.
- You belong here.
- You have a purpose on this earth.
- Everything you need is inside you, just as an acorn holds an oak.

Peter soaked in these new thoughts and reveled in this flourishing vision, smelling the flowers and tasting the vegetables.

Afterward, Peter told me he pictured green peppers, a favorite food, growing out of his head. He loved the idea of eating mind food and planned to make a drawing of his pepper head. We returned to this image often and it was helpful to him in choosing thoughts that served him.

Ultimately, no matter what trauma has led to a lifelong state of anxiety, the antidote must come from within. Thought seeds like Peter planted can grow more powerfully when a person realizes they are connected to the spiritual realm like Peter's divine energy fabric of love and grace. By its nature, this energy fabric is everywhere present. If you struggle with anxiety, consider grabbing your own rope and climbing into the safety of the unknown. This powerful image is not proprietary. Everyone has a rope, and all the ropes are connected to that divine energy fabric. And once you've connected, take a look at your mind garden. What will you pull out and what will you plant?

Fly Free

In this next story, Vera doesn't find a rope, but she climbs out of her situation on the back of a bird.

"Go to your room!" That's a common childhood punishment, but for Vera it meant both rejection and sanctuary. Vera was routinely banished to her room, feeling misunderstood and miserable with the lack of affection from her parents. She was drinking heavily of the "unlovable" story potion. But at least she was safe in her room, and she'd done what she could to make it cozy. She had pillows she could hide under when the noise of her parents fighting got too oppressive.

Vera got a strong dose of the "unsafe" story potion because the violence in her home was off the charts. One time she ran outside to get away from the screaming that had been going on for hours. Her alcoholic father was beating and choking her mother. Unfortunately, this wasn't uncommon. As Vera hid in the woods behind their house, another occasional sanctuary for her, the screams from Vera's mother seemed to get louder. Then she saw her father, carrying a hunting rifle, dragging her mother into the woods.

There were plenty more violent incidents that she told me about, but that's enough of a snapshot to help you understand that Vera would have trouble imagining a healthy relationship for herself. Her ability to trust love was at zero. The "unsafe" story potion and the "I'm not lovable" story potion were completely blended, resulting in the "can't trust love" story potion. At age fifty, Vera was tired of the struggle. She longed for love.

I suggested that Vera go through the inner woods to a welcoming tree, a portal to her inner world. A tree is an ideal opening into that inner realm because the roots naturally lead us down deep into the earth, which is like going down into our psychic depths. Vera's tree was one of the most lively and whimsical I've encountered. It had very wide roots, a short trunk, and extremely colorful trinkets and fruits hanging from it. It was a very inviting, happy tree. It was an entryway that felt safe.

I asked Vera to imagine a guide waiting for her at the bottom of the tree. If you are looking for a guide on your own, don't pre-decide what your guide is like. Wait and see what comes to you. Vera encountered a bird with a long thin neck and a wide and elegant wingspan. Soon she imagined riding on the back of this crane. She described the feeling of the feathers as lush, and she felt a sense of joy as they flew through a fanciful environment.

This uplifting experience prepared Vera for facing her dark struggles as she relived being banished to her room or hiding from her father's violence. She spent a bit of time recounting what that experience felt like and crying. When she seemed to have expressed her sorrow sufficiently, I suggested that she scoop up the child and talk with her. These were her words to the little girl.

> *Life is magical. It's safe to play in your wild and luscious imagination. It's good to run free and chase the wild butterflies and be a great wild butterfly huntress. When your feelings are hurt, you're welcome to be in my open, loving, accepting arms. Your tears and your cries are precious, too. The door is always open to be who you are and having fun is really*

right, exactly perfect for you. When you're having a difficult time, you can ask for help, and you can have help. I love you so much and my loving embrace is constantly with you.

Then I encouraged Vera to imagine flying out the window with the child, riding on the bird, away from the pain and oppression to the lightness of a world where she would be free to be herself. She flew into the cosmos to play among many colorful beings. She noticed her sternum and collarbone opening up, a contrast from her familiar hunched posture, as she stayed in the realm where she was free to be herself, to be light, and where she could and would meet the love of her life.

After, Vera felt peaceful.

My awareness is expanded. I'm less boundaried by my body. I feel more committed to feeling that freedom in all my relationships.

Vera returned to my office five days later with a surprising story of connecting at the Oregon Country Faire with a man she had just begun dating prior to our session. They had a delightful time together. She told me they had found each other in large crowds without using cellphones or making plans to meet. Vera believed he intuitively responded to her desire to see him. She told me she had made a conscious effort to ride the crane in her imagination and remain in that place of lightness. By practicing this vision, she was creating the conditions to embed the story potion antidote in her system. She was successfully using the fifth treatment, Steeping the Imagery.

In a subsequent hypnotherapy session, Vera dissolved easily into the cosmos. Her small self was happily investigating all the delights of her expanded world. I suggested that maybe she was experiencing a cellular realignment, and this seemed easy for her to imagine. Because our brains don't distinguish between literal and imaginative reality, Vera's time spent in the cosmos was in fact rewiring her consciousness. As she imagined feeling safe, her brain and body worked together to create that possibility for her.

As you read Vera's story, you may be inclined to wonder if that could happen for you. I want to assure you that it is possible. It may not happen overnight. Vera had to keep working with her crane freedom and lightness of being, using the power of her imagination, letting the imagery steep. This is the story of just one session, not a magic wand that changed everything forevermore. But with dedication to seeing and feeling her image, she had a powerful treatment for changing her experience. This can transpire for you, too. Your story potions can be antidoted, just like Vera's.

In the next story, another abused child who grew to struggle with relationships found a surprising antidote to her "unsafe" and "unlovable" story potions.

Lilac Medicine

The fragrance from beautiful lilacs outside Dahlia's childhood window transcended time, reminding Dahlia that she was precious. She struggled with self-confidence. Badly abused as a child, Dahlia had a long history of abuse and suffering as an adult. We had done extensive therapy together a few years back and her confidence had soared. She'd extricated herself from situations that were not serving her. However, a few years later, she was beaten down again. She'd had a head injury that severely affected her well-being on many levels along with a couple of abusive relationships. Dahlia felt depressed. She wondered how she had gotten back to this place.

Dahlia is not alone in the feeling that, despite lots of inner work, the same issues continue to surface. I think it's important that we realize that we are not here on planet earth to be ceaselessly happy but rather to excavate our souls. There is a light inside each one of us that is brighter than the sun, but it is dimmed by the residue of many lifetimes where we swallowed negative story potions that diminished our identity, our value, and our possibilities. As we go through life, the process of creating antidotes for the story potions we've been subjected to involves one opportunity after another to hollow out the space inside us, removing potion clogs and making more room for our beautiful light. Each time we deal with our big issue (and we all seem to have one), we go a bit deeper and become more hollowed out. Maybe it's no coincidence that hollowed, hallowed, and haloed are so close in spelling.

In continuing this excavation, we returned to the site of Dahlia's childhood. Despite the abuse she had suffered, the first thing she remembered upon returning to the bedroom of her childhood home was the big window and the two beautiful lilac bushes that grew outside. She could smell the fragrance in her memory and began to relax and feel lighter. I sensed there was an antidote brewing. There was certainly safety in that smell.

The next trauma memory Dahlia returned to was a time she was left sleeping at her church hall, one of those places where families spent many hours at a time in religious study and socializing. As she tuned into the child waking up in the dark, I asked her what the child was thinking.

She's scared and alone. She's wondering, Why did they forget me?

The questions we pose never go unanswered. We instinctively scramble to supply an answer, even if it's an incorrect answer. Dahlia's answer was not in her favor.

Because I'm no good and they don't like me.

This turned out to be the story potion that had defined her life so far.

She gave me a few examples of her history in that town that seemed to her to substantiate her belief. She also mentioned that her mother was depressed a lot because they had very little money and her father was often gone. Since Dahlia herself was no stranger to depression, I asked her about her own thinking skills when she was in that state. Not surprisingly, she admitted she was not too sharp, and her memory was terrible. She could see that her mother may have forgotten her child because she was so depressed that her memory was shot. The beauty of recognizing such a different explanation while in a deep state is that the subconscious mind accepts it and replaces the old story with the new one.

I asked Dahlia to speak to her young self and share this new way of understanding so she could affirm the truth of who she is. The words that flowed from Dahlia's wise heart were powerful, poetic, and healing. Exactly the antidote she needed.

> *Beautiful, sweet child, your mother loves you. She is not well, and she forgets everyone and everything. She is scared right now because she doesn't know where you are. You are very important to her. You are important to the world. You are a beautiful lilac bush. Every year you blossom more fully and confidently. The fragrance of your soul makes the world a more beautiful place. You are not defined by the ugliness of the world around you. You bring the medicine of lilacs to a world that desperately needs that medicine.*

No matter who you are or what you have endured, you hold the equivalent of a lilac bush somewhere in your psyche. As you focus on your light, you hollow out your darkness and your name and your nature become hallowed, a medicine the world is aching to receive.

Hidden Cracks in Relationship Foundations

Story potions that make us believe we are unlovable and unworthy affect our relationships. The next story shows how that can play out.

Kay almost had an affair. She felt done with her marriage of over forty years when she first came to see me. She had met a charismatic younger man who she thought was flirting with her. Kay was toying with the idea of stepping out with him. Ironically, she heard about me from this same young man, who was a former client of mine.

Issues around love and belonging show up in relationships with those we love and belong with. Relationship issues almost inevitably arise so that we can heal our hidden traumas and beliefs. Initially, most of us think the problem is with the other person. However, as we grow in life, experience, and wisdom, often aided by therapy, we begin to look within for the source of the conflicts in our relationships.

But until we do, the story potions from early trauma create cracks in the psyche that affect the foundation of our adult relationships and guarantee they will crumble unless the fissure itself is addressed. For Kay, the cracks came from her mother and her church, but an outside interaction was necessary to bring them to light. This was the real benefit of meeting that flirtatious younger man.

Unfortunately, most people deal with the issues leading to an affair *after* the affair has happened. Kay was willing to explore *before* she acted on her impulses and caused real damage. At least for the moment, we put the affair idea on hold and pursued the more pressing matters. This led her on a trail through her life story.

Kay suffered from chronic pain and depression. She had an unrelenting inner critic and a great deal of unaddressed childhood trauma from an emotionally abusive mother. She had a history of religious trauma from a group of well-meaning but judgmental, dogmatic "friends."

Kay had also gone through cancer and, having let her nursing license go during chemotherapy, lacked meaningful work in the world.

Kay and I worked together for a couple of years and dealt with all of this, using hypnotherapy, counseling, and art. We uncovered and healed her story potion of "essentially wrong."

Though we spent a long time together, after just a few months, Kay felt much happier with her life. She realized her husband was neither perfect nor the problem, and they were getting along much better. By this point, Kay had already concluded that an affair was a ridiculous idea.

By the end of our sessions, Kay was enrolled in school to renew her nursing license. Her health was much improved. Her relationship was satisfying. She had eliminated negative, controlling people from her life and set clear boundaries. For the most part, she had stopped picking on herself. She was engaged in creating a beautiful exhibit of original art. She felt focused and happy. Although I'm not getting into the therapeutic details here of how Kay found self-love, this snapshot, I hope, shows you how much is possible for a person who is committed to finding that love of self by addressing their own trauma and learning to love themselves. In Chapter 6, you'll read some of Kay's details and meet Nonna, the wild woman who helped Kay turn a corner in her heart and find true self-love and acceptance.

The Intuition Game

Let's pause to play. Answers come more quickly when we're playing. We all get stuck at times wondering what the right course of action might be. Should we continue a particular relationship, pursue a different field of study, have a baby now? We have so many questions and when we are anxious, it's difficult for us to tap into our intuitive wisdom and get the answers that are right for us. Since we've been talking about anxiety, here's a DIY end run on anxiety.

Clarify your question and come up with three to four possible answers. For example, you might have two different colleges you're considering, but you also might want to do a gap-year program in another country. Working for a year or two also seems attractive. You write each option down on a piece of paper. Make sure the paper is thick enough that you can't read through it when you turn the pieces of paper over. You also need a fifth piece of paper that has a question mark, representing an option you haven't considered. Shuffle the papers so you have no idea what's on the other side. Then number each one, 1-5.

Close your eyes and breathe in on a count of four, out on a count of six. Put your hand on your heart and speak to your inner knowing. "Oh, my heart, show me the best path." Pick up the first card with eyes still closed and hold it to your heart. If you have someone to assist you, this is even easier. They can hand you each card (not peeking at the other side themselves) and record your answers.

You imagine you are at a campground. From where you sit, you can see five paths radiating around you. For each paper, in turn, you imagine choosing a path. Keep moving from path to path until you have explored all five.

As you go down each path, let your imagination go wild. Usually, you'll start out on a path that seems like it could be part of a campground but soon it can change dramatically. You may find yourself climbing a steep mountain, close to the ocean, bushwhacking through brambles, or on a pleasant stroll through a meadow. Anything is possible.

If you have an assistant, they should write down whatever you are saying. Pay particular attention to how you feel on this pathway. Are you scared, excited, bored? Are you having fun or feeling pushed beyond your limits? Take careful note. If you're on your own, you can record your impressions on your phone as you go or pause after each path and write what you noticed on the back of the piece of paper. DO NOT look at the other side. Come back to the center of the campground in between and then choose the next trail to the left.

When you have finished your explorations, make a guess as to which path was connected to each of the options. Then turn them over and see what your intuition has shown you about your choices. If a trail felt very difficult, you might want to avoid taking that option. An easy path might be okay unless it was boring. It's a fun way to discover what your deep mind already knows.

What do you do next? You are free to choose. I will tell you from experience that you ignore these insights at your peril. One time I did this with my former husband. We were deciding whether to end our marriage. I can't recall my answers, but I've never forgotten his. The trail of continuing our marriage looked like climbing over lava rock for him. On the "ending the marriage" trail, he saw himself joyfully riding a bicycle over a grassy hill. Those seem like pretty clear answers, but at the time, neither of us wanted that answer, so we ignored the sign. Two years later, nothing had improved, and we got divorced. We could have saved ourselves some serious heartache and financial misery by listening to our intuition.

If you have a decision to make, try this game. You can't hurt anything by playing and you may find that instead of listening to the trauma-influenced voice in your head, you get some helpful guidance.

Here's one caveat. Following your intuition doesn't guarantee no mess or fallout will come your way. Your soul's desire is that you continue to evolve. That rarely happens on a flat, straight life trail. We build resilience and accumulate wisdom and compassion by handling life's challenges. But if you follow the emotions on the trails you are choosing from, even if growth is ahead, you will likely be able to experience the feelings you notice on that trail. Choose what you want to feel.

CHAPTER 3

Trauma Before "You"

L ong before you learned the word "me," trauma had a chance to infuse your cells. As soon as there was a cell that became part of you, everything that cell was aware of was being programmed into your future ego consciousness. Cellularly, you were aware when you were conceived, while you were gestating, and during the birth process. If you were adopted, even as an infant, that event and all the feelings around it are recorded in your cells. Pre-dating your ego identity even more, your parents' traumas got passed along with the DNA and so did traumas from your ancestral line. The fourth treatment, Going Beyond the Physical, accesses information from cellular reality.

Cellular Memory

How we were conceived makes a difference. Was it a loving union, an unconscious hookup, or even a rape? And who were those parents? Even when the conception was intentional, the parents can be carrying unhealed trauma in their cells from their own lives or from their parents or ancestors. When conception involves a sperm donor, so much is unknown consciously but can be discerned through cellular memory.

What happened in utero and during birth also matters. Of course, this is predicated on the belief that life is conscious, no matter the form it takes or whether we humans know how to communicate with that life form. If you can accept this belief, then recognize that just as little children are emotional antennas, picking up whatever energy they are moving through, a fetus is also picking up the vibes of the mother while floating in the womb. A mother who is delighted to be pregnant radiates a very different energy from one who is ashamed and scared about the pregnancy. A baby who moves through the birth canal with relative ease has a much different first experience of the world than one who struggles for long hours and is finally yanked out by forceps. A child who is welcomed into the arms of a mother filled with gratitude, awe, and love has a different start than one who is whisked away to the neonatal intensive care unit or to a foster home.

In the stories that follow, you'll get a window to all these traumatic life starts and how the hypnotherapy treatments helped transform potions that were instilled from those rough beginnings. Perhaps you will receive an insight into trauma that you or a loved one are carrying and begin to realize that you could also be free.

The Toy

Chloe's struggles went all the way back to conception. This came as a surprise to her because there was so much trauma in her childhood that she believed was responsible for her challenges, even though working on it had failed to make a significant difference.

Chloe's troubles with men had been going on for her entire life. Her father attempted to fondle her as a child, though she was able to push him away. Her brothers loved to torment her, and so did her father, enjoying her reaction of tears or even terror. She recalled an incident as a child of ten where she had been frightened by a *Twilight Zone* episode about a two-story-tall man who roamed the city streets. That night, as she lay in her bed on the second floor, she heard a tapping on the outside of the window. She was petrified. It turned out to be her father, who had climbed a ladder in the dark for the sole purpose of scaring her.

As an adult, Chloe had been brutalized by a boyfriend while living in Yugoslavia, barely escaping with her life. The boyfriends who followed were disrespectful of her and always took advantage of her. She had been working on her need to speak up and set boundaries, but she sensed there was a deeply embedded pattern, some story potion like "I'm not safe" or "Use me" that caused her to attract such men into her life. She wanted to change it. We headed into the inner world to find out why she was set up to be treated like a toy for a man's amusement. Here is the dialogue that ensued.

I'm seeing all pink with yellow around it. Everything seems puffy. There are no lines. No borders. No definition. Just space, and it's all pink.

"What do you feel?" I asked.

Nothing. I'm just an observer.

"Can you walk more into the pink?"

I don't have arms or legs. I think this is all happening before I was born.

"People have subconscious memory of preconception, conception, and their time in utero. Does what you're experiencing right now remind you of any of those stages?"

It seems to be when I'm being fertilized. I can feel a fighting to merge, for the sperm to come inside of me. I'm feeling invaded, an intrusion, that something got inside of me. But now it's over. I'm just this big mass of pink.

"Imagine you are watching this on a video and rewind until you have an awareness of your parents. Put your attention on what they're feeling about conceiving you. You have a memory of this."

I don't think my mother wanted it. My father was forcing himself on my mother. Dad wanted it. He was one of three brothers. They all wanted to have babies at the same time. The wives of the other two had already conceived and he wanted a baby, too. He didn't care about my mother's wishes. I was conceived for his game with his brothers.

Chloe was quiet for a long time, absorbing this information.

Then I guided her through a visualization of being conceived and bringing an angel with her. Immediately after conception, I had her imagine telling her father that she was aware of his game, and she did not intend to play. Then, at every abusive point in her life, I had her visualize the angel coming between her and whoever was mistreating her, picturing the person being repelled by the powerful light of the angel.

I suggested further that, in the present, people who were approaching Chloe to use or disrespect her would be repelled. People who were approaching with kindness and respect would harmonize with the angelic light and move easily toward her. After that, Chloe seemed peaceful. When she came to consciousness, she shared her feelings.

I feel I made a tremendous journey, and I understand more—a lot more.

Chloe is a perfect example of acting out a story potion that was swallowed before she had any way of understanding what was happening. Without a conscious memory of how the pattern was set in motion, or understanding the impact, a person can't really make a fundamental change. But when the subconscious root is uncovered, then healing can happen as it did for Chloe. I was delighted to get a note from her a couple of years later telling me that she had met a kind man, and they were getting married in a month.

In the next story, the trauma originated at conception, but that wasn't evident at first. And the healing required more than addressing the trauma from conception. Jody had to shoot a few spitballs to complete her process. Wouldn't it be great if you could reclaim your self-esteem by shooting spitballs? That's what Jody did. Here's what happened.

Spitballs

Jody, a recently widowed grandmother in her late seventies, learned that shooting spitballs could get her back on track. Jody had had a good life by most standards. She'd raised several children and enjoyed a long marriage. She'd also had a satisfying career in the high-tech world while pursuing art as a hobby. She'd been an avid hiker, completing a large portion of the Pacific Crest Trail. Many years into retirement, with health issues confining her to home, reliant on caregivers and taxis to get around, she felt restless and trapped. Even more, she felt bereft of purpose and unable to motivate herself to follow through on inspiration. Jody suspected that lack of worth was the true culprit.

Jody had three older brothers. She knew her mother had her tubes tied after giving birth to the third boy and had always believed she was unwanted. She unconsciously thought of herself like an undocumented immigrant who had snuck across the barrier designed to block her from enjoying a new life. Jody had conception trauma.

Her mother's critical nature had always seemed to confirm that Jody was unwanted and didn't belong here. Jody assumed that's why she felt unworthy. Story potions that are consumed before a person is even born are particularly insidious because there has never been a time that the person didn't have that belief.

Whenever the client or I have an idea about the root of a concern, we may be correct, but I practice an open mind. A session often takes surprising turns. While sometimes the inner journey is like an express train, leading directly to the true start of the problem, other times it's more like a downtown bus, with frequent stops along the way, before arriving at the healing station.

In Jody's case, we took the downtown bus. The first stop was in a refreshing springtime garden where she smelled wonderful lemons and heard a scolding voice telling her not to pick them.

So many don'ts.

Jody was whimpering softly. She felt like this was just another "don't." Maybe "Don't go down that tube" was the first.

Somewhere in me, I know what's right for me. I know the right time. But everyone kept telling me that my mother didn't want any more babies.

I was curious about the identity of "everyone" and where she was hearing this message. I encouraged Jody to make a trip in consciousness, back before she was conceived, to explore the agreement her soul had made with the soul of her mother. Jody heard something that surprised her.

My mother doesn't want any more babies—unless it's a girl. She wanted a baby girl but gave up on that dream and had her tubes tied. I have to be a baby girl.

That mandate implied to me that Jody's soul didn't necessarily *want* to be a girl, so I asked about this.

I don't think I did.

Jody believed that showing up as a girl meant she had to give up rowdiness and spontaneity and determination. Jody was incarnating into the US culture in the early 1940s, when girls had tightly scripted options.

"But you didn't give those qualities up, did you?" I asked.

I was thinking that one very determined soul got through a tubal ligation.

No. I was all those things.

Jody made another bus stop to explore her non-binary wholeness. She liked perfume and lace and pearls. Her mother crocheted her a skirt that formed a perfect circle when she twirled in it. How she had loved that skirt! Jody also played with the neighborhood boys, building forts, and nailing boards to their skates so they could race down the steep hills, getting banged-up knees and tumbling in a happy heap. She also remembered loving the alley cat that allowed her to dress him in doll clothes and put him in her baby carriage. She lingered a moment at this stop, filled with all these pleasant memories of childhood.

Back on the bus, it was time for the final destination. Jody began recalling her brother Ronnie, the youngest of her three older brothers, shaming her.

"You'll always be a big crybaby. You're spoiled!" he told me.

Jody felt bad as she thought about Ronnie and how she had robbed him of all the attention he would have had as the youngest if she hadn't been born. Jody said her brother grew up and got in trouble with drugs and police and had relationship issues. I asked Jody to consider that his problems were part of his wiring and destiny and not her responsibility. Her worth was not tied to his ability to value her—unless she gave him that authority.

I also asked Jody to imagine that Ronnie had given her something concrete that symbolized the idea that she was unworthy. She told me he gave her an "unworthy" sticker that covered her forehead. I let her know that she no longer had to wear this label and could peel it off.

We are the authorities who get to decide what is true for us. We just don't often realize we have been tagged or that the tags are removable. This is just another way of thinking about story potions. In Jody's case, a label was a perfect image because she could reclaim her power by taking it off and repurposing it.

As Jody attempted to peel it off, this sticker proved difficult to remove, so I suggested she use "Goo Begone." It worked. The label came off and then she rubbed some lovely rose cream onto her forehead to soften the spot that had been sticky with glue.

Next, I instructed her to pick up all the soggy pieces of label and wad them up. I had her imagine she had a thick straw and then shoot the wad like a spitball back at Ronnie. That made her laugh. She confessed she'd been a terrific spitball shot as a kid. She sent that spitball off with sharp aim and great joy. Jody felt so much freer—and valuable.

The next time I spoke with Jody, she had completed several art projects and was feeling more satisfied with her life.

Nobody is destined to hold onto a lie forever. If you are still hanging onto one of those malicious potions, like Jody, you can convert them into labels, peel and wad them into spitballs, and get rid of those lies for good.

Strung Out

Lisa's lack of confidence, which affected her business, started before she was born. Have you ever considered your professional challenges could have begun so long ago?

Lisa felt blocked about being more public with marketing her business and speaking about her work to groups and generally showing up as an expert in her field. She was mystified and frustrated by her inability to move forward on those fronts and had no idea what was behind the problem. She would discover prenatal origins.

I led her down the stairs that wound along the roots of an ancient tree. When she reached the bottom, I had the thought of those strings of colorful plastic shapes that might adorn the doorway of a teenager or a hippie. Although I usually trust whatever ideas come, I admit I censored this one a bit and my subconscious offered another image of old moss hanging in strips and forming a similar (but more organic) curtain. I suggested that image to Lisa and the next thought that came to me was that she was entering an opium den. I mentioned that to Lisa, but thought it was a weird image. She didn't immediately relate but she was seeing vague shapes. I suggested she pretend it was an opium den, and the shapes represented visions. If so, what were the visions about? "Judgments," she replied immediately, "and jealousy."

As she explored this idea, she began telling me about people in her life who she had thought were friends but who became jealous of her, causing the friendships to fall apart. This was painful for her. The fact that these friends had also been colleagues helped her to realize that part of her fear of taking a lead spot on the professional stage was about losing friends because she feared they would resent her success.

I invited Lisa to bring in a wise woman to help her understand why she was attracting jealousy. When you experience something from others, often it can reflect a quality in yourself that is hidden in the shadows of your consciousness. As Lisa imagined the wise woman explaining, she started to feel numb. The sensation was concentrated in her stomach. She felt as if she were floating in the numbness. Her limbs felt very heavy.

I'm completely secure. I'm in aqua water. I'm surrounded by fluid, but I don't feel wet. Oh! Wow! Okay, this is about being in the womb. Wow! I feel so numb in there. I almost feel lifeless—like some part of me has died. It's the connection to my mother. It's missing.

As soon as she was born, Lisa was given up for adoption by her teenage mother, who, she later learned, had used drugs while pregnant. That explained the numbness and my impression of an opium den. Lisa went on to connect the dots about jealousy.

Jealousy plays a role in this. Even though I have a mom, a part of me has always been jealous of the moms and daughters who are biologically connected and close to each other. Just today, as I was putting on blush, I thought about my birth mom and wondered if she had cheekbones like mine. In this womb I don't feel frightened, just numb, and disconnected.

As she continued exploring this idea, Lisa realized that in the past she had unconsciously chosen friends who ended up being threatened by her rather than those who would encourage her. Jealous friends were a match vibrationally for her own hidden feelings of jealousy.

I asked Lisa to reimagine the uterine waters as the love of the Great Mother. She had previously made a deep connection with the Holy Mother of Guadalupe and so as soon as I made this suggestion, Lisa felt her body relaxing and she was able to get cozy.

I'm completely comfortable, like I'm in a big bed of down comforters, wrapped up and sleeping peacefully.

I continued to describe the love and delight of the Holy Mother for her and told her that she was encouraging Lisa to give her gifts to the world. Lisa felt the jealousy dissolve in the presence and connection she felt with this loving mother. Lisa began to picture herself doing a demonstration on television. At the end of the session, she felt like she had been through a real transformation.

Shaman's Child

When the mother who birthed you can't raise or love you, all is not lost. Lisa, the woman in the last story, given up by her sixteen-year-old mother who already had a child, had been adopted by loving parents. Their love was formative but could not entirely erase Lisa's loveless start. In the story that follows, it's significant that Lisa was unaware of her origin story at the point of this journey.

Lisa was aware of a pattern of resistance throughout her life to anything people wanted her to do. We had decided to explore her fear and resistance. Surprisingly, we were led back again to her start in utero. The journey led us first deep into a forest where a healer showed up. Lisa described her in detail.

> *She has tan, wrinkled, leathery skin. She's a Native American. She is wearing a cloth shawl and carrying a stick with a wooden handle. Her gray hair is pulled into a bun. She has a satchel around her that is colorful, with zig-zag patterns, and is filled with stones. She has very kind eyes and warm energy.*

The healer gave Lisa an herbal potion to calm the fear in her chest, which the healer said was fear of the unknown. Lisa was afraid to swallow it because she didn't know what she would feel when she took it.

> *I'm afraid to fully give in to the healer because then she could persuade me to believe what she believes.*

As we explored the root of her issue with being persuaded, Lisa became aware of how she had persuaded herself that her birth mother had loved and cared for her in the womb. Now that she realized this was a lie, she could see how the lie had created a crack in her foundation. The underlying story potion was that her mother didn't love, care for, or keep her because she was unworthy and undesirable in some way. That belief was so painful that convincing herself of a story she wanted to be true allowed her to survive. Lisa hadn't had the resources to handle the truth until now.

Once we saw the real issue, the repair process could begin. I suggested that Lisa begin to recognize the healer as her true, deep mother, the same Holy Mother she encountered in her last journey, just dressed differently. I suggested she think of her birth mother as a conveyance, and that idea resonated with her.

Lisa imagined the deep mother attuned to the growing fetus self, sending love and a cradling energy to her. As she imagined this, Lisa had the awareness that she was a shaman's child and that, on some level, she had always known this.

Lisa and I worked together on a regular basis for a long time. She came to really own her shamanic gifts and to step into a powerful healing practice. You'll read her story in her own words in Chapter 7.

Finding a mother figure who can provide the love that a human mother was challenged to offer is a powerful antidote, the work of the imagination and the heart. The key is recognizing that love flows through creation. You can pull it forth and shape it into a form that works for you. In the next story, that love took the form of an egg.

The Healing Egg

A pregnant woman, Ginger, came for therapy, and her son later showed he'd been paying attention to the work she was doing. She was pregnant with her second child and feeling depressed. Her first daughter had been a Caesarean birth, and it had been a very difficult experience for her. She'd felt violated, and it took her a long time to recover. She was afraid of having a similar experience. Instead, she desired to have an easy home birth.

As we explored the violence of her childbirth experience, Ginger told me she had grown up in an angry home. Her father was controlling, her mother passive. Her big brother took out his frustration and anger at being yelled at all the time by beating up Ginger and calling her names. Molested both by her maternal grandfather and a neighbor, Ginger got no help from her mother when she confided in her and so had no way to be safe. She expressed her anger through art but allowed others to scream at her because she felt powerless.

To fulfill her dream for the second birth, Ginger had to find her power. But first, she had to find safety. During hypnotherapy, an image emerged of an egg. It was a motif that came up over and over again in our sessions. Sometimes she held it, sometimes a healer held it, and sometimes it held her. The most powerful way it showed up was as an egg that she could climb inside where she could experience safety, nurturing, and sanctuary. This egg also became a place of transformation.

Because Ginger specialized in art installations, she later described this egg in detail as an art installation she planned to create. This is her vision, in her own words.

> *There is a spacious gallery with white walls. The only piece of art, in the center, is a giant egg. The viewer/participant gets into the egg and assumes the fetal position—or any other comforting, relaxed, curled-up position. Then the door is shut.*
>
> *The inside is lined with crushed purple velvet. There is a low glow of light, sort of pulsating. Once relaxed, the person hears the sound of a mother's heartbeat, as if hearing it from inside the womb. Soft new age*

music plays. There are sounds of breathing lungs, womb sounds, and a soft woman's voice singing angelic, abstract sounds.

After being in the egg for a period of time, one emerges and is somehow transformed. The transformation might be spiritual, physical, or mental. Somehow, the heart is full.

Ginger imagined this egg during hypnotherapy, and she spent plenty of time inside it, feeling love and light being radiated into her body and her psyche. Over the months of her pregnancy, she worked on the emotional pain she'd been packing around, and she began the forgiveness process. The light from the egg seemed to help her lighten her heart.

Interestingly, after her son was born safely at home, he grew up to be a child who was fascinated with eggs. He would find and collect egg-shaped stones everywhere they traveled. He displayed his eggs in each room in the house. The field of energy that a person enters in the hypnotic state clearly does not have borders. Ginger's son evidently experienced the safety and light of the egg in his own fashion.

Being Born

Beyond conception and time in utero, birth experiences affect us significantly. It is a form of entanglement that's in our cellular memory but never consciously remembered. This is true for you, true for me. No exceptions. These few examples that follow illustrate what birth memories could look like.

During hypnotherapy Rose was imagining having assorted adventures with the help of a shaman when she became aware of a sharp pain at a point to the left and upward of her third eye.

I'm going through a dark passage. It's taking a long time. Something's pulling on my head.

I felt instinctively that Rose was reliving her birth and wondered if she'd had a forceps delivery. I asked her how she was feeling.

It's bewildering, annoying. I don't know what it is.

Next, she described how she was getting pulled into something shaped like a flower that felt softer. She could feel it in her neck.

I still don't know where I'm going and it's still pulling on my head. Now it's slippery and I'm going faster. There is dark blood. It's not scary. I don't know what it is but it's enveloping me.

This was a small segment of a much more complex journey that she later told me felt like she was in the birth canal. She was unaware of whether forceps had been involved in her birth. She did not experience a radical shift because of this fragment of birth memory because it was just a slice of a bigger issue she was focusing on in the session, but her experience beautifully illustrates the kind of memories our bodies hold.

Another client, Lindsay, was feeling grief over the loss of a relationship that had ended three months prior and she had difficulty letting go of her hope of restoring the relationship. She was feeling very uncertain about the future. She had no idea what was next for her. Her language was full of birth terms. For example, she told me she was *stuck*, but felt that something new was *opening up*, and she was starting to experience *flow*. I suggested she needed to go back in time, to experience freedom in the present. She regressed into a womb space and stayed there right up until the onset of labor.

I feel joy. I feel my heartbeat. It's a strong heartbeat. Quietness. It's my being—just quiet. I'm feeling aware throughout my body.

Lindsay was smiling happily. I could sense her contentment in utero. Then she began to be more agitated, her body twisting.

I'm not sure how I feel about this motion—it's new. I'm calm again. My head feels heavy. My head's uncomfortable. It's big and heavy. I want to pick it up and put it straight. It's such an effort.

Her breathing became more rapid, and she kept twisting her head.

I'm sure there would have been more cellular memory available, but Lindsay didn't need to revisit the whole labor process. She needed to get a body awareness that contentment, disruption, and a new cycle of being are a natural process. She skipped ahead to after her birth.

I'm seeing myself as a baby. I have slanted eyes—almond-shaped eyes. I'm a little old soul with hospital beads around my neck. I'm kind of frowning.

I asked Lindsay to hold the baby in her imagination and speak to her from the heart. Lindsay began to sob.

You're very precious and I love you. I'm going to take care of you.

I suggested that she talk to the baby about how to handle the unknown.

Always take time to listen, and no matter how painful it feels, follow what you hear.

I told Lindsay I suspected the baby self might need some reassurance that the pathway does open when least expected. When Lindsay spoke again to the infant, her words were filled with love and poetic reassurance.

Life is very beautiful. Always appreciate the time on this earth. Feel the nuances of the wind—the way the air caresses and the clouds float so carefree. There's so much richness in growth and experience. Stay open to that and be a part of this life as fully and as richly as you can.

You may wonder about the value of recalling your birth experience. It's inherently traumatic to make that birth passage, and it can affect you in surprising ways. But once this cellular information is in the open, it's possible to spin a new tale. A small but pivotal adjustment in what is being experienced can create a major shift in the person's life experience. Remember, time is an illusion, so you are making a change in the present.

Even though birth was just a detail in Rose's session, it seemed to bring her more peace to recall it. Lindsay found an understanding within herself that allowed her to begin moving forward with trust, despite not knowing the details of what lay ahead. Shifting Lisa's perception from numbness and disconnection from her mother to being enveloped by the love and delight of the Holy Mother allowed her to relax and open to her potential and own her shamanic gifts. Ginger not only felt safe enough to have a home birth, but she also passed that safety—and the love of eggs—to her son. Jody found a greater sense of wholeness and self-acceptance. Chloe was able to keep disrespectful men out of her life and find a kind husband. In each of these cases, disentangling themselves from their parents' emotions and their own uterine and birth experiences opened these women up to a freedom in the present that they had not been able to find previously.

Let yourself simply wonder if your own birth experience may be having an unresolved influence on you in the present. If you are resonating with this idea, you have a starting point to explore with a professional.

The Epic Story

I have found that most of us receive a core wound at an early age that shapes the story of our lives, creating prominent story potions. One person is given up for adoption; another loses a parent to divorce, death, prison, or addiction; a third experiences horrendous abuse; a fourth experiences a critical health challenge; a fifth has a parent or

71

sibling suffering with mental illness; and yet another has no home or becomes a refugee.

Others have less dramatic but still potent wounds. A parent's mobile career means a child never feels a sense of belonging in a neighborhood or school; dyslexia makes schooling hard and the student prone to the "I'm stupid" potion; a child grows up in a poor area where nobody's dreams survive; or a perfectionist parent is impossible to please. And sometimes, these circumstances are combined.

The Odyssey, The Lord of the Rings, Shogun, One Thousand and One Nights. These are just a few of the epics we have grown up reading. They are stories that either transcend a single life or a single episode. They seem bigger than life somehow. They involve perilous challenges and heroic people to look danger in the face. These tales are seared deeply into our psyches once we have read them. Yet they pale in significance to the epic story of our own lives.

Sydney was a successful, assertive woman who told me she didn't have any big traumas. She was frustrated that she hadn't been able to attract a healthy partner. Her companion of ten years was the nicest man she'd been with. He listened to her and shared his feelings. But he had bipolar disorder and couldn't keep a job. His health was poor, and he drank too much. He no longer contributed financially and spent most of his time in bed, and their sexual attraction had fizzled as she assumed a parental role. He surely had some story potions that were at work, but Sydney had a belief that she didn't belong and wasn't worthy. Her family had lived all over the world, her father was a perfectionist, and her talented mother also had bipolar disorder. She may not have had a world-class trauma to contend with, but she was coping with toxic story potions, nonetheless.

Whatever our wound, we move through life unconsciously re-creating or being drawn to situations that resemble our original experience, so that we have a chance to work through the unfinished emotional business and gain the maximum growth and learning. When I've been the client, I've found a tendency to think, "Oh, not this again! I've worked on this so many times."

Many clients have expressed the same frustration. It's true. We have been through this before. Again and again. But because this is the core of our personal epic, we need to revisit it repeatedly, each time gleaning something new, each time able to access more of our wholeness.

The nature of these wounds, especially the deepest traumas, is such that we try to make sense of them but fail to do so. There is no way a child can comprehend pain and horror. This is where souls and humanity collide. But the child still makes an attempt to find an explanation, clinging to toxic story potions such as "I am not worthy or not lovable," "It's all on my shoulders," "I'll never amount to anything," "I'm not safe," "Bad things that happen are my fault," or "I can lose everything in a heartbeat—and I will."

These story potions are like inner dragons that we come to earth to slay. The struggle to overcome them is the true hero's journey recounted in all the epic tales. If we succeed, we gain the holy grail—our own brilliance—which becomes a gift for all.

Even if we don't succeed, perhaps the battle has a value. We develop character as we put our energy in service of the greater good. I believe the possibility always exists that we can overcome these dragons, although the timing may not be what we hoped for. In the next pages you will read about one woman's epic story and the way she needed to approach her dragons from many angles. But you will also learn that she was entangled with her mother's guilt. The following three stories involve other people whose issues were tied to the trauma of their parents. None of these clients could fully release their own trauma without addressing the ancestral pain.

Lila's Dragons

Adopted from Vietnam as a toddler, Lila had a complicated connection with her mom and a physically abusive father. She had lost a beloved sister to addictions and had issues in relationships. Lila had a number of dragons to face. As it turned out, they all stemmed from adoption.

I know that some of you have been adopted and many of you have had addicts or abusive people in your lives. May you find mercy for yourself as you see how complex life can feel when you are faced with multiple challenges and the story potions that result, especially when the root of the trauma is hidden.

Lila came to me with insecurity issues. She had unresolved issues from her previous marriage. She told me that her wife had always made her feel like she wasn't good enough. Now she enjoyed great chemistry with her new partner, Tish, but didn't trust her. She wasn't confident that Tish really wanted to be with her. She wondered if Tish would go back to her husband or maybe find a new boyfriend. Despite Tish's reassurances, Lila didn't feel that Tish was committed. We used hypnotherapy to get to the root of Lila's insecurity, traveling directly to a very poignant image.

> I see a child standing on an old wooden chair by the window. She's three. She's wearing a dress and has chubby legs. She looks dirty. She's scared, worried, sad, because she's all alone. Somebody left her there in a big room. There's kid stuff in the big room. It seems murky and dirty. There are two others in the room, but they aren't kids. They're much older. They're wearing gowns—maybe robes? They're working.

As she focuses on the scene, Lila begins to identify with the little girl standing on the chair.

> I don't belong here. It's an orphanage.

Returning to looking at, rather than being, the child, Lila tells me the child is waiting for someone. Lila wants to talk to the child but is afraid to do so. She doesn't know what to say. She realizes that she's had an ongoing belief, stemming from this time, that she's not good enough and if she disappoints people, they will leave. This turned out to be the core story potion as Lila will come to understand. For now, I encourage Lila to talk to the little one and give her a sense of value. After some silence, she gathers her courage and allows pure wisdom to flow.

> *You have this ability to call forth what you want. You are super-powerful, but it goes away when you're afraid. You have to learn not to look to others but within. You weren't abandoned. You were chosen to be part of this situation to grow.*

Afterward, Lila felt amazing. However, she continued living in what seemed like unrelenting drama. Tish was an alcoholic and, as had been true with Lila's former wife, expected Lila to take care of her financially while she refused to work. Lila had tremendous creative energy and was always coming up with new ideas. These occupied her attention, and she'd tune out the discord of being used along with the lack of safety and affection she was feeling. Our work together examined various traumas of Lila's life.

One aspect of her trauma involved abuse by her father and the failure of her mom to protect her. In the present, Lila felt judged by her mom, and they hadn't talked in over six months. But in hypnotherapy, she remembered crawling into her mom's room and sleeping on the floor beside her bed, with a hand on her mom to feel comfort. I asked Lila to focus on her hand and that feeling of comfort. As she did, she went back further in time to being a baby in her birth mother's arms.

> *I can see her looking down at me. My brother is here in this space. Grandma's in the corner. I'm three. My mother is sitting in a wooden rocker,*

*holding me, and my brother is holding my hand. I feel love. My brother loves
me and wants to take care of me. My mother feels sad because she can't keep
me. She's telling me this, but I still feel so much love.*

Lila told me after the session that she'd seen herself in a small shack in
Vietnam. She told me her Vietnamese grandmother told people's for-
tunes. Her mother took in laundry. They were very poor. Her mother
had taken her to the orphanage, where she was looking out the window and watching. Her mother changed her mind and went back to
retrieve Lila.

After this experience, Lila began to feel more love for herself than she
had before and seemed more comfortable in her own skin.

In another session, we were examining her pattern of unreciprocated
caring with addicts in her life. Tish's alcoholism had gotten worse, and
she'd had two suicidal episodes. Lila was exhausted from the drama.
We went into hypnotherapy to explore the root of her enabling addicts.

Once again, Lila returned to that small village in Vietnam. She saw herself sitting on her mother's lap and wiping a tear off her mother's face.

*My mother is saying, "The only reason I'm giving you away and not
your brother is because he'll be able to take care of me and you won't."*

Even though her mother had repented and brought Lila home from
the orphanage, it was too late because the woman who would become
her mom had already seen her photo, made a deal with the orphanage,
and was on her way to adopt Lila. Her mother had just learned about
this arrangement and felt she had no choice. She needed to let Lila go
but felt terrible about it.

Lila realized that in every relationship, she would immediately
start taking care of her partners, above and beyond any reasonable

expectations, so they wouldn't abandon her. This scene has been on repeat, repeat, repeat.

Again, Lila spoke to her young self. This time, she started telling her about her higher purpose.

> *You're here to teach people how to trust themselves because God is a multidimensional power moving through you. Be led only by that.*

Then she turned to her young Vietnamese mother and shared words of wisdom and permission.

> *It's okay to let me go. You're doing this for me. It's my destiny.*

This was a turning point for Lila. She soon left Tish and all her drama.

We still had another piece of work to do around her adoptive mom. Lila told me she had written an angry letter to her mom, which she never sent. As she reflected on their connection, Lila said that her mom always told the story that all she remembered about the adoption was how much she wanted Lila. She sat with that story of being wanted.

> *I'm feeling a random rush of release. I'm letting go of all the diseased energy I've held toward my mom.*

Lila experienced light filling the room. As she looked at her mom through eyes of light, she felt her mom's love. Leaning into that, Lila felt adored.

Shortly after that session, for the first time ever, Lila's mom told her she was proud of her.

> *"My prayer for you every day has been that you will see that God is in you and that you are amazing, and God has a huge purpose for you," she told me.*

Two years later, Lila and I met again. She was happy to report that she now had a very close and loving relationship with her mom. They talked daily. Even more to her satisfaction, she was happily remarried.

You know, without the deep work we did together, I would never have been in a space where I was able to have a healthy, honest relationship.

Lila had moved back to her home state and had married a woman who adores her and takes care of her financially. Their relationship is creative, playful, and loving. Lila told me that being provided for has stirred up her control issues and her trust issues. She has had to face again the false belief that her worth was based on her providing for others. Now that she wasn't the breadwinner, did she still have value? She knew the true answer, but doubts were still rumbling around.

In this session, Lila wanted to explore more drama that Tish had caused by spreading rumors about Lila and taking over a business that Lila had created. While having no desire to defend herself, Lila was hurt that people with whom she thought she had strong bonds would believe Tish's lies. I led her into the tornado of pain that she was feeling, and she went right back to the three-year-old.

I'm not worth keeping.

This time, once she linked the current drama to this old story, she was easily able to hold the child and remind her she was loved.

We also explored her relationship with Tish, now from a distance. Lila had known for a long time that Tish was a replication of her relationship with her beloved sister, who was plagued by addiction most of her adult life and had died of an overdose. Lila had enabled both of them. She knew that. She'd felt guilty for enabling and guilty for failing to save her sister. But this time, she got a deeper awareness.

Lila realized she had hoped that by being the one who would never abandon her sister, she herself would never be abandoned. She felt great remorse for that, so we brought her sister into her consciousness. Not surprisingly, her sister held nothing against her. Lila realized her guilt with her sister overlaid a guilt she felt from her time leaving Vietnam.

Lila wondered if she felt guilty for not protecting her brother in Vietnam from the challenges of living in that situation. If she had been saved from a life of poverty, what about the brother left behind? Obviously, this was not the responsibility of a toddler, so I challenged Lila on this.

"Whose guilt is this, really?" I asked her.

Suddenly, Lila realized that as an empathic little girl, she'd taken on her Vietnamese mother's guilt at letting her child go in the hopes of a better life, as well as the guilt of her adoptive mom.

By then, Lila had learned more about the story of her mom coming to take her. Her mom revealed her memory of seeing Lila's brother, who looked so much like Lila that he could have been her twin, staring with big eyes. Her Vietnamese mother was holding Lila, and they both were crying. Her mom had gently, but firmly, pulled Lila from her arms and then hurried to the boat. She held her close, trying to comfort her. Meanwhile, her mom had lived with that hidden guilt that she had taken something (this child) that didn't belong to her just because she wanted a child so badly. Lila had internalized and lived with the guilt of both her mothers.

This deep story underlay the old conflict between Lila and her mom, and beneath her upset that Tish had taken a company that didn't belong to her. Lila felt a wave of energetic release at this big revelation. Because she had done the deep work already, this time she was gleaning another level of freedom from her epic story, and she was able to disentangle quickly.

Lila's story is a hero's journey, an epic saga that involved slaying inner dragons and finding her way to be able to live her purpose and abide in love and joy. As you read this, perhaps you are wondering about your own story. Be assured, we all are heroes. We all are living an epic story. Trust the light within you to guide you and enter bravely into your inner world. You will find the freedom you were born to enjoy.

Time Loops

Time is a slippery idea. We think it is linear, but it is not. It spirals endlessly, moves back and forth freely, and layers over itself. This means that we have opportunities at any moment for healing relationship hurts that came before, and we can heal on multiple levels at once.

Zoe also had an issue that seemed to be about the present but looped way back to her start in life. Zoe wanted help from within to let go fully of a man who she knew wasn't good for her. She had met him as she was getting out of a marriage where she felt stifled. They had one of those connections that get the juices running and the sparks flying. She felt compelled to pursue it even though she realized this relationship was never going anywhere. He was much younger and clearly had a lot of growing up to do before he'd be ready for a meaningful partnership. Zoe had four kids already, aged two to eight, and was now a single working mom. It took her a year to push him out of her nest, but when he decided he didn't even want to be friends, she was heartbroken. Her "not enough" story potion got activated.

As we began unpacking her heartbreak, Zoe confessed that she'd gotten pregnant almost as soon as they had gotten together. She had known he wasn't ready for fatherhood. The COVID-19 pandemic had just begun and there was no way of telling where that would lead. She worked in healthcare and already had that bunch of kids. She didn't have the bandwidth for another child, so Zoe made the choice to have an abortion. But as soon as she did it, this deeply spiritual woman felt she had made a huge mistake. She had packed that pain inside and only now, as her child would have been about two months old, was it coming fully out. She felt ashamed. She didn't know how to forgive herself.

In hypnotherapy, we went deeper and found the time loops that begged for healing. Her self-judgment had begun with her mother's disappointment in her. When I asked what she had done to disappoint her mother, Zoe traveled back to infancy. At two months of age, her father had left. In the wake of that event, her mother didn't really want to deal with a baby. It's easy to imagine that a woman with lots of postpartum emotions flowing, newly single with an infant, might not be thinking too clearly. But the baby didn't understand that. The story potions the baby absorbed were "I'm not good enough" and "I'm not worthy of love."

It really is possible to change this messaging by imagining the adult self who, in Zoe's case, was a very loving mother already, tending to her infant self and speaking words of love. As Zoe was doing this and allowing her baby self to soak in the caring and appreciation, I realized there was another time loop at work. She needed to speak to the child she had aborted, to reassure the little one that her choice was about the timing, not about the value of this being.

As she spoke to that unborn soul, Zoe felt the chains of judgment regarding her mother's choice letting go. Her mother had also been in a situation where it was hard to imagine nurturing a child. It had nothing to do with Zoe personally.

Although we didn't get into Zoe's history with her mother, I can well imagine that this difficult start led to a lifetime of challenge in their relationship. We could go back and patch over each place where hurt happened, but the most powerful step is to address it at the point where the misunderstanding began. Afterward, Zoe said she felt much freer.

Repairing that original hurtful impression opened the door for forgiveness for her mother, greater self-confidence and appreciation, and forgiveness for herself. It also liberated Zoe from her obsession with a partner who was long gone and still inappropriate. Once she could appreciate that her need for him to validate her worthiness had kept her tethered to him, she could snap that string.

No matter where or when the hurts have occurred or how many hurts are looped together, we have the ability to journey through time and space and start anew with a story and beliefs that serve us and allow us to be the blessing we came here to be.

Whose Voice Is It?

Sometimes trauma is interlaced with a relative's, as it was with Lila and Zoe, and sometimes it totally belongs to someone else in your lineage. That's what Pam discovered.

Just as Lila realized she carried her mother's guilt, Pam discovered that her pain belonged to her mother. She experienced it as her own because of cellular memory. Pam didn't know that when we started working. She was just very upset with herself. Once again, she had messed things up. Badly. She had unwittingly put others she cared about at risk. She had committed to something she knew wasn't right for her and then immediately started running around with her super-cape on, never pausing to listen for direction from within. This was a pattern in her life, and she was weary from it. Truly exhausted. And humiliated by the fallout.

As we went into the inner realm, Pam saw a witch with scraggly hair, clutching a vial of potions. Pam was scared. The witch seemed evil.

Dangerous. Screaming with a weird voice that had two sides—dark and light. The voice insisted Pam had superpowers and that she *must* use them constantly.

At first, Pam thought the witch was screaming at her. This sounded like the familiar voice in her head, always pushing her to do more. But she found herself thinking instead about her mother. She realized the witch was screaming at her mother. Most puzzling, Pam was seeing her mother as a girl of eight.

> *Something happened to her. It's like she was the bad seed. I think she had a mental breakdown and from that time she was different.*

Because Pam was present as an egg in her mother's ovary, she had access to a holographic knowledge of her mother's experience.

Pam continued to explore what may have happened. She sensed the setting was the big house where her mother's family had lived. She saw pieces of furniture like a working bathtub up in the attic and an old trunk with stuff belonging to her great-grandfather. She had the sense that the household was very rigid, and her grandmother, whose own mother had died early, seemed uncaring. Suddenly, Pam was hit with an insight.

> *My grandmother wanted my mother dead. She was jealous because her daughter was a daddy's girl.*

Her grandmother didn't try to kill her daughter physically, but her spirit was fair game. Her daughter couldn't do anything right. She had to improve her table manners to get to ride a bike. She never succeeded and never learned to ride. Her father was a minister and so she had to play a certain role. She was never good at that role. There was no single incident but rather a toxic environment that Pam's mother tried to escape with alcohol.

Somehow, just recognizing that this driving voice in her head was really in her mother's head gave Pam some breathing room. She voiced her desire.

I just want to be separate.

"Exhale consciously and imagine that you're breathing that voice into a big glass jar," I instructed. "Once it's all out, put a stopper in it."

It's scary to look at. It's angry and screaming.

I felt it was important for Pam to reclaim her power. Now that she could see herself as separate from the screaming, scary voice, she had the power of choice as to how she would relate to it.

One choice was fear. Pam could continue to see the voice in the jar as something that could hurt her. A more powerful choice was loving acceptance and forgiveness.

Forgiveness is not approving of a behavior. It is seeing beyond the behavior to the being caught in that expression and remembering that a deeper truth than our many trauma-based actions is the oneness from which we all emerge. The big bang released all that would ever be into time/space. We are truly all formed from that and so are kin on the deepest possible level.

There is a Hawaiian prayer known as Ho'oponopono. It is based on the idea that another's actions could be our own because we are all one. If we step into the other, we can speak powerful words of alignment that set us, and the other, free. These are the words of this powerful prayer:

I'm sorry. Please forgive me. Thank you. I love you.

I encouraged Pam to offer Ho'oponopono to her maternal lineage. As she did this, she pictured angels holding the jar and it dissolved in their hands. Pam sunk into a very deep place in her soul, imagining a new criterion for any undertaking she would accept: the spaciousness and freedom to be herself.

I checked in with Pam after this session. She was much quieter than she'd ever been and was, for the first time she could remember, not saying an immediate yes when asked to do something. Instead, she was taking time to discern if she really wanted to do it. She felt peaceful and curious about where she'd be led now that she was listening to her voice of wisdom instead of the voice of that inherited witch.

You undoubtedly have cellular memories, too. While some memories are positive, others are linked to destructive story potions that have been there from the beginning of time as you have known it. For now, I just encourage you to open your mind to the idea that whatever may plague you in your darkest times may not belong to you. Not only is it a story potion, it's a potion that may have been swallowed by someone else in your lineage. Even more importantly, let yourself imagine that you could feel free, peaceful, and empowered to be the person you were born to be and manifest the dreams that matter most to you. Your unconscious mind holds the keys to freeing you from any story potions that imprison you.

Discover Your Inner Archeologist

Sometimes life feels like an archeology dig where a rusted chamber pot can turn out to be a healing artifact. So much is beneath the ground of our awareness, and often there are layers and layers to what we will discover. On the surface, a complaint with our lives is an indicator that shows us where to begin digging. Under that surface layer, we may find sensations, emotions, images, or wisps of memory. If we focus carefully on these, they will lead us to discoveries that are buried beneath them, entangled in our subconscious minds. The treasure at the bottom layer is always a part of the self, a dirty specimen that feels unloved and worthless, contaminated by terrible story potions waiting to be transformed. As we take hold of this dusty relic in our imagination and tenderly scrape away the rust and scum and polish it with love and truth, this self will begin to shine. Just as we need to remove the dirt in order to polish the artifact of our soul, we have to separate our identity from the issues of our parents that have clung to us. The next story illustrates this process beautifully.

Debbie grew up in the South in a very poor family. Now in her sixties, she was dealing with an assortment of health challenges, plus insomnia, depression, and anxiety. Debbie felt stifled in her work and marriage, and she was overweight. The excavation we did together, like many archeological digs, required many sessions. We worked monthly for close to a year and she did lots of processing and took action in between our meetings. In one session, the image of God as an archeologist came up. Debbie found it very helpful to imagine the divine examining the pieces of her life tenderly and seeing the good in them even when they looked dingy and broken.

The dig started out with her bronchial symptoms. Underneath those, Debbie found sadness. She was sad about her relationship with her children. One was needy and the other was distant. She hadn't seen either in a while.

As Debbie stayed with the sadness, she went deeper and started remembering the sorrow of her parents. Her father was depressed; her mother was depressed and oppressed. They lived in a damp cinderblock garage with an old scrap wood box for an outhouse and cold running water. There was barely enough money for food, and her parents were always fighting. Debbie just wanted to get away from it all. She could not know at the time how entangled she already was with their emotions.

She began to focus on her parents' story potions. Her father never talked much. He had a low-paying job and was sad because his first wife had left him for another man. He'd swallowed the "not good enough" potion. Her mother was grieving because her second child (born just before Debbie) had died at birth. She'd swallowed the "unsafe" potion.

Her father coped with his sadness by numbing out. Her mother shut down in her own way. She didn't want another child because she was so afraid of losing it. Debbie was very aware, in the hypnotic state, that her mother had not wanted her. Her mother's fear of loss was far bigger than any desire for a child. Debbie was also aware of her own reluctance to be born into that energy.

Once born, Debbie quickly swallowed her parents' potions. So began her dance of trying to escape while her mother tried to keep her safe by confining her. They were playing out a drama that did not begin with Debbie. She was like an understudy who had stepped into a role created when her infant brother died.

As an adult, Debbie had traveled to many parts of the world, yet the specter of poverty and the feeling of being confined seemed to follow her because the potions were part of her.

On the day of this dig, I suggested Debbie think of poverty as an artifact. Immediately, that made it smaller instead of all-encompassing. She conceived of it as a chamber pot, old and rusted. She did not want to touch it, but she imagined the divine archeologist picking up the pot. It crumbled to pieces, and what she called "the nasty, dirty, rusted, bacteria-ridden fragments" fell to the ground. The archeologist gathered these bits in his hands and added his own energy to them. As he held them to his heart, he began to cry because he could feel all the pain they contained. Debbie tried to stop him from doing anything with those pieces, but he shook his head, smiled, and opened his hand, revealing gold dust that he let fly into the wind. She heard these words.

You are my precious child. Healing is your birthright. You just needed to know how to see.

When Debbie came in the following month, she'd been sleeping better, was more disciplined about getting on the treadmill, and was wearing fewer layers now that she felt more secure and had less to hide. She'd been able to connect with the archeologist to address issues as they came up, and she was focusing on building an art studio, a creative project that had her very excited.

Other issues arose each month as we dug deeper and deeper. At the end of our time working together, she was painting regularly and loving the work. Her medications had been radically reduced. She was sleeping eight hours a night without a sleeping pill. One of the most significant changes was that she was no longer taking on drama that belonged to other people. Today, a good ten years later, Debbie is happily making art for a living.

Each one of us is a magnificent dig just waiting to be explored. If we are willing to see ourselves as a treasure rather than a mess, we can start by connecting with our inner archeologist, that highest self vibrating within, just waiting for our attention. If we decide to follow the lead of the archeologist, we will find helpful diggers and be led, layer by layer, to the artifacts that make us unique treasures just waiting for a shine. This is how we transform our story potions from poisons to pure gold.

House of Secrets

Secrets and betrayal bounce from one generation to the next. Scarlett and Andy were unaware that their parents' hidden trauma was affecting their own relationship. Their ten-year marriage was a second for both, and they were very much in love. But in the past year they had been pulling away from each other, burdened financially, and busy with other friends and activities. This pattern of drifting away came to a head when Scarlett had an intuition to check Andy's phone. She found texts back and forth to another woman, Emily, who Andy had said was just one of a group of golf buddies. In fact, Andy and Emily had engaged in a brief affair during Andy's previous marriage.

When confronted, Andy assured Scarlett that even though Emily was in love with him, he had chosen Scarlett. He claimed he was a man of integrity and agreed to call Emily, in Scarlett's presence, to put an end to the emotional affair that was happening. Scarlett felt relieved when he made that call. A day later, Scarlett again felt the instinct to check his phone. She found a text warning Emily to expect a weird call and that he still loved her. Scarlett was livid. She went outside where Andy was practicing his golf swing and gave him back her wedding ring. He protested and apologized and said he'd take Emily's number off his phone, which he did right in front of her. Only later did she find out Emily's contact was still on his phone, but now her name was listed as Pro Golf Shop.

Bereft, Scarlett came to see me. She felt like she was losing the love of her life and didn't know what to do. She wanted to try hypnotherapy to see if there was something in her own background that was influencing this situation with all the secrecy and betrayal. She discovered a strong influence. She was entangled with secrets from her childhood and so was her husband. This is what came out. Pay attention to how often she chooses to keep a secret from her mom.

Scarlett began talking in a soft, childish voice.

> *I'm in a shed next to our house. We lived in a rural part of Oklahoma. My daddy used the shed for skinning deer. There's a little old couple who live next door. I call the woman my Cookie Gramma. The man next door is in the shed cutting a deer. I'm watching in horror. He sets me on the bench and pulls my pants down and puts his finger in me.*

I'm petrified. Frozen. He tells me not to tell my mommy. I'm five or six. I ran over to his house and told my Cookie Gramma what happened. She said, "Never go in that shed again."

Now I'm in the bathroom. I'm in the tub with Daddy. He's taking his penis out and rubbing it against my clitoris, in and out and up and down. I'm scared and confused. Why would he do that? I keep quiet. I don't tell my mommy.

Later, Scarlett told me that many years ago, she'd had a wisp of a memory of this bathtub scene. She thought she had dealt with it. Often clients feel that they've already healed an issue because they faced it before. I find there are many layers to trauma, and we need to address them over time as we are ready. The experience Scarlett was having during this hypnotherapy session was far more intense than what she reported about the earlier memory where she had seen the event but had not felt the emotional intensity of it.

During our session, Scarlett's memories continued to pour forth.

Now I'm in my house. There's a strange man peeping through the window. I'm seven. He didn't stay long, but he scared me. He had mean eyes.

She paused again for a while before the next memory emerged.

Oh, no. There's more. I'm in a camper. My dad's been out drinking. I'm not more than seven. He comes in the dark and wakes me. He's rubbing his hands over my chest and poking his finger in me. I get away and sleep in the camper booth. He passes out. I don't tell my mom.

After these memories, Scarlett is sobbing. She speaks to her younger self directly.

Why didn't you tell your mommy?

The child responds in Scarlett's imagination.

I was afraid to upset Mommy. Then she'd leave him, and I wouldn't have a daddy, and I'd be different from all the other kids. Broken.

Scarlett realized she had taken in that "broken" story potion anyway. She felt defective because of the molestation, plus her mother had ultimately divorced her father. Because Scarlett thought she was broken, deep down, it made sense that her husband, Andy, wouldn't want to stay with her. Scarlett realized her child self still needed to feel safe.

I got you, little girl.

Scarlett thought about the correlation between these past experiences and what she was going through with Andy in the present. Her strategies had been to keep quiet and not rock the boat—then and now—until she found his texts and began speaking up. She saw how she had been afraid to set clear boundaries. She would put up with Andy's protests and minimizing of what he was doing and would turn quickly to forgiveness and love. Then, inevitably, she'd get hurt again.

We slipped back into an expansive and peaceful blue-sky image. I reminded Scarlett, while she was in a suggestible state, that secrets make us sick, and truth leads us to safety. "Nothing anyone does impacts the love that you are," I told her.

Scarlett repeated aloud what she was realizing.

I am safe because I am love. The Divine within directs me to love and safety and forgiveness.

When we talked about this experience, she realized that she and her husband had both grown up in a house of secrets. His father was a closeted gay man who snuck around having affairs. This was now public information in the family, but Andy had never had therapy. He didn't know if he or his brother had been molested. Later, after Scarlett had this session, she and Andy started couples therapy, and Andy agreed to therapy on his own. He came to recognize the legacy of living in a house of secrets and how it had affected his marriage.

It's key to understand that entanglement is happening even when a conflict seems to be a straightforward transgression by someone else. Maybe it's straightforward. But the story potions that we and others involved have swallowed cloud our perceptions. The legacy of the past is not behind us. Realizing that past and present are entangled is crucial to disentangling and making space for the life you desire.

Ultimately, Emily would be completely out of the picture and Scarlett and Andy would enjoy a much closer and more treasured marriage than what they'd experienced before. But there were more secrets to be revealed before this happened.

Scarlett came back to see me several months after this first session. She told me that Andy was working hard to demonstrate his love, being very accountable and compassionate about her ongoing trust issues. But Scarlett was exhausted by her inner detective who seemed to be on the clock day and night.

In our session, Scarlett found her inner child curled up in a ball, trembling with fear. Scarlett picked up the little girl and held her close. As she did, a memory of her stepfather came to her. He was holding her on his lap, sitting in the rocking chair. This was when she was fifteen and was experiencing a broken heart with her first boyfriend.

He's trying to comfort me, but it feels creepy. He's fondling my boobs.

She was quiet after this revelation. She later told me she had always thought her stepdad was a good guy.

The next memories had to do with different boyfriends she'd had. One slapped her when she came home from the grocery store, and she broke up with him right away. Another boyfriend was killed by a drunk driver, and she saw herself lying on his tombstone and sobbing. She noticed a heavy sensation in her chest. Then she remembered running through a hotel looking for some guy she'd picked up at a bar. She was feeling rejected and that heavy feeling in her chest had moved to her stomach. I told her to focus on these sensations, hoping that whatever was hidden in them would come to the surface, but it didn't seem eager to come out.

"Scarlett, you need to claim authority over whatever is hiding."

I choose freedom. I can handle it.

Now the heavy sensation moved to Scarlett's knees.

Come forth now.

As she made her demand, the heavy feeling moved again. Her knees felt lighter but now her ankles and feet were heavy. Finally, the memory began to peek out.

> *I have an old memory of having sex with Elvis Presley. Maybe it was a dream, but it's always felt like a memory even though that doesn't make sense at all. Elvis was much older by the time I was born. He didn't live in Oklahoma, and we wouldn't have had the money to go to Memphis. But now I'm realizing it wasn't Elvis at all. It was my dad.*
>
> *I'm in my little house in Turley, Oklahoma. I'm about five years old. I think there is penetration happening. I know I was a virgin when I first*

had sex in high school, so maybe this memory isn't accurate. Ewww. He's dry humping me. He seems very abusive. Manic. Dry-humping craziness.

"Can you smell alcohol?" I asked.

I already knew that her father was an alcoholic.

Kind of, yeah. Like a drunk dude. I haven't seen this before. He turned me over and held my arms while he dry humped my butt.

She was silent for a long time as if her brain were on fire and she couldn't douse the flames.

"What's going on?" I nudged gently.

Scarlett replied with what sounded like a stream of consciousness.

Help, help, Mommy, Mommy. Drunk abuse. Limp dick shit. It's basically a dry rape. Roll over. Roll over. I roll over to the other side of the bed and curl up, and he passes out. I slide off the bed and crawl under it. My heart is pounding. I crawl out and run. I jump into bed with my mama. I'm crying. "What's wrong?" Mommy is asking me, but I can't talk. Mommy puts her arms around me.

There's another long pause, and then the scene moves forward in time.

Dad is leaving. The twins are so little. They're in the playpen and don't see him go. I'm standing at the screen door. Before, when I remembered this, I was so sad. Not now. This time I'm thinking, "See you later, motherfucker." Maybe Mommy figured it out.

I've skimmed over the details all my life. That's really why he left. What he did to me. I turned it into a dream of having sex with Elvis

Presley. That's when I got addicted to sadness, so I wouldn't have to feel angry. I see myself pulling my hair and crying and rocking. I'm scooping the little one up. She's safe with me, no matter what. I'm safe with me. I literally don't need anyone except my connection with God. I'll always be safe.

I realize now how emotionally unstable I can be. I've put too much energy into loving others instead of myself. But once I see my part, I'm accountable and honorable—a cool person. I'm proud of myself. The child in me wanted to run away, but I said, "No. You're a mature woman now. Look at it." I have codependency issues I really didn't see before. They show up with my grown kids as well as with Andy. I'm deeply affected by what others think or do.

Again, Scarlett was quiet as she processed all this awareness.

I still feel a little worried. Andy has his own issues and I'm not his teacher. I need to stay on my side. I need to be there to love and support him through his healing and know that we have the same intention for a healthy, loving, forever relationship.

To close the loop, I suggested that Scarlett thank her inner detective for her work and let her know the case is closed. Then I suggested something that is often very powerful with overactive protective parts.

"What if you give the detective a promotion so she won't be tempted to go back to watching for issues with Andy?"

Scarlett was intrigued.

What could I promote her to do?

"Why don't you make her a money coach? Put her in charge of keeping you on track with your finances and business."

Scarlett loved the idea.

That's perfect. She's diligent. She'll make sure I am focused on accomplishing the things I need to do to make money.

I ran into Scarlett six months later at a downtown event. She came running up to me and gave me a big hug. "You saved me!" she exclaimed.

Scarlett told me that things were really good with Andy. She'd even been able to be calm and friendly at a big golf event when Emily had made an appearance. She noticed that without her anxiety in the mix, there didn't seem to be any energy to hold Emily in the picture and Emily had wandered off after a brief exchange. Andy was continuing his therapy and learning so much. Scarlett now focused her attention on growing her business instead of monitoring Andy's behavior. She felt free.

Scarlett's story illustrates the layered nature of trauma memories and the entanglements that keep us bound to our formative story potions. But once those memories are in the open and we have brought forth the antidote of love, we can experience real freedom. Even though the behavior of others can be troubling, it also can be a doorway to our liberation, if we are only willing to explore our upset with curiosity, courage, and compassion.

CHAPTER 4

Let's Get Weirder—Because We Can

The challenge with trauma is we experience its effects in our bodies and minds, but the causes may not originate there. In this chapter, I'm inviting you to answer a strange question: "What is me and when is now?" Hint. You won't find the answer using your physical senses. You are so much more than you seem.

Even without your fingerprints, you can find traces of your awareness in elements of the earth. You can also catch yourself walking around in different bodies at alternate times and places. This makes no sense from the material plane, but the Going Beyond the Physical treatment involves pulling consciousness from other realities to effect healing. According to indigenous wisdom, trees and rocks and rivers have voices, and you are not as distinct from them as you might think. If you can open yourself to the idea that you are kin with all that lives upon the earth, you may be surprised at the remedies available to you.

There are also teachings that indicate we are multidimensional beings who are living in several places and times at once. Others argue for more of a sequence of lives. Of course, still others argue that it's one life/person and we end up in heaven or hell. If the last option is your belief, you probably should skip this section because the fourth treatment definitely finds medicine hidden in other lifetimes.

In the stories that follow, the lines of identity will get quite blurry and the medicine very deep.

Meadow Mind

Past lives usually refer to human lives, though some feel they've been an animal. I once had a psychedelic glimpse of being a jaguar, and a girl in my grandson's class claims to identify as a fox, so maybe we have been animals. But until I met Steven, I hadn't encountered someone with a past life as part of the earth. Before I share his story, I want to remind you that reasoning will not help you understand the deep medicine of moving beyond the physical. You have to jettison that prefrontal cortex for now and leap into the boat of your imagination. This is Steven's story.

The trauma caused by Nazis wasn't limited to humans. Steven voiced the earth's trauma as he came to terms with his own. As you experience this story it may seem like it's all happening in his imagination. Or perhaps he had become the mouthpiece of the earth. Maybe he slipped dimensions and had become the earth. To me, it doesn't matter which is true. Steven's experience provided the shift he needed to release his personal trauma.

Steven came in for a past-life regression. Because he'd had a difficult childhood, he told me he was spiritually aware but also exhausted with life. His intention for the regression was to clear up whatever karma he had that would bring him back to another human incarnation. He wanted to be finished with earth school.

Steven believed he might have been a Nazi soldier and indeed we did travel back to a beautiful meadow in Germany. He turned out to have been a young boy of ten who took in the horrors of what the Germans had done. Evidently, he had also taken responsibility for those horrors because he was German.

That sense of responsibility may indeed have been the place from which his trauma grew, but the healing he received in the session was not typical. We did not address the boy or the Germans directly. Instead, he identified with the earth that had held the horrors and, *as the earth*, he went through phases of resistance, acceptance, forgiveness, and peace. I'm going to share this part of the session as he shared it with me. There were long pauses between each section of his awareness.

He began by seeing himself as the boy with his arms open wide to the beauty before him. He described a meadow ringed by mountains all around and a forest behind the meadow.

> *I'm trying to take the presence into me. I don't want to be alone in this beauty. I want to be part of it. I want to dissolve into it.*

He must have succeeded, because he experienced the soldiers from the meadow's perspective. For the rest of the session, different aspects of the earth were narrating.

> *There are men in uniforms. They're destroying the whole earth. My beauty is gone. It's gone. It's like the earth has been ripped up and folded over on itself. It's gone.*

His tone was incredibly sad. Empty and lost.

> *They tore me up. I can't go back. It's never going to be there.*

Steven pulled away from the desecrated meadow and took a higher view.

> *I'm the sky. I don't want to go back. The tops of the trees are beautiful. The meadow is smaller, encroached on by the forest. The souls of the soldiers are trapped and cannot move. I keep getting higher. I touch*

the souls with forgiveness. They arise like balloons. I release them all. I know not where they go but they are free and I'm happy.

The earth grows and heals. It becomes covered with foliage. Animals are filling in the spaces. The forest is full.

Steven seems to just shift his consciousness with ease. No longer taking a sky view, he is back to being part of the ground.

I'm not warm, but I am not cold. I fear the coldness. I feel a cool gentle wind blow over me. I'm earth and grass. I fear the wind will make me cold. Sunshine comes over the mountain, touching the top of me and I feel warmer on the front of me.

"See if you can allow the seasons to change while you remain conscious of them," I suggested.

I'm fine—even in snow. I'm completely covered now. I see nothing but darkness. I'm like a seed in the ground. My center pushes up through the ground like a beanstalk. I still feel the presence of being in the ground. I feel a large part of my body growing roots, growing out of the ground, like a large trunk of a tree, arising from the ground.

As he describes this growth, he begins to panic.

My awareness is upside down. I've grown very strong and tall, and my consciousness is at the base of the tree. I'm scared. I'm growing like a child standing on weak legs. I'm so tall. I'm so high. I'm the tallest thing in the forest but I have no foliage on my branches. I'm just very tall.

"Do you want foliage?"

I won't stand out in the forest if I have foliage.

"Why do you want to stand out?"

I want to be noticed.

It seemed like as soon as he paid attention to that ego desire, it dissolved.

The foliage is taking over. I've grown very bright. So many things amuse me—birds, butterflies, my leaves. I don't want to be more than the forest. I love holding life in me—birds and their nests, squirrels, and chipmunks. I absolutely love it. I know I'm part of the forest. I have life in me. That's all I care about. I am one with the forest.

Our leaves have all fallen—stripped to bare branches. You can't tell me apart from the others. I'm fine with that. I can grow my leaves back like all the others. I'm not as brilliant as I was. I'm the same as the forest.

I feel a slight sadness because I can't differentiate between me and the forest. I have no individuality anymore. It is what it is. I don't care anymore. I don't have care in me. I'm just part of the whole. Boring acceptance. No creativity. We are all the same.

From this place of non-attached being, he again shifted consciousness.

I'm being chopped down. I'm not upset. My leaves wither and die. My branches are bare. I'm too strong to rot. I grow hard. My bark starts to peel. My branches become stiff. I've rotted inside but my outside is still hard. I'm holding strong. I don't want the rot to take me back to the ground.

"When you were in the ground, you didn't want to leave it."

Now I don't want to be part of it.

That feeling seemed to pass quickly.

> *My branches are still hard but most of me has deteriorated. The very top of me has reached the meadow. The grass has grown where I've rotted. The meadow has expanded. My meadow is back. It's not as big as it was, but now I'm truly part of it.*

Steven subsequently felt very peaceful and surprised. Our deep minds are so wise. Preaching to Steven about forgiveness, the futility of resistance, or the benefit of going with the flow would all have been nonproductive. He, like all of us, needed to experience these qualities for himself. So his wise mind gave him a new story where he got to see himself as the forgiving, resilient, creative earth in its many forms. And the issue of completing earth school never came up.

The Great Tree

Do you ever wonder what makes a person feel safe? We could say that our environment is key to safety, and it certainly is a big factor. But I would argue that the main influence is our mind. This next story includes both a past life and an entanglement with the earth, made possible by the highly imaginative mind.

A coffin isn't a typical transport to safety and freedom, but for Angela it worked. She came in hoping for enlightenment and relief from a theme of betrayal she'd been experiencing repeatedly all her life, no matter what work she did to heal it—and she'd done a wide variety of therapies. Once we got into her inner world, the "something is wrong with me" and "unsafe" potions turned out to be at the root of her issues. Angela had already done significant inner-child work. We thought a past life might be a factor. It was. But the healing came from a mystical realm where she experienced herself entangled with a tree.

Initially, by slipping inside a tree, Angela traveled back in time to a medieval period when villagers were milling about the tree looking for her. She was a waif with no home or even a name. She was honest but they thought she was a bad seed.

I'm "a Joseph," like the Bible character who could use dreams to fore-tell the future. I see things. Mostly I see what's true about people—the lies they've told, their dishonest acts, the upstanding selves they present that mask their true intentions. People can feel that I see through them, and they don't like it.

The villagers succeeded in finding the waif and they locked her in a small room that was like a prison cell. After a long time, a heavyset woman prevailed on them to set the child free. It wasn't that she cared about the little waif or intended to take her in. She just thought it was wrong to imprison a child.

This unwanted child grew up like a tumbleweed, finally becoming a prostitute because that was the only means she could find to survive. The waif felt shame about this and eventually she contracted a venereal disease and died. Angela felt hopeless recalling all this. She wondered why she was even alive—then or now.

Here's where editing the story in the subconscious has transforming power. I suggested that Angela imagine the villagers placing her in a wooden coffin. But inside the coffin, I told her, she was still alive—her life force would never die. I prompted Angela to connect with the wood of the coffin and imagine it came from the tree she had sheltered safely inside. This was a story that bubbled up from within me. The voice was speaking. As she took in these powerful words, Angela began to feel safe.

I know that tree.

"It's the great mother, the tree of life," I explained.

Angela rested in that idea, and then she imagined herself having a new life *as* a tree.

> *I'm a happy tree. I'm thriving. I live long as a tree. My branches spread way out. People picnic under me. I'm a joy in their life—just being strong, being so much a part of the earth. I belong with the trees around me. I feel alive and animated, even though I'm a tree. I'm communing with the other trees and with the people, even though they don't all know I am. The descendants of the people who were so horrible to me—their children, and their children's children—are sitting under me and appreciating me.*

Angela had found her goodness and her worthiness as a tree, but it translated to her self-esteem and that brought her true hope and peace. It didn't matter that she was a human, not a tree, because through the power of imagination she had entangled herself with tree energy and from there she was able to experience herself as good.

Notice that safety was a key element in this story. What we believe and tell ourselves creates our emotions and our sense of security. A blanket or a teddy helps a child feel safe, although they have no innate properties of safety. Angela could have believed she was trapped in the coffin and freaked out. But she accepted the belief that she was being sheltered by the great mother tree and so she felt shielded and peaceful. If you struggle with safety issues, or lack of worth, here is another possible antidote. Imagine yourself entangled with something that represents security to you.

Past Lives

Soldiers, monks, and captives are just a few of the characters whose lifespan doesn't end with death. In the last two stories, both Steven and Angela experienced elements of what was likely their past lives, even though their healing antidote involved entanglement with nature.

Lives from long ago often influence our current experiences because we seem to be written into stories of bygone days, complete with characters and emotions. The story potions we take with us from the distant past can be treated in hypnotherapy, whether we go looking for them as Steven and Angela did, or they arise spontaneously.

Not everyone believes in past lives, and even among those who do, there is more than one theory about how they work. Hindus and Buddhists believe we continue to be born and reborn, evolving as we go, sometimes balancing out mistakes through experiences in a subsequent life that could be seen as punishment or a chance for understanding and compassion. Those raised in the West, who have been heavily influenced by Christianity, tend not to subscribe to the idea of past lives. However, many Christian leaders did believe in past lives until as late as the sixth century, when it was rejected as a Christian belief because reincarnation was seen as detracting from the medieval belief that resurrection meant the corporal body was being taken to heaven.

As we've already discussed, in the third dimension, we buy into the idea of time and space. Yet if time and space are illusions, what is the past? I have read explanations that we share soul experiences as a pod of beings. One soul's experience becomes everyone's experience. Sometimes people have had past life recollections that overlap chronologically, and this theory explains that anomaly. The teachings of Seth, a channeled entity from the Great Beyond, say every life is happening at once in multiple dimensions.

Past lives that we recall are rarely lives of the rich and famous. A memory of being someone notable from history is far more likely to be an archetypal story, so if something like that comes up for you, hold off on getting autographs. All the regressions I have done with folks involve memories of nameless servants, harlots, soldiers, merchants, farmers, orphans, healers, rulers, thieves, priests, and so forth. The benefit that comes with these stories is that we can see our blind spots, the story potions we have swallowed, in someone else's story. Once we see a blind spot and notice the harm it is causing ourselves and others, it becomes possible to make a change in the present, which is the point of hypnotherapy. We want to antidote harmful story potions so our brilliant light can shine in the here and now.

Whether you believe in reincarnation or not, think of the stories that emerge through hypnotherapy as healing stories, perhaps stories pulled from the collective consciousness, perhaps unique to you. What matters is not whether they are historically factual, but whether by identifying with them, you find insights that lead to healing for you.

Here's what I absolutely know to be true. People can tap into memories of other lives in detail. By dealing with issues of these other lives, they can heal their own. In this section, I will be sharing examples.

The first example I'll share did not come from hypnotherapy but from seeing the evidence with my own eyes. When my youngest daughter was four and developed enough fine motor coordination to be able to draw, she spontaneously began creating detailed scenes of totem poles, tee-pees, and native people while chanting in a style that sounded indigenous to me. One of her most dramatic pictures, which still hangs in my office, showed a large snake, with a peace pipe in its mouth, arched over a tee-pee. At that time, we did not have a television, and I had never chosen storybooks about Native American life, so she had no way of coming up with these images except from deep memory. She also dreamt of the snake, as well as a white wolf. These totems offered her protection.

Two years later, her first-grade class made a trip to the fire station. She went into such a panic, talking about how afraid she was of fire, that I had to escort her outside. I wondered where her fear of fire came from. By then, I had read the book *Children's Past Lives* by Carol Bowen, so I decided to experiment. I held her on my lap and said, "Tell me the story of when you were in a fire before."

Holly instantly began talking about being a little girl in a pink dress and there was a big chandelier with candles. It fell from the ceiling, a fire started, and she died. It was a simple story, but her fear of fire seemed to dissipate after that.

You're about to read just a few of the many past life recollections that have emerged over the years. Some memories are my own, and others belong to clients. As you read these stories, I encourage you to keep an open mind and consider the possibility that story potions affecting you, or people you care about, may not have originated in your present life.

The Treacherous Abbot

The first story I'll share is my own. This past life emerged at a time when my family was getting ready to move from Houston, where we'd been living for ten years, to Bend, Oregon. Although I'm a native East Coaster, I was very happy in Houston. I had a large community of friends, a good school for my daughters, and I was just starting to teach classes and have a following, which I was really excited about. But my Californian husband had always hated Houston and working in an office, and a field engineering position had just come up in Bend. It was fair for him to have a chance to do work he loved since he was the one supporting our family. I agreed to the move, but I was still unhappy about having to leave a community where I was so integrated and happy.

At that time, although I received regular chiropractic care, I suddenly started experiencing pain in my mid-back that was unresponsive to my chiropractor's treatment. So I went to see a healer who did something like hypnotherapy. As she worked on me, I returned to the nineteenth century in the Western United States.

I was a rancher with a wife and child. One day, three men came to my door and offered to buy my land, but I wouldn't sell. A few days later, my family and I were ambushed by these same men as we drove home from the market. They shot my wife and son fatally and beat me nearly to death with the butt of a rifle. The pain and rage I experienced while recalling this episode were intense.

After the beating, I awoke in an abbey. Having lost everything that mattered to me, I stayed on and became a monk. It was my job to tend the garden. The back pain from the beating never went away. Eventually, I lay dying in an alcove with an open door that was near the front entrance. Three men came to the door carrying a wounded man. The abbot took the body and handed them an envelope. Suddenly, a buried memory flashed back to consciousness. Those were the same three men who had ambushed me years earlier, and the same abbot who had paid them off for their villainy. I realized the abbot had wanted my land for the church and had hired these men to steal it when I refused to sell. All these years, I had served this church and this abbot. I began screaming and choking with impotent rage.

Although the woman who guided my journey suggested a new way to think about the experience, I wasn't ready to accept it. I don't remember her helping me make the connection between what was going on for me in the present and the details of the story. I also, unknown to her, had spent my first nine years as an adult in the convent. I'm pretty sure I've had numerous lives in church service of some form. There may have been multiple layers to this pain besides my frustration at having to leave a home I loved in the present.

The next morning, when I woke, my back was so sore I could barely drive. I felt every bump in the road as I took the girls to school, and I couldn't turn my neck enough to feel safe about merging on the busy freeways, so I stayed on back roads. I went to see my chiropractor, but he couldn't find anything physically wrong with my body, which was very confusing. I had a friend who did psychic energy work, so I went to see her next. Without even hearing the story, she detected massive past-life issues flooding through me. After several hours of intensive energy work, the pain in my back was all gone.

I had never had such an intense experience where my body was expressing the pain of my emotions. This was also my first past-life experience. I didn't have a way, at the time, to understand what had happened; I only knew I had moved through something powerful.

As I reflect on this episode, I suspect that my emotions about leaving Houston were stronger than I felt comfortable expressing. Because I believed it was the right and fair thing to do for my husband's sake, I couldn't give myself permission to feel angry about having to move, especially just as I was starting my own career. The part of me that felt victimized was relegated to a hidden room in my unconscious, where it seemed to have stirred up a fellow victim who was only too happy to be the spokesman for our collective sense of injustice and rage.

I like to think that if the seasoned channel of divine healing I am now had been working with my younger self, I might have been able to take her even deeper to the "not fair" and "I can't have what I need" story potions underneath these experiences. Those story potions have shown up throughout my life in other ways, most notably with my mother's sudden death when I was seven. An antidote at that point might have helped me understand earlier what I know to be true now. There is a principle of order at work that we can't always see at the moment. Even though I'd never heard of Bend, Oregon, at the time of my move, it has been my home for over thirty years and feels more like my place in the world than anywhere I've ever lived. My husband and I parted ways two years after our move, and he enjoyed a long career of field engineering jobs across the world while I chose to stay in Bend and have flourished here with both career and community. However, there was one more past life I had to address before I could begin to experience the success I've enjoyed in Bend. I had to reclaim power that I'd left behind in ancient Rome.

Who Is My Lord?

I don't have an opium addiction, but when I lost my power, I found out I'd had one before. This past-life memory emerged at a time when I had really gotten distracted following in the charismatic footsteps of a friend. I had abandoned my own fledgling business and gotten caught up in new and bigger ideas of a business I could do with her. I was all too ready to place her in the role of guru or lord, even though she wasn't asking for that. With the wisdom of hindsight, I realize I didn't have the confidence in my own light to develop gifts that I'd been given. The past-life memory helped me to see what I was doing. The "I'm not enough" story potion was certainly activated.

In this memory, I was a young lord of a Roman city-state. I had a friend named Claudius who seemed so much wiser than I. Increasingly, I listened to all his advice and ideas, and I leaned on him to make important decisions. At the same time, my visits to opium dens became more frequent. Ultimately, my life ended in an opium haze, and I died realizing I'd stopped living long before my last breath.

Once I had that past-life insight, I was able to make a dramatic halt in following my friend around as if she were the Pied Piper or the true lord of my life. I returned to cultivating my own business and trusting my own intuition. This was a straightforward memory and life adjustment. They are not all that easy, as you'll see in the next story.

Castle Horror

Love is not an option. That's what my client Maureen believed. Her experience with love was complex. She'd had a very abusive childhood, on so many levels. She was unsuccessful with most relationships and had decided she was not a candidate for romantic involvement. However, Maureen reached a point where she began longing for a partner and wondering what she had to sacrifice to have one. When she came for hypnotherapy with that specific question, she ended up remembering a very grisly past life. Was it actually a past memory or a metaphoric illustration of the horrors of her childhood? I don't think it's important. Recognizing the "love is not safe" story potion and having a way to express the depth of her pain is what mattered.

In this memory, she and her mother were taken to a castle after a group of men on horses had burned down their village and killed all the men. This was a horrible environment where rough men raped the women at will and the children were treated as servants until they were old enough for the same treatment as their mothers. There was more detail that I'll spare you, but Maureen's character died by slitting her wrists to escape. This certainly explained another layer of her aversion to a relationship with a man. Recalling it brought the wound out into the open, but she needed more.

I asked Maureen to travel to a memory of a loving relationship. In this memory, she is married and young and very much in love with her husband. Their sexual relationship feels wonderful to her. This is critical because Maureen herself could not imagine this possibility and yet inside the regression she was able to feel the joy and deliciousness of healthy love. Her husband died when he was still young, but she and I were able to travel into a dimension between lives and imagine them dancing together still. Returning to that lifetime, she saw herself as a sage old woman to whom villagers came to learn the secret of the love she'd known with her husband. This was her secret.

> *You have to open your heart. Let your hearts touch. Never be afraid.*
> *You can experience light and flow together. Trust each other and always*
> *be kind.*

Next, I had Maureen imagine the sage and her beloved in the light re-parenting Maureen. They touched her forehead, and a darkness came out of her—a vapor that dissolved in the air.

111

It leaves a space for light, a pink, glowing light that fills every space inside me. My eyes are open and shiny. I'm not crouched and huddled anymore. I see myself spinning around and happy.

Finally, I told Maureen to fast-forward to the present.

I see the chains breaking off my heart. My heart is cradled in loving, protective hands. I feel unafraid. My life is overflowing. I'm walking up a mountain by myself, but the earth is sparkly, and I see it differently. Somebody's waiting for me at the top. He reaches for my hand and says, "I've been waiting for you all your life—waiting for you to be free." We hold each other. We both look down to the valley below—the valley of our lives. We each had a different path and needed to live the way we lived.

Maureen described a vapor of love surrounding them and bells chiming—but not on earth. This was in heaven (which is code for expanded consciousness). She was filled with peace.

On earth as it is in heaven. I have my whole heart—not just half. It's not wounded but glowing and vibrant.

After this regression, she was able to have a relationship with a man to whom she'd been somewhat attracted. Although short-lived, it was her first adult romantic relationship. This was a significant start.

We didn't continue to work together, so I don't know what other steps Maureen took on her healing journey or whether she found another boyfriend. Her journey illustrates how story can both illuminate the depth of pain to be dealt with—inviting self-compassion—and offer a way to imagine another possibility.

Each person has their own timeline, over lifetimes, for the deep work of healing. Sometimes a session like this one is a taste of what is possible, a seed that will grow in the ground until it pokes through, ready to bloom. It's important, I believe, to respect the soul's timing and love ourselves and one another at whatever point we find ourselves.

Singing Crow

Stories heal. Remember the second treatment, Using Language of the Deep, involves speaking in story to reach the subconscious. The fourth treatment, Going Beyond the Physical, pulls the stories from other dimensions, including the "thin air" of imagination. Because the stories that come up in regressions reveal toxic story potions, they require antidotes and those don't have to be factual. The important element is that the new story is believable.

Betty had a heavy smoking addiction. She had begun using cigarettes as a teen and now, in her fifties, was eager to stop. She felt like the habit and the smell made others reject and avoid her. Although she knew about the peer pressure that had motivated her to take up cigarettes, she also had a strong suspicion that there was a past-life aspect to her smoking, and she was correct. Through hypnotherapy she shed that "unacceptable" story potion and found her value.

> *I lived in the United States during the nineteenth century. My name was David. I was a young mixed-race man and I followed my white father's ways. I worked as a ranch hand, herding other people's horses, but my heart hurt. I longed to follow my mother's indigenous ways but saw the white men ruling the land.*

It sounded like David had swallowed a story potion that convinced him that survival depended on being like the white men. "If I'm myself, I won't be acceptable. I won't survive." That was the potion. Betty continued to remember what happened in that lifetime.

One day, I was falsely accused of stealing horses and sentenced to hang. Dangling from the noose, in the last moments of life, gasping for air, I bitterly regretted my choice to ignore the call of my heart and follow the white man's ways just to survive. Now the white men were killing me anyway.

Betty lay in the chair choking while recalling this painful end. As she grew more peaceful, letting that lifetime go, I suggested a different story. This was an unusual experience for me. The story simply came through me. I told Betty this new tale as she lay in the receptive, hypnotic state.

"A young mixed-race man named David, who was also known as Crow Boy, grew up living in two worlds. From his father he learned to tame wild horses and whittle wood. On his mother's lap he learned stories of the native ways. His father taught the attitudes of white men, but Crow Boy didn't listen. His heart belonged to the traditional ways.

"When the boy reached the proper age, his father allowed the mother to take Crow Boy to her people for initiation. During the ceremony, he began to sing the songs of his tribe. When he sang, they felt the light of the stars and the heat of the earth in his music. The people were deeply moved. Even the chief began to cry. They gave him a new name: Singing Crow.

"Singing Crow and his mother returned to the ranch. Several years later, his father died. Singing Crow sold the property and brought his mother back to the land of their people, where they both made a new home. Singing Crow continued to heal and inspire his people through song. When his mother lay dying, he sang her across to the other side. She went with a smile of rapture on her face. Singing Crow lived a long and satisfied life."

Betty realized, as she choked with the noose around her neck, that smoking, and her chronic smoker's cough, kept the shame of that past life going. Once Betty accepted the new story and replaced shame with a sense of pride, she never smoked another cigarette. Her ability to walk completely away from addiction was a testament to the power of a past-life release to make space for new life in the present.

While Betty's story dealt with conflict between races, the next stories center on warfare.

I've Seen the Enemy...

Past-life regressions often involve warfare, maybe because the nature of war is filled with struggle and sudden death, leaving a soul with unfinished business. Surprisingly, the resolution opportunity shows up in personal relationships where we may be involved with the enemy or because we left a part of ourselves on the home front in a war and aren't available for a relationship.

Ben couldn't seem to commit fully to Carly. They'd been in a relationship for three years, with two breakups in that time. He questioned whether she was the person for him. Ben noticed that he was drawn to music with a theme of loss, and he wondered if he had a lost love in the past that he was holding onto. In hypnotherapy he returned to the American Revolution.

Ben found himself standing by a "ridiculously tall" waterfall in a forested area. He climbed down the cliff to a valley below and felt his emotions growing stronger. He took a little wooden boat and moved along the river, through the woods.

It feels swamp-like. Slightly haunted. Misty. I hear birds calling.

Then he realized he literally was traveling through a swamp in South Carolina. He recalled the story of the Swamp Fox and a group of local South Carolina rebels. He believed he was part of that team.

As Ben slipped into the memory, it seemed like an ordinary day. There was a fire crackling and crickets. He was milling around with others, traveling from one campsite to the next, checking in.

I'm not the leader, but close. I head up a special ops group. I feel young—maybe late teens. I think I'm male. I feel tenderness. Is this fight personal?

He suggested the men sleep for the night but then noticed that he felt a swell of grief.

Have I already lost her? It feels out of my control. Something happened. There was nothing I could do.

Ben was silent for a long time. I suggested he rewind to an earlier point where that "something" had happened.

I'm walking around on a crunchy surface—like burned embers. It's a small area. Not a battlefield. There's a fence. Nothing else is left.

Ben was feeling intense grief. I asked him to rewind a little more, before nothing was left. He went to a farmhouse.

There's a small plantation. I hear sounds of life. There's an outbuilding, hay, horses, livestock, a field with crops, an orchard with apples and pears. There are some slaves, but it's a good energy. They're happy. They have a good relationship with the owners.

Note that when these regressions happen, we return to the consciousness of the person at the time. The idea that slaves were happy with their situation and their owners jarred my modern consciousness and may not have resonated with Ben's either, but the character he had reverted to had that impression of the slaves.

I might work there. I spend a lot of my time there. They feel sort of like family. There's a father—he's the authority. He's concerned for his family but doesn't show it. There's a mother. She's quiet, loving, a little lost in her own world of grief or fear. She's afraid of the British.

There's a daughter—she's significant. We respect each other. She seems brave, wise, and courageous beyond her late teenage years. She's very strong in an inner way. Not closed. We were meant for each other.

The dad knows it's not just their farm that's at risk. A group of locals are organizing to fight. Even though the dad wanted me there to protect the farm, the greater good was to protect everyone.

The daughter is brave enough not to show me her fear. She knows I'm fighting for them. I had to go or feel like a coward. Despite her brave face, she intuitively knew the destruction and separation ahead.

I suggested that Ben imagine this lost love was also aware that love would hold them together over time, that her comforting presence was accessible to him now to soothe the young soldier who thought he'd failed, to help him see a bigger perspective and feel good about it.

After this regression, Ben was able to be more honest in his current relationship. While his girlfriend felt all they'd invested in the relationship would be lost if they split up, Ben realized there was a bigger picture—his life and happiness. It took him a few months, but he decided that something essential was missing from this coupling, and he found the courage to leave for good.

In past-life regressions, often the memories that arise are stories of victimhood at the hands of an enemy. In Ben's case, he lost his love at the hands of the British, in the interest of saving his country. These victim memories help us see, and hopefully get free of, our victim tendencies in the present. Ben had to step into his power to make an enlivening choice in his relationship.

However, for every victim in a story, there must be a villain—or at least an antagonist. It can be helpful to actively look for our villainous antecedents.

Candace was also having relationship struggles. In regression, she saw herself as a Mongolian soldier on a rampage, slaughtering peasants without thought or remorse. Just before she killed a small boy, she happened to look in his eyes. Candace recognized the soul of the husband she was currently so disgruntled with. This left a strong impression on Candace. Her perception of herself as the victim in the marriage came into question. If she had slaughtered him in another life, maybe there was more to her husband's resentment than she realized. This possibility led to her offering more compassion, and their relationship improved. Ultimately, her marriage also ended, but not before she had claimed her role in its demise.

It's fascinating to me how often there is a war theme in the background of relationships. Enmity was a huge factor in the next story, too, but the enmity wasn't between the couple.

Unending War

Warfare is widespread in our world, and has been for millennia, so it makes sense that there would be many people suffering trauma that's a carryover from a war experience. My client Dan was definitely one of those individuals.

Dan was at war in every aspect of his life, beyond anything that made sense in the present. Dan and his wife came to me because of marital conflict. Dan was temporarily out of work—another cause of marital tension. He spent his time glued to the TV, watching news about the invasion of Iraq. Their relationship was troubled enough but was compounded by a disagreement with his parents involving a lawsuit over property.

Dan was constantly tense, often explosive, and unreasonably controlling of everyone and everything. His wife, who had engaged in an affair but was trying to work things out with him, was dismayed because he was trying to keep her constantly under his watchful eye.

Dan's life seemed like a battlefield. At one point, he made a provocative statement.

Never let your enemy survive.

I was very curious about where that belief originated, and who the enemies he was trying to conquer might be. He was behaving like deadly foes were all around, yet they were certainly mostly in his own consciousness. Perhaps the enemies he wanted to kill had been long dead physically but living on, like vampires, sucking the joy and peace from his life. We decided to explore the issue of enemies through hypnotherapy.

I guided Dan to the River of Time and suggested that, out of the many bridges spanning the river, he choose one that seemed to call to him. He chose a bridge that had an Oriental look to it. Either Dan fell off the bridge or was pushed off. He wasn't sure. He got scared right away, to the point of panic and crying. Then he began to narrate what he was experiencing.

I'm around bamboo. I fell off the bridge into a really dark area. The bamboo is thick. There is a bit of smoky light, like a shadow light. It's daytime. I want to move, but I can't. There's something out there. I'm not sure what. My feet are in the water. I'm on an embankment. I'm wearing lightweight clothes. I'm wet and muddy.

There are people in front going through the shadows. Two of them. They're talking. I can understand some of what they're saying but they're mumbling. I'm waiting to see if there are more. I don't see any. I wonder if it's safe to come out.

Ow! My leg hurts below my knee. It's in the water. I don't want to make any sounds but there's a tear behind my knee. My arm hurts, too. Something went in through the front of my arm and didn't come out. There's not too much blood. I can still move. Where is everybody?

There are reeds over to the side. I'm moving toward them. No, it's very thick grass hanging over the bank. I think I'm okay in here. I can't see behind me. My leg is starting to hurt more. I'm barefooted.

"What happened to your shoes?" I asked.

I don't have any. I have short hair that sticks straight out—maybe a couple inches long.

"Where did you come from? Where is your home?"

This feels like Vietnam. I'm not an American. I come from a village nearby.

Dan went back to the village in his memory.

I see rice paddies and a small hut on the edge of the forest. It sits six feet off the ground, and it's made of thatch. I know people who live there but I don't think anyone's home.

Suddenly Dan panicked.

They are there—they're dead! Someone older is lying on the floor and somebody is outside next to the trees. They were running away but they

120

were shot. The old man inside is lying on his side with one arm pointed above his head. Blood is going out onto the steps toward the young woman lying by the tree.

Because they were from his village, Dan knew these people, and he was overcome with sorrow. He didn't know why anybody would shoot them.

I don't know if I'm safe either. I don't have any guns. I don't know if the enemy is still around. I see the road out of town and I'm running down it, leaving the scene behind me.

Although this memory is short to read, it was long in coming out. Dan was very immersed in this lifetime and was terrified throughout the session, so there were long pauses in his narrative. Even though we were not at a healing point, he couldn't do anymore, so I suggested his character find a safe place to rest until the next time.

When Dan returned the following week, he told me that he had stopped watching the news and felt more at ease. He realized he'd been constantly worrying about all the casualties. Dan had been in the Navy for four years, and then, after a four-year hiatus, returned as an Army Reserve Scout. Scouts act as the eyes and ears on the field, gathering information about enemy positions, vehicles, weapons, and activity. They determine whether to call for reinforcements and when to order a retreat. Dan said that his training taught him to keep pushing, to never slack off. "There's always more in you," the officers told the Scouts.

When we returned to hypnotherapy, at first Dan recalled the earlier scene, but quickly shifted to another scene in a different war.

My clothes are tan. I have a dark brown leather belt.

"Are you a soldier?" I asked.

I'm not sure. I remember being trained. There's a long barracks—a foot off the ground. There are lots of people. Wait, these aren't barracks—we're locked up! There are guard towers around us. We're all together, but we're not from the same country. Our clothes are different, but none of our clothes are very good.

I'm wearing a pair of shorts. I wear a British uniform. I'm British with brown hair. My hat looks like I sat on it forever. I'm wearing calf-high socks. My shoes are brown and worn out. My uniform is in pretty good shape compared with the others.

We are walking in formation. Somebody in front is telling us stuff, but I'm not paying attention. I'm looking at the people with my eyes. I can't turn my head because I'm supposed to be paying attention. I'm in a group with Americans, British, and Australians. The person talking to us is wearing jockey pants, polished brown boots, and a riding crop. He has a star on his hat. He's Oriental.

We're all really sick. The man in charge walked away and we're breaking ranks. I just sit down. We're allowed to walk around inside. I'm very hot. I'm not as sick as the rest of them. They're not doing good.

"Fast-forward to the next important scene," I directed.

I'm counting vehicles going in and out of the gates. They come down from the jungle. Something is happening. Everyone in the camp is agitated. The people guarding us are agitated.

The trucks have wooden boxes in them. I think they are taking the boxes away from the camp. They're in a hurry. More trucks are coming. They're in a hurry, too. They're leaving both gates open. There are still guards in the towers and by the gates. They have helmets on and wrapped cloth netting. I think they are Japanese. Now they're all leaving. We don't know what to do. They left the gates open but we're all too scared to go.

We're going to stay for a while—it's too hot to go. We'll leave at dusk. The British and American officers are arguing about tactics. They're making a couple of us mad. We walk up to them. The British officers outrank the Americans because there are more Brits. We don't want the Americans telling us what to do. They want to run everything.

Now they're splitting into two groups. They can't agree and won't stop arguing. None of us are in good enough shape to go far. The argument is about taking the easy path or the steep terrain. Someone suggests splitting into small groups.

It's been decided—five groups—two American and three British. There are just a few Australians. The ones who are sick will take the easy route. We don't have any water or food. I've got a bad feeling. I tell them we should stay. I say the Japanese wouldn't have left unless there were troops nearby and they were afraid the camp would get bombed. Those wooden boxes must have been filled with mortars.

There's a lot of scrambling. We're disorganized. We can't get all the sick out and everybody's scared. I'm directing people. "Put the real sick in the tree line. Let's go now." We're starting to work together.

Now there are only a few of us left in the camp. We're checking the barracks to be sure everyone's out. We're so scared. We didn't get a head count before we left.

It's the next day. We didn't leave yet. We stayed in the tree line with the very sick men. Then an American sergeant showed up. He came down from the hill and is talking to our commander. He says the Americans are gonna send trucks and take us. "Actually," the commander laughs, trying to give us the bad news the easy way, "only the sick get to ride in the trucks. You have to walk out."

We're walking in a different direction—through a valley to a beachhead. It's supposed to be safe here. They're not going to arm us because there aren't enough weapons. They just have a few to spare. We are getting water—one or two canteens. We're not getting much food. It's all in cans and none of us have a can opener.

Now we're split up and moving again. I'm taking the second group— about twenty soldiers. We're each given a compass but no maps. Some of our group can stand, but they are really sick. They're not going to make it.

We're following a stream. I only have five guys left now. The others didn't come. I don't know why. We've lost sight of the first group. A couple of guys are really scared. They want to go left and circle around, but we were told to go straight.

It's dark here. Suddenly it's quiet. Get down! Something's wrong. The third group is still behind us. I don't know where the first group went. There are no birds, no sounds. I'm gonna wait for the third group to catch up. They don't know why we stopped. The jungle is getting thicker. We make it to the edge of the beach, but there are no signs of the first group.

Someone is running down the beach. He's screaming hysterically. He says they're all dead—they were butchered. I'm looking at the massacre now. There aren't even body parts to take back. It's a small area. I'm confused. I don't know what to do. We've gotta move. We've gotta move back next to where these guys were killed but not so close the enemy can see us. This isn't safe.

My chest hurts. Sorry. My mouth's really dry.

Dan starts making choking noises and then he dies.

I encourage Dan to linger above his body. From that perspective, he can see that something hit him in the chest. The others made it. His soul was having trouble finding the light, but then he did, and everything was okay.

My lesson was that I can't control everything.

Dan came out of the hypnotic state abruptly, squirming, hot and sweaty, and he ran to the nearby bathroom and threw up.

These very dramatic past-life memories were only a portion of the counseling that we did, but they helped Dan and his wife understand that the intensity of the stress he had been under was not just coming from the present.

Even though we didn't create an antidote to this unsafe, out-of-control story potion, just releasing it through the recounting—and even the vomiting—created more space and ease for Dan. It became apparent that his statement "Never let your enemy survive" referred not only to his inability to control what his enemies had done to him in the past but that he had carried that fear forward and was living as if the enemy was still hiding behind every bush.

Sometimes past-life memories are simply enriching, sometimes they give us new insights, but in situations like Dan's, they can offer an explanation and an escape route from unknown trauma when nothing else seems to work.

Ultimately, stories of the past are primarily just that. Stories. Stories full of potions. But because they allow us to step outside our own skins and narratives and excuses, they offer us a different perspective and that can provide the antidote we need for true healing and freedom.

When the Wheel Falls Off

The next story has nothing to do with war but it illustrates how we can find resources in our past lives.

Ed's work life had blown up dramatically and suddenly. A lying co-worker convinced the boss that Ed had done something heinous. He was fired and now was having trouble finding a job. He was closing in on retirement age but didn't have enough savings to retire. Word had traveled in his industry, and he didn't think people would give him another chance. He felt victimized and defeated. He had trouble thinking about anything except what he'd lost. He was definitely having trouble loving himself.

Ed had spent plenty of time in our sessions expressing his grief. He had every right to his feelings. He had been wronged. The challenge for him was that as long as he remained stuck emotionally, he was unlikely to come up with a winning idea for work. Also, he was energetically an unattractive candidate for any job because he was radiating misery and lack of confidence. I started to wonder if there could be a past-life element that was trapping him, so I led the way to the inner realm, but I didn't say anything to him about exploring past lives. I just remained curious.

I'm aware of low-lying hills. The colors are like an old painting that's faded with the years—muted green colors. There's a stream that is only a trickle.

"What happens if you step into the painting?" I asked.

The colors seem to get brighter, and the stream has more water. There's a horse drinking out of the creek. There seems to be a carriage.

"Touch the horse. What do you notice?"

It feels content. I also notice people from the carriage are cooling their feet in the water. I know them. I'm not sure how.

"Rewind the scene a bit and see yourself sitting in the carriage. Where are you sitting?"

I'm the driver. Someone is sitting beside me, and two more are in the carriage. I think it's my family. My wife and kids. A girl and a boy. They're around ten or twelve years old. It's a warm, mostly sunny day. A little wind. We're having a fun day out riding. Everyone is happy, joking around.

"Fast-forward the scene. Does anything happen?"

On the way home, a wheel comes off the carriage. I'm trying to fix it by using a piece of wood for leverage. It's not working, but I'm not upset. We're all just taking it lightly. These things happen. I'll figure something out. We'll get the carriage going again.

"Notice that this man is confident, competent, connected, and good-humored. He's part of your psyche. What would happen if you let him take over this challenge with your work situation?"

I continued to talk to Ed in the hypnotic state, suggesting that he was confident, competent, connected, good-humored, and able to fix this situation. Even though he didn't yet know how he would do that, he could trust that he would fix it.

Afterward, Ed felt positive. He could imagine having a better attitude and finding a solution even though he still wasn't sure what it could be. We talked about memories of times that seemingly miraculous, unexpected results had come about in his life. Such memories serve as touchstones to help us remember that surprising and fortunate outcomes are possible even when situations seem grim. When we focus on such possibilities, we open ourselves to being pleasantly surprised. I encouraged Ed to keep imagining himself as a man undaunted by the wheel falling off the carriage of his life, knowing he'd find a solution.

When we began this session, I had been wondering if there was trauma in another life. But instead of turning to a past incident that had unraveled him, Ed dipped into the treasure chest of experience to find a memory that served as medicine to propel him forward. In most every life we master certain useful qualities. Hypnotherapy can help us remember and realign with those dormant traits that can help us in the present.

CHAPTER 5

Healing Traumatic Disconnection

Trauma creates a barrier between our bodies and souls. Before trauma, we have access to a healing force. Just like a cut to our skin quickly seals over and is soon forgotten, we have an innate ability to heal, but most of us are disconnected from that power. In many cases, specific traumas have caused diseases or unhealthy conditions. In other circumstances, the cause isn't trauma based but we are still disconnected from our innate healing force due to the way we have been trained in our culture to see healing as a separate force. Disconnection from the love-light we are can be the root of what ails us, body and soul. In that sense, the trauma is societal rather than personal and affects us deeply. But the first treatment, Embracing Yourself, reminds us that we are not a symptom or a disease. We are love-light, whole and complete. In the hypnotherapy journey, we are embracing ourselves and remembering that wholeness.

Physical Healing

By the time we have symptoms, most of us have trouble imagining being healed without a long process and medical intervention. This inability to imagine such an outcome is a societal trauma that most of us share. There have been other times and cultures where complete "miraculous" healings were common. In the late nineteenth century in the United States, there was a wave of healing happening. Part of the Transcendentalist movement and the New Thought movement, people were being cured of terminal disease and physical conditions that seemed irreparable. They were doing this by changing their minds. They were embracing their identity as divine emanations and using the language of the deep to create healing results.

I know healing is possible. Because I'm also a product of a society that puts its faith in mainstream medical solutions rather than possibilities from beyond the physical dimension, I can't pretend to have mastered the consciousness that makes healing inevitable. So I never promise that hypnotherapy will heal a person physically. Yet I have seen powerful transformations in a person's body. Usually there is an emotional or spiritual component involved in what ails the person, and this is particularly malleable to the treatments hypnotherapy offers.

Dr. Joe Dispenza has also popularized the idea that physical healing can be achieved by a change in consciousness. The remarkable stories of people who attend his healing retreats prove the correlation between mind and body. In the following stories, which vary in length and detail, you will read examples of physical healing through consciousness change, which were accomplished using hypnotherapy.

Crowded Again

Ann was eighty when she came to see me at the recommendation of her doctor. Ann was desperate because her shoulders hurt badly, and none of the medical interventions she'd tried were helping. As we focused on the pain in her shoulders, she traveled through the pain back to her childhood with a controlling father. She felt like there was no room for her to be herself.

Then she saw her present situation with her husband, whom she had married when she was twenty. In the ten years since he'd retired, he had been hanging around the house most days and had been increasingly vocal with suggestions and instructions about how things should be done around the house. Ann realized the present situation was exactly the way she had felt with her father as a girl. She had no space to be. These cramped emotional quarters were being expressed in her shoulders.

Once she realized what was going on, Ann found the courage to tell her husband that she needed a room of her own to spread out and make art. He was more than willing to help her reclaim a room in the house for that purpose. Not surprisingly, her shoulder pain went away.

Get Off the Carnival Ride

Those who've had morning sickness will understand viscerally the feeling of being on a carnival ride that won't stop. Adrienne came to see me one cold January day when she was twenty-six weeks pregnant, looking very pale and weak. She had been in the hospital for two weeks undergoing a variety of procedures to stop her nausea and frequent, daily vomiting. So far, nothing had worked. Her midwife suggested she give hypnotherapy a try.

Some of Adrienne's family members had experienced positive results with hypnotherapy, so Adrienne was willing and hopeful it would work for her, too. It turns out she was highly suggestible, which was fortunate, given the urgency of her situation. While it's possible there was a medical cause the hospital staff hadn't found, it was far more likely the cause was emotional, based on some belief held in Adrienne's subconscious mind. Either way, the most pressing issue was to stop the vomiting.

I didn't do an elaborate induction. Instead, I simply asked Adrienne to choose an image that described how she was currently feeling. She said she felt like she was on a carnival ride that kept spinning. I wanted Adrienne to shift from being at the mercy of this sensation and image to recognizing herself as the powerful creator of her experience. I asked her what she wanted to create instead. Her answer was immediate. "I want the ride to stop so I can get off." I encouraged her to imagine exactly that.

Adrienne pictured herself getting the attendant's attention and having him slow the ride to a stop. Then she visualized getting off the ride and taking a moment to steady her legs again. This whole process only took a couple of minutes. While picturing this scene, Adrienne became visibly calmer. "I can breathe again," she said. We magnified that feeling of being able to breathe with a spacious image of clouds. After that, the nausea was completely gone. We were all delighted—and astonished—by the change.

Adrienne was able to maintain the state of calm for a couple of weeks, but then I received a call from the midwife who had referred her to me originally. She told me that Adrienne had gone up to Alaska to visit friends and ended up back in the hospital for the same condition. Again, she was undergoing tests and procedures that were failing to make a difference. She was losing weight, and the hospital team thought they'd need to start intravenous feeding. I suspected she'd forgotten about steeping the imagery. That fifth treatment is not optional. It's essential, as Adrienne's situation was clearly demonstrating. I asked the midwife to remind Adrienne to get off the carnival ride. Adrienne began practicing right away, and once again, the vomiting stopped completely.

The next day I spoke with Adrienne by phone. We focused on the pain in her stomach that was left from all the vomiting and her inability to eat. This time she imagined a knot in her stomach that was preventing the food from getting through. She pictured her guardian angel untying the knot. As soon as she did this, she felt a desire to eat rice with butter and sugar for breakfast.

Adrienne also realized she needed to stop worrying. She was going to be a single mom and didn't have a family that she could lean on. It was understandable that such a situation would cause anxiety. But rather than focus on how to solve her circumstances, in the trance state, she described a painting in the sky that the rains washed away. She subsequently felt relieved. I assume the painting represented her worries. While she was hypnotized, I also suggested Adrienne see herself weighing more (a condition for being able to get out of the hospital) by imagining that the angel would step on the scale with her. She felt a lot better after this session and intended to go eat as soon as we hung up.

The report that I heard from her midwife two weeks later was that Adrienne had gained nine pounds and was out of the hospital. I didn't get another call, so I assume she had no more pregnancy complications. Since we didn't stay in touch, I don't know how her life went, but I do know that she had a taste of being the creator of her reality instead of the victim. I hope that was an experience that she remembered throughout her life, one that helped her get through hard times. That's certainly a power available to all of us if we claim it.

From Front-Page News to Back-Page Mention

Drifting in a boat, having a wolf companion, and holding a special stone were some of the medicinal salves Suzanne found during hypnotherapy. She did not receive a miracle cure, but she did experience transformation that brought her peace of mind, even amid painful medical conditions. I worked with Suzanne for a year altogether, with a nine-month pause. Her story illustrates the complexity of the healing journey and the distinction between a cure and recovering your wholeness.

When she first came to see me, Suzanne had physical pain that was out of control. She'd had two hip replacements, a ripped rotator cuff, bone spurs, and arthritis everywhere. She'd had jaw surgery for TMJ worsened by arthritis that required a year's recovery, and eighteen months later she had to have the surgery again. She'd had to stop working because the pain was too much. Her thyroid had been removed, so she had a compromised immune system. She had always been thin and active but had gained forty pounds in the past several years. She had tried both physical therapy and acupuncture, but the relief was minor. She had to resort to morphine when she got a headache. Her doctor told her they had run out of options. She'd have to learn to live with the pain. That's when she called me.

Suzanne told me she had a sweet life. She had two adorable little dachshunds, a devoted husband of over thirty years, a beautiful home, and she was comfortable financially. When her pain was a ten, suicide had crossed her mind, but she believed that was a selfish act, and she could never do it. She served as the family glue.

Suzanne came from a total jock family. She said that her very controlling mother had no patience for weakness or tears. As an adult, she realized her teenage mother had felt out of control and that led her to compensate by trying to keep a tight rein on her offspring.

I asked Suzanne about her spiritual beliefs. She didn't believe in God as an entity, but she did believe we went in and out of expression as energy and so live forever. Her practice was to lie and watch the cloud shapes and quiet her mind.

Suzanne described herself as a type A who used to keep her house immaculate but now was able to watch movies and ignore the dust. She had been a cheerleader in high school and still had that personality, cheering everyone else on. She had gone from being a waitress in high school to being the chief operations officer of a company.

Suzanne started experiencing pain in her thirties. At that point, she was able to manage it with biofeedback, Feldenkrais, and yoga. As her pain intensified over the years, she'd tried pretty much every treatment and practice—except being good to herself. She lived with the real and imagined voices of her mostly male doctors and people in general saying, "Are you sick again?" She believed they were implying she was seeking attention through all these medical conditions.

The first time I saw her, after the long intake, we did a short hypnotherapy journey to help her explore the house of her body, beginning with her feet. I asked her to breathe out a blessing of sunshine and acceptance to every part. I talked with her about the stories we tell ourselves.

The next visit, she had been reflecting on stories and told me the story of her birth. She had been due at the end of October but wasn't born until December 3. She came out butt first with the cord wrapped around her neck. She had to be taken from her eighteen-year-old mother right away. Breech births are difficult and often signal a life of struggle.

Suzanne said she used to be a dreamer, walking in the hills, loving her alone time. She was "touchy-feely," bringing home interesting rocks and pieces of wood. Her younger brother was very much like her, and they were quite close. Even though they were both touchy-feely, they were also both afraid of their emotions and she'd hang up the phone if she sensed tears coming from either of them. She told me her birth father was a jerk. Her evidence for that was that her mother told her he was. She didn't want to explain more, but she vaguely recalled being attached to him when she was small. Her stepdad came along when she was seven, and she adored him. He had died at fifty-eight from a life of cigarettes and alcohol.

This time, we repeated the breathing exercise as a breath transfusion, and then we went spelunking within. I asked Suzanne to imagine an opening in her pain.

> *The pain is really deep. The opening is bigger than I first thought. The air is cool and it's a good smell. I'm afraid to go further but I know I*

will. I always do. I can walk down here. The walls are cool. I'm moving slowly.

I asked her to imagine someone was with her to protect her and she described a gray wolf. That made her feel more assured. Suddenly, the hairs on her arms stood up as she approached a mossy covering. She began to cry. She wanted to touch the moss, but she was afraid of what it might be covering. She realized she had to go forward. I reminded her that the wolf was with her.

The fear Suzanne was feeling seemed to be lodged in her chest, so I also asked her to place her hand on her chest to comfort herself. This gave her some relief. As she calmed, Suzanne realized there was a memory hidden under that moss.

This sounds so trite, but I keep seeing my biological dad leaving. We loved him so much. I remember him leaving us at the house at the scheduled time even though our mother wasn't home. He went to the neighbor's house. I couldn't understand how he could be so close to us and want to talk to someone else. I pretended I hit my head and went over there crying. I needed a justification to go over. I felt like he dismissed me. I went home to my bedroom. I couldn't get why my dad didn't love me as much as I loved him.

I asked Suzanne to imagine holding her child self and allow the wolf to bring father energy.

It feels great. Even though the little girl is crying, at least she has someone. I think I'll be taking a lot better care of her.

When Suzanne returned the next week, she was feeling better generally and had spent a good bit of time with the little girl and the wolf.

This week our hypnotherapy journey involved a voyage to Avalon, a mystical, mythical British Isle. We were specifically hoping to find help for the inflammation in Suzanne's hands. The Isle of Avalon was known for its healers, so I invited Suzanne to find her personal healer and ask for relief from the pain in her hands. The healer gave her the gift of a large, smooth stone. It was a translucent white agate that filled her palm and was cool to the touch.

The healer told Suzanne this stone was to cool her inflammatory thoughts. She could also draw on its inner light to fill the dark spots inside Suzanne that had been damaged. The healer had wise and loving advice.

> *There's no need for you to hurt. Just feel the goodness inside you and let that fill you up and light the darkened corners with the real you. There's no reason for you to keep holding onto those hurts. Your life will be so much better if you let the stone show you the light and cool the inside of your heart and chest and throat. Let it help you to grow softer and not worry so much.*

Ten days later, Suzanne reported that her arthritis had been diagnosed as menopausal and so it would heal, which had given her hope. She'd been relaxing, meditating, and holding the little girl, which had been very helpful. She was feeling good, cleaning out clutter and fixing small appliances. She said the fear factor with her jaw had lifted and now served more like an alarm system, alerting her to pain she needed to attend to. She said the elimination of guilt for not "doing" was huge. Her jaw was no longer ruling her life. She was saying no when she felt like it and she wasn't staying in a funk. At this point Suzanne felt so much better that she took a break from hypnotherapy, knowing she could return as needed. That return happened nine months later.

When Suzanne came back, she was very depressed. The arthritis in her hand was worse. She'd had surgery to rebuild one of her thumbs as well as carpal tunnel surgery, during which a couple of nerves in her wrist got cut. As a result, she was now on a twenty-four-hour morphine drip, which also meant she could no longer drive. The drug left her drowsy but didn't eliminate the pain. Her jaw was a big problem again, too. She seemed disconsolate.

I'm fifty-three, and all I have to look forward to is a life of pain and more surgeries.

She'd been put on an antidepressant but still didn't want to go anywhere. She said she was hiding from her family, who were all worried about her. When they'd ask her how she was doing, she'd just cry. Suzanne's mother was being supportive but didn't know what to do when Suzanne broke down in tears.

Suzanne was still practicing with the white stone, and the wolf was still with her. She told me that I'd be amazed at how much wolf paraphernalia was in her house. I felt sad to see her in so much pain again.

I never would have thought I wouldn't be able to control something.

That was a light bulb moment for me. I asked her to consider if perhaps being in control was not a good thing. Her face registered shock. The idea seemed completely foreign to her.

You can't just go through life willy-nilly.

But then Suzanne began to reflect on her experience traveling. When she and her husband went on trips in the RV, he was all about the destination and she was about the journey. She loved to make spontaneous stops and explore surprising nooks and crannies. Suzanne began to consider the idea that control might be a teacher. This thought proved both startling and resonant.

Why am I trying to control my pain? It's controlling me. I hate when people tell me that I can control my pain because it's all in my head.

Why do I think I need to control something I can't control? Why am I afraid of it controlling me? Especially when I'm an "against the rules" kind of person. My need to control my illness is taking away both my planning and spontaneity.

Something profound was stirring in Suzanne's consciousness. We ended that session with a visualization of drifting in a boat on the ocean, being free of pain. She was able to imagine it and promised to practice steeping that drifting boat imagery.

A week later, the news was not good, with more dire medical developments. She'd found out she needed a root canal, a second new crown, and she had two cavities. Worse, she'd also been told she might have a clot in her lung so she needed a nuclear test on her heart to see why she couldn't breathe.

But she had practiced the boat visualization and had decided to join a pain management group I'd told her about. She'd been reflecting on control.

I've never been a go-with-the-flow kind of person, and yet I always thought of myself as a hippie free spirit.

We did another hypnotherapy session, continuing with the boat imagery, to practice letting go of control. I had her put down the oars and embrace the journey as her soul's longing for transformation. She told me after that she saw a butterfly emerging and this brought her to tears. She also realized during the session that things don't always turn out as we want, and maybe that's okay.

The following week, Suzanne had recognized that she'd made all her diagnoses the front-page news of her life and perhaps she needed to relegate them to back-page stories. As a result, she'd been focusing more on her nephews and nieces recently, and the joy they represented.

She'd found out that she had bronchitis, rather than a clot in her lungs, and that an inhaler and steroids were helpful. She was feeling better physically, which was helping her mentally.

We spent most of the session focusing on her relationship with her mother. Suzanne said her mom had worked in a man's world. She got the Realtor of the Year award in her city two years in a row. She was dynamic, attractive, and healthy and everyone loved her until they got close. Then they saw that she was always critical and complaining, saying horrible things about her friends. Suzanne had a scathing description of her mother.

> *She lies, is a hypocrite, is self-centered, uses people, has to be right, and her way is the only way.*

Suzanne used to be unable to say things to her mother but now she could.

> *My mom has made me sick to my stomach because she knows what buttons to push.*

As soon as the words came out of her mouth, she began to feel the buttons dissipating. Suzanne hadn't realized how personally she'd taken her mother's attitudes. Even though she may have been on the receiving end, these were her mother's issues, not hers. She was also startled to realize that all the sickness she'd endured could have been connected to internalizing her mother's treatment of her.

The next week was Suzanne's last session. She'd deeply taken in the message that she was not the one with the issues. It was her mother. She'd been able to spend five consecutive hours with her mother and it had gone well. She'd let things slide and they had had fun. Suzanne discovered that by ignoring comments or changing the subject, her mother would forget, and they'd just move on.

She'd also reflected on her mother's life and all the ways she had been a good mother. For example, using flashcards, she'd taught Suzanne to read and write cursive by the time she got to kindergarten. She'd painted murals on their walls, and their house was always clean. Suzanne could see that changing which story about her mom she focused on made a big difference in how she felt and how they got along.

Physically, the steroids were helping significantly, and pulmonary tests revealed she hadn't been getting enough oxygen at night, so with a new oxygen tank, she started sleeping through the night. Suzanne was, once again, feeling physically better even though her journey with pain was probably not over. But she had come to a point where she was committed to being good to herself and where she was allowing her feelings and her spontaneous whims to have free rein. She had somehow made it full circle to the dreamer child she'd described at the first session, who liked to wander among the hills and find cool stones and bits of wood.

As I reflect on Suzanne's journey, I think that letting go of control was the seismic shift for her. Perhaps the same would be helpful for all of us. Though we may not have to deal with the level of physical challenges Suzanne had, we all have circumstances we don't particularly like that we may believe should not be happening. Suzanne's story illustrates the connection between our thoughts and our body's expressions of those thoughts. By changing our minds, we can change our circumstances. Sometimes we can completely uproot the pain. Other times, as with Suzanne, we can live with it by letting it be what it is and placing it on our mental back page, while making the people we love and the gifts in our lives the stories we focus on.

Healing is a process rather than an outcome. Each journey is unique. Some are part of a longer series of transformations, and some journeys stand alone in their power. What I can say for sure is that there is a healing force inside of you as well as inside each of these clients whose stories I have shared. If you connect with that force, you will receive guidance that will accelerate your own restorative process in the best possible way. Healing isn't restricted to our bodies. The next stories are about soul connections where healing is needed to restore the fundamental relationship with a higher power.

Divine Disconnect and Reconnect

For many people, the connection to a higher power has been corrupted by story potions like "on my own," "can't trust," or "not safe." Reconnecting to that power is critical to finding healing and wholeness. In the following vignettes, you'll read about people who were terribly traumatized as children, resulting in a loss of divine connection.

Mark had an aunt he loved dearly. He was ten when she got cancer, and he prayed to God every day not to let her die. Evidently God didn't listen, or didn't care, because she died. As if that weren't bad enough, his beloved dog Sparky, who'd been around Mark's entire life, was poisoned by some dog-hater in the neighborhood. Sparky had been Mark's best friend, his one reliable source of unconditional love. With these two losses, Mark cut ties with God.

This is a common response to death. When my mother died, I was seven. I didn't cut God out of my life, but I stopped trusting, and I buried my hatred. I remember writing to my dad: "I hate God." I also remember scratching out those words so nobody would know, because that feeling was taboo. It was only as an adult, when my idea of God evolved, that I was able to align with the divine in a trusting way. In the single session I had with Mark, he recognized the buried bones of God but wasn't ready to resurrect that relationship yet.

Tara died at age three, when her mother tried to drown her in the tub, a memory that came through in hypnotherapy. As she remembered this incident, Tara could see bubbles but couldn't hear any sound under the water. She realized her child-self had given up and left her body.

Tara also remembered what happened after she left her body. There was light everywhere. She recalled all the people in the light and having the feeling that she belonged there. A woman in white touched her and spoke gently without words. For the first time, Tara felt loved and filled with joy. But then they told her she had work to do and so she couldn't stay. Tara felt betrayed. They didn't tell her what the job was. They said she'd have to discover it for herself. Tara was angry. She was too little. It wasn't fair. She closed her heart.

But now, in the session, Tara became aware that the woman in white was in her heart. She'd been there all along, trying to communicate, but Tara had been too angry to listen. Suddenly the channel was open again, and Tara began to feel a sense of love and joy flowing through her body.

Samantha grew up in a very unstable and unsafe environment. Her father was violent and even robbed a bank. The family lost everything. Her mother regularly tried to kill herself, and Samantha ended up being the caretaker. As a result, Samantha didn't trust anyone, but especially men. In hypnotherapy, she saw the house she had lived in when she was very young.

My feet are small. I'm wearing a nightgown and I'm standing in the doorway. I'm looking at a crib against the wall in the corner. It's mine but I'm too old for it. I was put in there a lot—every time I made a sound. My father didn't want to hear me. I didn't like it.

Since Samantha had told me she was very religious, I suggested she ask God to comfort the child. At that point she surprised herself as well as me. She started pushing God away and screaming.

Where were you? Why didn't you stop them?

Despite a professed devotion to God, Samantha's deep feelings were not aligned. Finding this unconscious resentment was fundamental to her being able to make a real connection with God.

Kelly came in feeling angry, bitter, powerless, and lacking purpose. They were only fifty-three, but their body had given out on them in so many ways. They felt broken and dead inside and just wanted life to be over. They were living on a small amount of money in a duplex shared with their dad, as well as an older sister who was an abusive alcoholic.

Despite being a highly educated person, Kelly was now isolated, lonely, and agoraphobic. They had rejected the religion of their youth and had no spiritual connection but remained terrified of hell. After two weeks of intensive treatments, Kelly turned a corner. They seemed softer and more appreciative and peaceful. They were even starting to feel a sense of purpose. Soon after that, Kelly made a powerful angelic connection that kept guiding them as their new story continued to unfold.

Gina and her little sisters were severely abused. As she was reliving one of the many scenes in hypnotherapy, I suggested she imagine getting help to get away from the abuser. As soon as I made this remark, a Native American woman showed up. Gina began to laugh with surprise and delight.

> *She's got long black hair, wings, and eagle claws on her feet. She's lying beside us. I feel real safe with her.*

After this, Gina began sleeping better. She found herself turning to the native mother for comfort on a regular basis. She felt much more peaceful. She told me that both of her paternal great-grandmothers were full-blooded Cherokees.

Patricia had been disconnected from any religion or sense of God but loved time in nature. In hypnotherapy, she found a connection through nature.

> *I am in a field of flowers. There is room in this field for many flowers. I see myself as a pink tulip with petals stretched to the sky and I am radiating light. I am drawing incredible nourishment from the earth. As my roots get deeper, the flower opens wider, and I see a Buddha figure sitting in the center. I feel completely peaceful. There is a strong correlation between the roots underground and what happens in my life above the ground.*

Angela was raised as a Jehovah's Witness in an exceptionally strict and violent family. She had been thinking about suicide since she was eighteen, and she lived with a deep sense of emptiness, worthlessness, and isolation that was directly traceable to the story potions she had imbibed since childhood. The "unsafe" potion informed her perception of the world. God was not safe. People were not safe.

Like Patricia, Angela was able to find a sense of safety and worthiness by turning to the ensouled divinity she found in nature. Using her power of imagination in hypnotherapy, Patricia became part of a hive of honeybees. She felt like they were emissaries of sweetness, and she pictured herself as the queen bee, here to be nourished. She experienced a single drop of honey as pure joy, feeding her as a queen so she could birth more bees. For the first time, she was experiencing home as a place of sustenance and empowerment.

The divine connection, understood in myriad wonderful ways, is very important in reversing harmful potions. Peace, love, safety—these are all necessities that emanate from a higher plane. When we are estranged from God, we lose full access to these necessities. If you feel disconnected, I encourage you to pray. By that, I mean set an intention that you are open to connecting. Then put the burden on that very capable higher power to reach out to you. Be open to seeing what kind of difference that can make for your life.

The next set of stories stretches the idea of healing to include emotions. There are many people whose bodies seem healthy, and who may also have a spiritual connection, who are unhappy. Without full access to our emotions, we can never be fully happy—or truly healthy. Our emotions impact our physical health even though we may not perceive the correlation.

Emotional Disconnects

Keeping feelings at arm's length is common and hazardous to our health. Besides feeling disconnected from the healing force and the divine of our understanding, many of us are disconnected from our emotions. When asked what we are feeling, we don't always know. Our bodies hold that information, but we cut ourselves off from our bodies, too, because they often have not been safe places for us. Since trauma often involves hurt from raging people who pressured us to accept their inappropriate behavior silently, anger is the most common emotional disconnect we experience.

Many people have grown up in a home gripped by anger. Survivors of such an environment sometimes become loose cannons scattering shots of wrath everywhere. Others grow up to be so terrified of their own anger that they can't even make an effective boundary when people are treating them abusively or are out-of-control and raging at them. They simply freeze or run away, too frightened to confront the angry person. Whether the person is fighting or fleeing, their story potions are all safety related. "Only anger will keep me safe." "This fury is deadly, and I am not safe." "Hide your feelings and keep your distance."

Jenny

Jenny had been hit often and hard by her mother with a severity born of jealousy. Jenny's first-grade teacher routinely spanked the children and made them stay in the coat closet. Jenny's reaction to this abusive treatment was to freeze up and remain silent. In the present, people often took advantage of her, but she never presented her needs with insistence, and she never said no. Jenny told me that she was more and more frequently experiencing a sensation in the space between her throat and her heart that she described as "a weak opening" but couldn't imagine what it signified. She also described current life circumstances with frustration. "I just can't do this," she said.

In hypnotherapy, I guided Jenny to imagine a door before her and to run her hand along the line on her body where she was experiencing the weak opening, imagining that this was the doorway she was seeing in her imagination. Then I suggested she walk through the door. That turned out to be more difficult than she thought.

I'm blocked. I can't move through it.

"Say the words aloud, 'I want to come through,'" I suggested.

I want to come through.

Jenny kept repeating this phrase and, as she did, she began to cry—softly at first, but soon she was sobbing.

I want to come through. I want to come through.

She was choking through her sobs. I encouraged Jenny to keep repeating these words louder and louder.

I want to come through. I want to come through. I am going to come through. I will come through. I will come through.

"Do it. Go through," I commanded.

Suddenly Jenny was laughing and shouting.

I'm here.

She later explained that during the session she'd been reliving childhood experiences of being hit by her mother and her teacher. She had been floating in the silence of her frozen response and that's what she had moved through.

I came through the silence of never fighting back with my mom. I felt like I swam through that into my voice. I found my willpower.

The body is so poetic. Describing her throat (seat of the voice and one's power of dominion) as a weak opening seemed to embody both Jenny's challenge making strong boundaries and the ease others had in invading her space. In subsequent sessions, Jenny was proud to report her progress with speaking up and setting boundaries.

Bill

Bill was the opposite of Jenny. His anger was out of control. He'd grown up all over the South, the son of an army ranger. His mother's family was in the Cuban mob and his paternal grandfather was connected with the mob in the US. Although his father shunned any connection with the mob, he believed you must push to succeed and that there are dangers everywhere, so you have to be on guard. His father was adamant that vigilance meant striking before you can be attacked. He made sure there was a gun in every room.

Bill's father trained his children to always be prepared to fight by dragging them out of bed in the middle of the night for drills to defend the house.

We had to be able to go from a relaxed state to armed readiness at any instant, so I forgot how to relax.

Bill's older brother resented him because Bill was his mother's favorite and got lots of attention as a baby. The brother beat Bill mercilessly and daily. When his mom complained to his dad about her inability to stop the brother, his father dismissed her concern. "It'll toughen Bill up," he'd said. "He's too sensitive."

The brother would hold Bill under water until, terrified that he was drowning, Bill would fight his way free, screaming and punching. His father labeled that behavior as overreacting. Not surprisingly, Bill never felt safe as a child, so he had to learn to fight.

As an adult, Bill found antagonists everywhere. When he started seeing me, he was embroiled in a dispute with a corrupt developer that involved all his neighbors and the city as well. He came in week after week, surging with adrenaline. He hated his anger but couldn't stop himself or find a way to stop all the persecution he experienced in life. His wrath was affecting his marriage, his peace of mind, and his creativity. We set the intention to take an inner journey to find that elusive peace of mind.

Bill found himself in a dark cave looking at a child crouched in the corner, holding onto something.

"Can you tell what the child is clutching?" I asked.

He doesn't want me to see it.

"Breathe love in the child's direction without trying to force any outcome."

He has a doll in his hand. It has red hair, a horizontal striped shirt, and a white sailor's cap. He wants me to hold his doll.

Bill's eyes were flooded with tears and then he began to sob and speak sometimes directly to the child and sometimes to me.

I do love you.

I forgot about him. His only friend is his little sailor doll. My God, he's lonely.

You shouldn't be alone. You shouldn't be in the dark.

"What would you like to do?" I asked Bill.

I've been holding the child for a while. He's curled up in my lap. He wants to go home with me. I'm gonna take him. He wants to see the light but he's afraid of it. It's noisy and too chaotic.

"Is there anything you might do to ease the boy's transition?"

Maybe he'll trade his loneliness for support, even if it means a little chaos.

He has something else he wants to show me. It's a secret world. He has been out in the light before. There's a doorway that opens out into a child's world. It's beautiful. There's an owl in a tree that he talks to, who is wise and knows everything. I know that owl, too. I forgot about him. There's a treehouse with lots of little people—either children or owls—I'm not sure.

Suddenly, Bill sat bolt upright with his eyes wide open.

A voice just said to me, "Wake up—this isn't Wonderland."

"Who does that voice belong to?"

My father.

"Lie back down, close your eyes, and listen carefully to this important message."

"This is not your father's world. You don't have to live in your father's world. Your father's world is fine for him, but not for you. Everyone has their own world to create. In the book of Genesis, God creates a world of his own. As children of God, we are creators, too. Each of us has the job to create a world of our own. Return to that world now. Accept your world. It's okay for you to choose to live in a world of peace."

Bill spent a luxurious long while exploring this world and basking in the peace. Afterward, he told me he had not felt such calm in a long, long time. This serenity stayed with him throughout the week, even though the chaotic circumstances of his life didn't change.

Mike

In contrast to Bill's outbursts, Mike's anger was trapped inside a cold space in his heart. Mike was a middle-aged man who had been married for over twenty-five years to the same woman. They were not especially close. He kept himself busy and hid emotionally. He regretted having married at such a young age and resented his wife's desire to get close to him. He told me he guarded a part of himself that he wouldn't share with anyone. He described it as a sealed box he couldn't open. We explored this further in hypnotherapy.

I'm in a warm, green, comfortable room with windows, but the curtains are closed. I smell roses but there's no furniture. How strange. It seems familiar but I don't recognize it. There's no door. It feels peaceful, warm. It's a safe place.

I'm examining a box. It looks like a box for a top hat. It's velvet with silk. The lid comes off easily. Inside the box is a smaller version of the room I'm in. I don't see any dark corners or cobwebs. There's a sunbeam that shines on a trunk inside the box. It's beautiful, made of gold, with jewels on it. The lid is heavy but I'm opening it. Oh my! How wonderful. It's so beautiful. I can't believe it.

"What happens if you imagine showing your wife what's inside?" I asked.

I close the lid immediately. She's going to take it.

"Who is she really?"

Mike took a deep breath.

My dad. He sold him. He sold him while I was gone. He sold my horse, Copper.

Mike dropped completely into the memory.

I'm twelve years old. I go to the barn but he's not there. I can't get my breath. I go to the back porch. I can smell the dog. He's an old dog and he's on the porch. My dad comes through the door. He says, "I sold your horse. I traded him for this shotgun and some money."

I felt numb. I wanted to cry, but I didn't. I acted like I was really pleased to get the shotgun, but I didn't want the shotgun. I let Copper down because I wiped him from my memory. I didn't want to feel nothing.

I saw Copper two years after that. He had a wonderful home, but he was mad at me—wouldn't come to me. He'd forgotten me. He was the only thing I had ever loved or allowed myself to get attached to because I knew what life was about. Anything that mattered got sold. Emotions didn't matter. I bought Copper. He was mine. But that's what we did for a living—bought and sold horses. After that I closed myself off because anything I owned was for sale. After that I never got attached to anything. I knew it could be sold.

Mike's anger was trapped under a layer of detachment, and both prevented him from experiencing intimacy with his wife—or any real joy and faith in life.

Mike had further work to do. He needed to see that the beautiful life the box world represented could only be accessible to him if he cut the ties of resentment toward his father and began to trust life. This would require many more sessions, but at least now Mike could see the hurt and the anger and the hope.

The anger that buffets us as children seems to have long arms, reaching into adulthood and continuing to wreak havoc, through us or to us. But when we go within, we all can find our power and generate a field of safety, just as Jenny, Bill, Mike, and so many others have discovered for themselves.

Anger-Fear-Grief Swirling Together

In this next story, there is no one emotion that is disconnected. Instead, the client is swimming in a river of emotions. Emma's task was not to be aware of her emotions but to express everything she was feeling and then find a way to calm herself. You'll notice how the second treatment, Using Language of the Deep, is critical to helping her find the peace she needed.

Emma was scared. Her husband, Johnny, was scheduled for surgery for swelling in his neck, which was very similar in appearance to the cancerous swelling in the neck that had killed her beloved father. They had three small children, and she was afraid of losing him. Grief that she thought she had dealt with had reared up again. She was alternating between crying and shaking and couldn't find a way to peace and faith. The "unsafe" story potion was dominating her. This is what she wrote about her experience.

Johnny's surgery is scheduled for August 12 and my goal is to release some "Little Emmie" pain and grief so I can be there for him and our family. I lie down on the soft couch with a blanket on my legs and an eye mask on. Jane tells me that, during the session, if I'm in the dark and don't see anything, I can reach out and around with my hands to "feel" for things like a blind person.

Jane tells me to focus on my breathing, feeling like the sea, in and out, and steady. My chest is heavy, and the breath is heavy at the start. It gets smooth and relaxed, and I feel myself fall into a deep relaxation state. Jane says she is going to say a sentence and I'll fill it in with the word that first comes to mind. She says, "I feel as relaxed as a _____" and the word "pumpkin" pops into my mind. She tells me this word is the key to get down into my deep relaxation state and I can use that key again.

She counts down from ten and tells me to walk down a stairway into the depths of myself as we get to zero. (Jane has the best voice for this type of work and it's exactly the meditation tone that feels so calming. I can feel her mouth linger on the number five as she stretches it out and think how cool it is that I can trick my mind to relax like this.)

For a bit after we get to zero, I don't see anything. It's cool, calm, and dark. She asks what I see. Nothing. Just dark. Jane asks me to use my hands to reach out and feel. I try for a bit and still nothing. I tell her my heart is so tight and heavy and that I'm scared. She asks who can help me feel safe. I say my grandma. Grandma reminds me that I'm one of her favorites. She feels so soft and comfortable. She helps my heart open and feel safe and calm again.

Jane asks if I'm brave enough to see my dad. I say yes. Jane tells me that my grandma is going to stay with me and wait while I see my dad. My dad comes in like a big, heavy energy. He's so big and I feel myself inside of his energy field. He's vibrating and so big. Then lots of crying and emotion come out. I'm saying I'm so mad and the thought about his affair comes into my mind.

This surprises me, but not really. I found out about his affair when I was nineteen and it was a huge loss to my young psyche. I tell him I'm mad about the affair and how bad it hurt me. Jane tells me he is big enough to handle my pain and that I can tell him how it felt and that it's safe to let my anger out. More crying and moaning.

My dad is there now like a blanket of sky above me. The sky is lowered right over me, and it's made up of layers of wings and feathers in dark purple and grays. I know it's my dad making this sky and he's telling me I can let all the pain go. I can feel the air moving and I know I want to let go of the pain in my chest and heart, but I don't really know how. Now my hands, arms, and legs feel like they have a deep vibration and almost like the fell-asleep feeling. I shake my hands and arms around, breathing deep and letting out deep breaths like horse's breath in yoga where your lips flutter. The horse's breath is helping to release the tension in my jaw. My hands continue to shake vigorously up toward the sky. I can feel the emotion releasing and moving from my upper arms down to my hands. Now I go from crying and moaning to calm periods and back again.

After moments of calm, Jane reminds me it's safe to let it out, all the anger and feelings. Lots more shaking of hands and arms. It just feels like the thing to do to move the feeling out of my body. I get messages of love from my dad. He's so proud. He loves me so much and he loves my girls. This makes me smile and cry. I can feel his love for me.

I shake and shake my hands until it's just my thumbs that are still vibrating. I tell him how much it hurt, how mad I was, and how much

I love him. My body gets calm, and I have the sense that he's holding me. I'm his little girl again. I roll over on the couch and bring my legs and knees up like I'm curled on someone's lap. My face is on his chest, and I weep and shake with all the feelings of loss and grief. For missing him so much. It's as if my dad's lap is the whole couch, and he's holding me like I'm his little girl again.

After a while, he lays me down in a field of wildflowers surrounded by mountains—the perfect mountain wildflower field, just like the one I was backpacking in last week. I don't want to say goodbye, but I can also feel I am ready to come back.

My dad said he'll be in the mountains and always there with me. The breeze is cool and sweet, and I can see the flowers blowing in the light breeze. I feel the deep, tired feeling after crying and having him rub my cheeks and brush my hair away from my face. This was the best feeling. So much love and tenderness from him.

Jane told me it was time to say goodbye soon and come back to the present. She reminded me that I could access this place anytime and that it wasn't going anywhere. Jane said I could use the pumpkin key to get back to my depths and that my grandma and father would always be there with me. She counted to five and said I'd be back present in the room and that I should pull my mask off and sit up.

This session was transformative for Emma. Instead of going through the experience with Johnny clouded by all the unresolved emotions of her past, including the anger that surprised her, she was able to be present. She was able to trust that her husband, Johnny, was not her father, and the outcome could be different, which it was. Johnny's tumor was benign and before long he was back to his healthy self. Of course, there was no way to guarantee this outcome, but energetically Emma couldn't even imagine a positive result until she could let go of the complicated feelings toward her father. Once she did that, she could steep in the image represented by her father holding her on a couch/field of wildflowers. Emma's job was to soothe herself. But in a quantum world where we are entangled, especially with those we love most, maybe Johnny's outcome was influenced by Emma's emotional healing.

You may be going through a medical scare right now for yourself or a loved one. Allowing yourself to fully feel and express all the emotions to someone safe is a starting point to open the space for healing. In the quiet that comes after you've given voice to those feelings, ask your soul for a calming image. Then apply the fifth treatment, Steeping the Imagery, allowing deep peace to create a healing container as you navigate the medical situation.

Chapter 6

Heaven Help Us

In this chapter we focus on the fourth treatment, Going Beyond the Physical, to release trauma and the resulting story potions with the help of friends from on high.

Asking for heavenly help does not mean pounding on the pearly gates or kneeling by the bedside wringing our hands in desperation. Heaven is not a location or a site of power but a state of expanded consciousness. When we turn to heaven for help, we are opening our minds to the sky of possibilities beyond the material plane. There is assistance to be found there and most of us need it.

Even without trauma, it's typical to have at least a sip of the "I can't do this myself" story potion. I think it's part of the human condition to feel we need someone to help us through life. As humans, we separate our ego self from our spiritual power, so, as we grow, we are more familiar with our human capacities—or lack of them. As a result, when we venture into the realm of healing, we want someone to accompany us. In the physical world, that may mean a doctor, a shaman, or someone with a convincing web page. When we are exploring worlds that are new to us, we seek teachers, scouts, and gurus. In the inner world, no matter what we are looking for, we turn to spirit animals, healers, angels, guides, and wise ones.

These supporters take many forms. Sometimes they reflect our upbringing or an area of fascination and study—a guide like Mother Mary, Albert Einstein, or Johnny Cash. Other times, they surprise us. Our wise subconscious minds know both the medicine we need and the one who can best administer it.

We reach out to heaven because we need help in the moment, but it's important to remember the first treatment, Embracing Yourself. You are wholly light in your essence. The help that seems to appear in a form outside of us emerges from that light. It shows up as a character in a story we, in our wisdom, are creating. This character, whether it stems purely from our imagination or vibrates in another dimension with a reality of its own, is not separate from us. We are connected to the source, as are the healers and guides that emerge from the one field of consciousness. Storytelling beings that we are, we access our own healing power and our own guidance more easily when we have a story that delivers it to us from heaven.

In the pages that follow, I'll share many stories of spirit animals, healers, guides, and wise ones. While I am not including angel stories here, there are several stories throughout this book—including "Dust in the Wind," "The Rope into the Unknown," and "Get Off the Carnival Ride"—that involve angels. Heaven is filled with helpers in many forms, eager to assist us. They travel through portals from our past, our future, our collective consciousness, our rich imaginations, and realms of higher consciousness.

Spirit Animals

Seagulls and cougars and bears, oh my! Animals are frequent helpers in hypnotherapy journeys. Native Americans and other indigenous people have long spoken of totems and the guidance that is available from the inner world through the energy of the creatures who share the earth with us. Animals offer medicine in the sense that their innate qualities are exactly what we need—protection, comfort, or freedom, for example—until we can find our own courage, strength, self-nurturing, wisdom, or whatever medicine the animal offers. A skunk offers a deterrent to unwanted attention. Fireflies speak of magic and hope in the darkness. Beloved childhood pets bring safety and comfort.

Your ego may have an idea of the animal that is right for you, but your wise mind may overrule. One woman received a seagull and struggled to understand why. Her ego was puzzled, even disgruntled. Then one day she had the insight that seagulls scavenge nutrition from discarded foods, just like she was learning to glean wisdom from her trauma, the kind of difficult life experiences that leave you scattered in unrecognizable pieces on the beach after a storm. She realized that her soul may have had a seagull element that inspired the choice to learn from such traumatic events.

Another woman had grown uptight about flying. She could have called in an eagle, hawk, or heron, but her wise self knew she needed to lighten up and gave her a humorous, imaginative bird. She saw herself as an egret stewardess wearing a long string of pearls, serving cocktails and laughing with the passengers.

I've had clients who have lion or wolf companions, a helper with eagle wings, or a horse that enables them to make a getaway. Sometimes the animal companions are regularly present and sometimes they make a single appearance to teach a lesson.

One man was struggling with an addiction to chewing tobacco until a coyote showed up to teach him to balance curiosity with caution. Before his coyote guide helped him understand on the subconscious plane, this man would stop chewing for a short while and then spot a tin of chew and feel tempted, telling himself maybe he could just have a little, unable to recognize its danger for him. Coyote is curious but knows to avoid eating poison and was able to free the man of addiction through that teaching.

Lauren was not a client, but she participated in one of my group hypnosis sessions. I told the participants to explore the spirit world without latching on to the first animal they encountered. There came a point where I rang a chime and told them to turn around and face their spirit animal. Lauren wrote the following poem to convey her experience. It illustrates the whimsy and the power of animal guidance as well as the importance of listening to the voice within. In this poem, sometimes my actual voice is referenced and sometimes it is woven into something that is happening within her imagination.

Homebound

Her voice calls me
to open the door.
Walk inside, she says.
The door, it isn't locked.
It opens silently, going around
to finally open on an ornate hall
with chandeliers and gold walls
and I laugh to myself at the pomposity of my imagination.
What part of this is me?
The turtle in clothes doesn't answer
but points to the fox at the desk.

And I hear my medicine woman's voice
Telling me to move along.
I walk to the fox and he hands me a gold key.
I compliment him on his pretty vest as he points toward the elevator owl
who comes to take my pack.

I notice what I brought with me
All my burdens and a couple sticks.
He takes my burdens, and he emphatically sets them down.
We get in the lift and it takes quite a while.

Just as I am questioning if this owl is me
her voice comes over the loudspeaker and calls out the floor.
Seventh floor, she says.
Is that really you, Jane? You sound like you are part of me.

My owl and I, we exit and I hop along behind him, down the hall
The door at the end is plain and doesn't fit the décor.
The owl, he uses the key that the fox had given me and then turns to leave.

I pull open the door onto an endless African savannah
—except it is brightly colored and filled with trees from my home.
There are ponderosa pines and aspen groves.
I know she has taken me to journey into my own heart
chock-full of juniper boughs and lava island metaphors.

I am anything but alone.

Her voice is here again and leads me to a pond with a single rainbow trout.
This can't be me; I don't understand.
I must be an elephant or a mama tiger or something else, so bold
and strong.
And then out of nowhere a giant green alligator comes up and eats me.
Wait, it ate the trout.
Okay, I suppose I can be an alligator, a bit aggressive, but I'll try it
on for size
fitting into my skin, trying to feel green, feeling okayish.

I'm in my own heart, safe
and here she comes again
my soft-spoken loudspeaker, my beautiful meditation guide.
She says,
You are here, Lauren, but this medicine is not you, not today.
She chimes, turn around slowly now, and open your heart's eye.

Oh, my heart,
There before me, in full animal glory
is my beautiful spirit,
arms held wide, my essence wraps its enormity around my body
and pulls me into its center
drying my tears on her matted, smelly fur
she welcomes me home

Lauren Kurzman

Neither Lauren nor I can remember, these many years later, what spirit animal showed up for her, except that it wasn't something big and ferocious. At that point in her life, Lauren had been in a situation that required her to fight to legally protect herself and her children. The fight was now over, but she hadn't yet released the adrenaline and the protective urge. I think that's why she was looking for a big spirit animal. But her wise self knew it was time to shift into a more vulnerable, receptive mode, and so the spirit animal that came was something gentle. When it comes to spirit animals, like the song suggests, you get what you need, not necessarily what your ego wants.

Animals Abound

Some people share a world with spirit animals. The specific animal they notice varies with the issue. My daughter Holly was one of those people. As I mentioned before, she had special animals she called upon as a young child of four: a white wolf and a special snake. They brought her a sense of safety. Her relationship with them began when she woke in the night, afraid of what was chasing her. I suggested she turn around and ask what they wanted. The answer was consistent. They had a gift for her.

When Holly was eight, I began using hypnosis to help her sleep. On the first journey, a deer showed up to accompany her. He was a reliable, friendly companion for many years. When she turned twenty, we did an adult exploration to help her find self-confidence. She relaxed by imagining a sheep. As she went more deeply inward, she found her deer. He was crying because it had been a long time since they'd connected. She traveled into a crystal forest in her heart. There she encountered her white wolf howling and telling her to "just be." It was a message of self-acceptance. She found animals all around her. A bird landed on her, a snake passed close to her, and a chubby black bear sat nearby. All of them seemed to be watching her peacefully. She got a deep feeling of safety.

Nearly twenty years later, I don't think animal guides are part of her reality, but perhaps they were there to help raise her when she needed them most.

Animal Re-Parenting

Max didn't set out to find a spirit animal, but two animals found him. Of the many sessions he and I shared, this one was the most powerful. As with Holly, it seemed to be a way for him to find what his own parents hadn't been able to give him.

Max was twenty-nine, ungrounded, and floating in emotional stew. He was going to college, pursuing a field that didn't really interest him, because his grandmother would support him if he seemed to be on the road to a successful career. She always saw his potential even when nobody else did, and she invested her hard-earned money in him. But only if he was also making an investment. She would pay for counseling and medical support, too. Max had several health concerns that all seemed connected to his emotional state. Although he hid behind his intellect, he experienced tremendous anxiety and had deep anger he was afraid to express. It would flash out in bursts but mostly seeped out slowly as frustration with his life. He drank intermittently and had used drugs in the past. None of this worked well for his body.

Max's relationships were unsatisfying. None of the women he'd been with had the depth or kindness he was looking for. His relationship with his grandmother was loving, but his mother was a toxic person for him. He described her as "self-centered and un-nurturing, constantly jabbering and bullying me." He was afraid to talk back. His mother had been married four times, and Max had only felt a connection with one of those husbands.

Going into hypnotherapy, we set the intention: for Max to feel freedom and strength and support to follow his passion, be able to set boundaries, and feel safe and whole. As soon as we began the session, right at the bottom of the underground stairs, a cougar was waiting.

He walks with grace and ease—so limber and fearless. He wants to walk into the dark and I'm to follow him. He takes me to a special place across a cold dark stream. It's an open grassy area. He has me sit and starts walking in circles around me, like he's guarding me. He wants me to sit and touch the grass, breathe in the wind, and absorb the power of this place. Dark figures lunge at the cougar. He wants me to trust that he has that under control and just stay calm. I do trust but my heart is still racing. The dark masses that lay on the ground are leaching into the body of the cougar. He's letting it happen.

Now we're walking away. The cougar has the same casual confidence as before. He absorbed the dark masses like a sponge. We're coming down off the plateau to the stream. The place feels familiar. I want to dally but the cougar keeps walking. The water in the stream is obsidian—so dark. My legs feel tired. I'm starting to float.

"See if any other animal has shown up," I suggested.

There's a bear. She's a loving presence. She seems to know I'm tired and picks me up. I'm cradled in the bear's arms. She's a mother bear. I try to wriggle a little. I'm uncomfortable with the touch. She's not letting me go, though. She's holding me firmly to her breast. She's not hurting me but I'm afraid to relax. I want to flail with my arms and legs.

"Breathe into your arms and legs," I told Max.

I'm getting comfortable with her. I've always known her. I'm starting to remember this warmth. The cougar has returned. I'm in awe of him. I love the way he walks—so at ease, lean, and muscular. Bear isn't putting me down. I feel comfortable in her arms now, cozy. It feels natural. I sense no fear around either of them right now. I feel like a little kid around them. I feel curious and free. It's been a long time since I felt that way. These are old friends. We're all one.

The cougar let me rub his belly. It kind of surprised me. The cougar is a warrior but at total peace. He has no fear, no anger. There's a haunting familiarity about all this—something about the place. My body feels much looser and more limber—like the cougar's. That's what I want when I look at him—to feel that way, too. I've lost my ability to think. I feel quite young. I'm frolicking in the grass and napping. A tree just sprouted out of the ground. I like the way it looks. It has an orange bark that looks like skin—grooved and smooth. The trunk is pleasant to the touch, hard. There are sparse leaves on the tree that are shaped like really green eyes. There's one apple hanging in the tree. I don't know if I should take it.

"Do you want the apple?"

I definitely want to climb the tree. They're the strongest branches I've ever seen. I love climbing trees. The fruit is way out there. I don't feel hungry—I'm just curious about that apple. I suddenly feel just a little scared. I don't know what that means. I can't make out the ground. I'm hanging from a branch. I'll have to let go of one of my arms to get the apple. I might fall. I want that apple. I don't know how I'll get down with that apple—or how I'll get down at all.

I feel divided. My legs are trying to pull me down toward the trunk—I know that feeling. I can see the cougar. He's looking up at me, pacing around. The bear has her arms out—she wants me to jump. I'd have to grab the apple and jump in one quick motion. I feel sick in my stomach and the sick feeling is working its way up into my diaphragm and chest. I can't figure it out. A voice says, "Just do it—don't figure." My arms are shaking so badly. I only have a little time left because I'm losing the strength in my arms.

"What would you do if you were the cougar? Can you get back to that feeling of being loose and limber?"

I can picture it, but I can't feel it. I'm not connected.

Suddenly, this feeling shifted for Max as he embodied the cougar's energy.

I expected a surge of excitement, but it's just easy. I reach out and grab the apple and fall, feet first, into the bear's arms. I knew that would happen. I don't feel triumphant or dramatic. I'm cradling the apple. It's like a prize. I'm pleased.

The bear is cradling me. I feel thankful. They were right there for me as soon as I looked for them. I can count on them. They're always there. It's just a question of me remembering to notice. I lose it when my thoughts are figuring.

Max grew quiet and reflective.

I don't understand the lack of anger and fear in the cougar.

"Anger comes from fear of getting hurt. What if you knew you couldn't be hurt?"

People really can't hurt me. I just saw that. It's a choice to be made. Bear and Cougar are always with me. I can draw on their strength in my body. I have a strong desire to be like the cougar. He doesn't have to prove his strength. He has assurance.

"Is he your true father? Maybe like father, like son?"

That would be great.

"Ask the cougar."

He is. He playfully knocked me down with his paw and licked my face. He told me he has already given me all those gifts. They're inside me.

I reminded Max that he had shown those qualities when he was running a construction project—an experience he had proudly related in a previous session.

I was bold. I had a clear knowledge of what needed to be done and no doubt about my abilities. I loved that feeling.

The cougar is my father, and the bear is my true mother. She's very strong, too. There's nothing she won't do for me. She's a nurturer. She never runs out of love. She's filled with it. I think that's where her strength comes from. I feel like a family with these two. That's why it was so familiar. I'm home and they're my family.

As he came out of the hypnotherapy session, Max was radiating peace and confidence.

I feel strength welling up inside my body. I don't feel just like that little boy anymore. I feel like a lean strong man as I stand up. My body is healthy and strong. No signs of physical disease. I feel clean and pure and capable. I'm starting to feel a rumbling of desire to be. To be alive. To reach out. To reach out my hands to others. I see myself confident and purposeful. I feel happy. I'm reaching my hands out to the heavens in thanks. The heavens are smiling back at me. I feel the earth at my feet and heaven in my hands. It doesn't get any better than that.

Thirty years later, Max has a successful business, is married to his soulmate, has four beautiful children, and lives in a place that sings to his soul. He had long since internalized the messages of his animal parents, as well as the love and faith of his grandmother. Today, he exudes confidence, caring, and strength and can model the qualities he gained from Cougar and Bear for his own children.

Whether the spirit animals are offering protection, nurturing, or modeling a needed quality, there seems to be a connection that our souls have to the animal world that allows us to receive this medicine. Maybe spirit animals help us return to a simpler state, our animal nature, where we aren't ruled by anxiety and complicated thinking. With the mental chatter and the emotional turmoil set aside, we can begin to connect with the essence of who we are and access the power that is always within us.

In the next section, clients find assistance not from the world of spirit animals but from helpers who show up in human form. They come from varied sources beyond the physical realm.

Inner Healers, Guides, and Wise Ones

We are natural-born bards who revel in stories. We love to listen to stories as children. We often tell stories to illustrate our lives and the meaning we are making of them. And, in hypnotherapy, we discover our story potions by recovering stories or inventing them. Dr. Pete's story at the beginning of this book was recovered. His experience with the mean boy happened in his youth, and he was now remembering.

The next stories include fragments of memory mixed with imagination. Each of these tales involves a healer who administers the antidotes necessary to deactivate the story potion. These healers come in many forms; indigenous and religious figures seem the most common. Sometimes the healer is a character you could easily imagine running into that has been endowed with healing powers by the imagination. Their methods vary widely, too. They may employ potions, food, bodywork, drums, crystals, symbols, and more. No matter the tools, the power of love and acceptance is prominent.

Some of the stories involve guides who show up to point the way or to accompany the person along their life's trail. Sometimes they show up from the past or the future.

You may wonder if these helpers are real or are *actually* present. Remember the fourth treatment, Going Beyond the Physical. There is a level of reality that is more powerful than the material plane. It exists within the realm of the imagination. This is a sacred, creative realm. The stories that follow happened there.

When I say it's a sacred realm, I also want to note that some people are afraid of hypnotherapy because their religion warns them that going within is the realm of the devil. In all the sessions I've ever guided, the devil has *never* shown up, although memories of some "devilish" acts by humans certainly have. What clients have encountered is a holy presence, a mystical connection, even a fusing with a spiritual dimension outside any common reality. Inevitably it changes their lives.

In these next stories, I will share some of these encounters. The sublime nature of the experience often prevents clients from fully communicating the depth of what's happening, but I think you will still get a sense of the wondrous nature of what can transpire. You have already read numerous stories of healing. There's something about having a healer or guide from the Great Beyond show up that takes the healing to the next level of awe and wonder.

Eskimo Woman

If you are working with a healing guide, you need to be open to unconventional methods. When Vanessa met the Eskimo woman you'll read about below, she experienced something far beyond anything Western medicine could conceive.

Vanessa, an Alaska native, needed some serious shaking to deal with her physical pain. She suffered from some inflammatory autoimmune issue, but the doctors had been unable to discover the exact nature of her condition or a cure. She and I did not discover the story potion that was at the root of this pain during this session, but she did have an experience to help her heal physically. During hypnotherapy, Vanessa connected with a beautiful healer in a garden.

> *She has dark skin and wrinkles all over, like a picture from National Geographic. She wears trinkets, bangles, and shells around her ankles, wrists, and neck. She has big brown eyes and wears an old dress, a very simple mumu style with Scandinavian patterns that reminds me of the clothing Eskimos wear. She's plump but it's easy for her to sit beside me. She looks happy, smells earthy, and feels so peaceful.*

Abruptly, the healer stood up and started moving her around. Vanessa described what she was experiencing.

She's looking under my arms, pushing my head down so I'm bent over, touching my back and my sacrum. It feels like she's reaching inside of me and pulling out a thing with octopus legs. She's pulling them off, detaching the thing. She's shaking me back and forth and pulling this thing off my tailbone. It's wrapped around my legs, spine, and the front of me. She has a rattle and she's shaking it. I don't know where this thing came from. It's hard to get it loose.

The healer mixes a potion in a clamshell to lubricate the suction cups so they can't keep sticking to me. She tells me to drink it. It's warm and slightly bitter but not bad tasting. Now she wants me to jump while she holds onto the octopus thing. It loosens and the tentacles come out, but the main part is still inside and hurts. My whole body feels hot and is throbbing. The healer bathes my body in golden light. I'm looking down on my body from above. I can see the light exploding over me and flowing inside of me.

Finally, the healer gives me some dark herbal resin to chew and some celery sticks. She comes behind me and holds me, rocking my womb. Then she disappears inside me.

Following this session, Vanessa had an epiphany about food that was right for her. She told me she had to listen to her body, not experts. She required tiny bits of meat and lots of vegetables pureed into a mushy sauce. Eggs were okay; so were kale, spinach, zucchini, and mushrooms. She said she couldn't have tomatoes, broccoli, or cauliflower, or anything in a box. No wine or coffee.

Reminding her that the healer was now inside, I asked Vanessa to envision her life a year in the future when the healer's treatments had taken full effect.

I'm seeing myself kayaking next summer. It's really different. How I think, how I am. I feel more normal now. I'm like a tribal woman.

Really simple eating. It's a real shift. I just can't run out for the day. My whole life is caring for my body differently. There's a preparedness. I see myself stopping to grab a box of berries at the store. Knowing what I need to eat. Never grabbing fast food or chips. I don't see myself going back to any other form of eating. Sensitivity is here to stay. I have to love and care for my body as it is. When I embrace it and what feels good to my body, I feel good. I have more energy. High vibrational eating. I feel lighter, healed, clear, and connected.

This session was an important shift for Vanessa in how she prioritized her self-care. Over the years, she continued to explore the right eating plans, which seemed to shift as her health demanded. She did have further physical issues, so I can't portray this session as a one-and-done fix. Yet, the experience was so vivid, and her reaction was so profound, that I trust it proved to be a significant step in her healing. I share it mainly to show the kind of healing experience that can happen in the inner world. There are many other possibilities, as you will see in the further stories.

The Sensei

Time is fluid. We can rediscover what we've left behind by returning to the past, and we can also find the guidance we need by traveling to the future, where we have the gift of age and wisdom. That's what happened for Eli. The guide he found was his own future self. Here's how it happened.

Eli and his girlfriend Sophie were considering a breakup. They were both twenty-eight and had been living together in Seattle since their junior year of college, when they met in a martial arts class off campus. They were both feeling like their needs weren't being met and had started couples counseling, but Eli wanted to dig a little deeper into his part. He'd had a needy high school girlfriend and had lost himself by becoming her support system. He didn't want to do that again, but he suspected he might be overreacting to any need Sophie expressed. Eli was interested in developing his musical career and his passion for martial arts. He wondered if he could be more open to Sophie's needs without abandoning his own. That was the question he brought to our first session. We set out to explore the creative tension between self-discovery and self-expression and caring for others.

Floating downriver, Eli reached an island that held a hidden portal to the inner world. When he reached that world, he was standing in damp grass just outside a cave. He could hear the dripping water and smell the dampness. The cave was dark and a little scary, but he was excited to explore it. His imagination provided a light, allowing him to see sparkling crystals on the wall, and inviting him to check them out.

I can feel the texture. They're clear and shining with the light. Sparkling. Some are very small with an intricate texture.

"Listen to the crystals with your fingers," I directed.

It's like a choir of soft, pure tones, gentle and soothing, like a magic hum. I feel like the hum is cradling me. I have this deep, crystalline knowing that I'll be okay, but it's hard to accept it. I want to, but there's a part of me that's unsure how to connect and let myself be embraced by the sound.

"I've listened to your music online, Eli. As I watch you play piano and I listen to the sound, you seem to be connected. You just lose yourself in the music, don't you?"

Yes. When I'm playing I do. But I see myself sitting at the piano and feeling distant from it. It makes me sad to feel separate from that part of myself.

"What's the earliest memory you have of feeling that disconnect? Go there now."

I'm singing opera as a little kid. I can feel the power and excitement in that ability of expression. I'm on a school bus at some camp. Suddenly I'm feeling self-conscious about singing. The other kids seem excited about hearing me sing, but they're also poking fun at me. I'm very aware of having an audience and I want to shrink. It feels easier to hide away. But I lose something—my power—when I hide. I lose my ability to connect. I'm comforted, though, by not having to worry about what others think because they can't see me. It's a relief of pressure. But I want to feel comfortable sharing that expression. It hurts to feel I've blocked it.

I left Eli to mull over that conflict for a few minutes and then asked him to find another memory where he felt connected to his music.

I see one of my teachers. We're sitting around the campfire singing. She had a unique voice. I remember her telling me she loved to hear me sing. How seen and accepted I felt in that moment. And the smile she gave me! Her name was Phoebe.

"What if you bring Phoebe along as a guardian angel when you sing?" I suggested.

I can take a deep breath. I feel a growing energy of confidence and support and joy in that sense of expression. I feel I'm getting closer to that. I feel good acknowledging that right now. As I sit with this, I can breathe deeper through my belly. I feel lighter and more at ease knowing and seeing that fear for what it is. I've been afraid to know that I have so much support and people who really appreciate who I am and love when I express myself.

"Think about Sophie from this place of lightness."

I feel her warmth but also this in-and-out pattern. When she backs away, it feels painful. Am I being selfish holding onto that lightness? If I back away from the lightness, it doesn't hurt so much when she backs away. Whoa! Maybe I'm setting the pace. That's painful to admit. When I back away from my own light, we both end up feeling more alone. As I sit with that idea, I feel warmth and calm. I feel clearer and I can see Sophie more clearly. I can really see her and be present. That feels connecting and peaceful. Still, I feel a twinge of guilt that in this peace I'm experiencing on my own, I'm not paying attention to Sophie.

"Where are you feeling that guilt?"

In my throat and the right of my forehead and the back of my head.

"Can you magnify that? It's like you're asking your body to speak louder."

It feels heavy and intimidating and shameful. I've lost connection to the lightness.

"Think of Phoebe as your muse. Try singing for her and see what happens."

I feel my chest opening. I feel the lightness again.

Eli stayed with that feeling of lightness until I brought him back to the room. When he came back, he said, "That was beautiful. I'm in awe of the sense of connection I felt to myself."

A month later, I saw Eli again. He had been able to maintain some connection to the lightness but had mostly been aware of when he noticed more challenging parts of himself that he had previously projected on Sophie, and he wanted to disconnect. He was practicing self-forgiveness. This time, he wanted to explore why he was doing the same thing with his music. "I feel like I have so much music that I want to put out, but it scares me, so I don't do it," he said. "Or I spend time perfecting it and I never get it perfect, so I isolate and don't share my music."

We dove into the inner world with the goal of connecting with the part of him that was confident.

"Imagine yourself opening to greatness," I recommended.

It's exciting. Also, I'm shrinking back.

"Imagine an energy of light flooding your chest and you're opening to it. It is leading you into a scene where you are completely one with your music."

I'm standing on a tropical shore, looking at the ocean, seeing the beauty of nature all around me. I'm incredibly connected to nature. I'm able to sing her songs and share them with the world—help people connect to her through music. I have a sense of freedom and empowerment, touching and exploring different mediums of art and music, and knowing that's exactly what I'm supposed to be doing.

"I'm sensing that the world is more linked in the heart to nature because of your music."

It feels important to play my songs back to Mother Earth—to give something back for all that's been given.

"Fast-forward through the sands of time to the end of your life. You are surrounded by family. There is a sense of a legacy you are leaving. You are a sensei, so respected by all. Imagine your twenty-eight-year-old self is standing there, and you create a love song to him."

I feel like I'm drinking the wisdom of the sensei. There are no words, just a feeling as I'm listening to the song.

Afterward, Eli was filled with quiet awe and appreciation. "It was beautiful to feel that vision of possibility and hope," he told me. "That I could make a difference. I heard ocean waves blending with the *guqin* (a traditional seven-string Chinese zither) while I was doing tai chi. I felt filled with wisdom, peace, and accomplishment. I had served Mother Nature well."

Reflecting on this session, I was surprised that the term *sensei*, which I last remember using fifteen years ago, popped into my consciousness for this young man. Eli had a definite leaning toward Asian culture, and he related to this term when he heard it. Perhaps in his future, he will be considered a sensei by those who know him. The future is still to be created in any moment, but we can visit our potential futures through hypnotherapy. When we do that, the future either serves as a cautionary tale or a guiding star to pull us closer. If you're feeling stuck, perhaps some time traveling will set you in motion.

Junkyard Shaman

How do you remember your life when it was something you'd rather forget? Jeanne's early years were marked by profound neglect. She believed she'd never have the resources or care she needed to be okay, and that was proving true once again as she struggled to remember. She had decided to write a memoir, but now her recall was fuzzy. Memories would tiptoe past the edge of her consciousness and run as soon as she started to look directly at them.

The year I met Jack, I walked on fire, traveled from Alaska to Mexico, was dating three guys, seeing channelers, dancing weekly, and in love with life. But I don't remember why I left those guys for Jack.

I do remember that everything changed once I moved in with Jack. He was a scary person to live with. I don't remember why I stayed.

Jack would yell and get angry and then, the next day, would say it wasn't that bad or that loud. "You're exaggerating," he'd tell me. Two days later I'd have blocked it out. I started keeping a journal because I didn't trust my memory. I just found a journal from year two.

One theme that I saw from the journal was that Jack would always lose it on my birthday or special occasions. On our second anniversary, he bought me expensive diamonds. I didn't know how to tell him that wasn't my style, and I didn't really like them. Turns out I didn't need to say anything because he saw the look on my face. "Nothing I do is ever right for you!" he shouted as he flipped a table over in anger. He broke a lot of furniture.

So Jeanne forgot. A lot. And that was happening more often. Jeanne wondered if this was because of her desire to capture memories in writing, or if she didn't really want to remember, or was afraid to reveal her trauma. To find out, we plunged into her amnesia about her own story.

Initially, everything was murky. Jeanne felt like she was floating in darkness. Then she noticed an odor that was strangely familiar. As she moved toward it, the smell seemed to vanish. She began walking faster and faster, hoping to catch the scent. She was moving so fast, she felt like she was moving through time. Everything around her blurred. Her heart was racing with the fear that she'd lost an important memory. Jeanne was distracted by all her forgotten memories. There were so many of them. She had the feeling of being lost in a dark fog. She sensed the recollection was in there somewhere, when suddenly she caught another pungent whiff.

Jeanne followed the smell to a junkyard. She heard animals scurrying and saw rows and rows of old vehicles with creaking car doors and piles of old tin cans. "What a playground!" she thought.

There's a little skunk stepping into view from behind an old brown Monte Carlo. The scent is filling my nostrils. It's not fresh skunk spray. It's the fragrance of the junkyard as a whole—diesel, oil, carburetors, old leather, rusty metal plus the wafting smell of that old skunk as it marches through the rows of old cars.

I reach out to shoo the skunk away and notice how small my hands are. I look down and see myself in a dirty cotton dress with yellow ruffles and eyelet lace hemming.

Jeanne's eyes welled up with tears as she sank deeply into this familiar childhood haunt.

> *This place feels like an escape—a place to disappear and forget—a place to feel good and excited about what I might find, like a pink plastic barrette and some old maps in the back seat of an abandoned car. I feel special here. Lucky. There's a cardboard box full of rocks and stones of all colors. Some are polished. The box is in the back of a pickup truck. There's even a piece of fool's gold.*

Jeanne was crying and embarrassed to admit that she had kept that piece of fool's gold for years, thinking it would be her ticket to having everything she longed for. Just remembering the fool's gold and the sweet innocence and hope of her young self deepened her heartache. She was starting to shut down from the pain when I felt a prompt to send her out of memory and into imagination.

"Jeanne, imagine there's a shaman somewhere in the scene," I proposed.

> *There's an older man with long gray braids. He's wearing blue jeans, an old leather vest, a cowboy hat, and boots. His face is wrinkled but his eyes are kind. I'm curious about him but I stay hunkered down in the bed of the truck to hide my rocks. I'm not sure if I can trust him.*
>
> *I'm surprised he noticed me. He's walking right up to me. I guess I didn't hide too well.*

Looking up at him from behind her messy bangs, she saw him smile and felt reassured.

The junkyard shaman opened the tailgate and sat down. He smelled like tobacco and leather. He just sat there, being a comforting presence for the little girl. His voice was soft, and he started telling Jeanne a story about a little squirrel. She scooched down to the tailgate to sit beside him because she loved stories.

> *Brother Squirrel forages and gathers nuts all over the forest. He jumps from tree to tree and branch to branch. He digs a little here, moves some dirt there, and pushes rocks around until he finds the perfect spot to dig a hole and then he buries one nut. He does this for hours, day after day, week after week, month after month. He buries nuts everywhere.*

Little Jeanne could relate because she often buried her treasures, too. She asked the shaman how the squirrel found all his buried nuts.

> *When the squirrel is ready for his nuts, he comes back and remembers the hiding places of all the ones he needs. The nuts he doesn't remember grow into magnificent trees.*

Somehow that made Jeanne feel better about her childhood. It took away the judgment.

Next the shaman lit a bowl of sage and blew smoke into Jeanne's eyes and mouth and ears and nose. He cleared everything out. He intoned three times.

> *You'll remember what you need to remember.*

Jeanne's head felt bigger. Vast. Uncluttered. Then the shaman put something in her hand, telling her to trust herself. It felt warm, flat, round, and soft. But, when she opened her hand, there was nothing there. It was invisible but she could feel it as part of herself.

> *Nobody else can tell you that you're doing it right or what trusting yourself is like.*

I instructed Jeanne to ask the shaman to drive her back from then to now in the pickup so she could retrieve the memories of her life along the way. As she did so, she began to imagine her memoir already complete.

Afterward, Jeanne mentioned that the shaman had told her that he'd see her soon around a campfire telling stories. She was surprised to think of herself as the storyteller, but he told her she'd been watching people do it for years and she already knew how. He told her to look at each memory and find the gift, and then she'd be able to tell the story.

Jeanne did begin working on her memoir after that. Although she hasn't published it yet, she's been able to incorporate her life stories into workshops that she leads. Most importantly, she stopped feeling like she couldn't remember. If you have trouble recalling your past, be gentle with yourself. Maybe you buried something painful that's blocking your memories. But like Jeanne, you have a guide who can help restore what's important and put it in a more healing light. Just ask.

A Happy Guide

Everyone in the family was shocked when Grandpa Jerry ended up in the ER one night and they sent him to detox. Jerry told me he'd never had a drinking problem, but he normally had a few glasses of wine before bedtime to quiet his mind. This hadn't bothered him until a situation occurred that he felt put his livelihood at risk. Panicking over that, even his normal three glasses didn't help. So he drank more. And more. That's how he wrote his ticket to the ER.

Jerry came to see me ten days out of detox. We'd worked together in the past, so he was confident I could help him. We talked for a while about strategies, such as having a meditation place and practice before bed. Jerry agreed that the real issue was finding a way to quiet his mind without substances. He went into his inner world with ease.

"Someone important is waiting for you," I said.

I see someone but not somebody I know.

"It's a guide there to help you. What do you notice?"

He has a human body but moves really slow. He's waving me over. He's a very calm spirit, a happy spirit, a relaxing spirit. He's waving me over, saying, "Don't worry. Let go of your worry."

I feel very relaxed.

The guide is telling me there's a better way. He says, "Let go. Don't be lost in the past. Be peaceful. Follow me. I'll show you a better way." The guide is always there. I just need to find him again.

"Ask your guide how to find him."

He tells me, "I'll be there for you. Just keep the light burning."

"Picture the setting where you are meditating and connecting with him. Where are you?"

I'm sitting on a nice reclining leather couch. My dog's climbing up on my lap and my wife is beside me. My daughter is there, too. The candle would be a good idea. That could be my guide.

"Maybe it could be a quiet time, even with the dog and all those people."

That's a good idea.

Jerry loved Glacier National Park, so I suggested he take the guide there so they could explore it together.

"Imagine that whenever you have a challenging situation, you and your guide can bring it with you to Glacier National Park. In the presence of such vastness and grandeur, the challenge will shrink to manageable proportions."

It turned out, Jerry told me, he just had to remember that the guide was really him. Because he felt like he'd let his family down with his detox experience, I suggested Jerry might be a positive influence by getting them all meditating with him. He liked that idea. He told me this meditation practice was sure to get him to the thirty-day post-detox mark.

Suspecting he thought this was a short-term solution, I decided it was time to bring up Steeping the Imagery, that crucial fifth treatment. I suggested Jerry might make the meditation a lifestyle change, not just a band-aid. Jerry was surprised by that idea. He admitted, "I usually just go from problem to problem, fixing as I go." He really could see the value of making this a lifestyle.

We all have access to a guiding aspect of ourselves. By relaxing and asking, you can find the one for you. Spending time with this higher self is a lifestyle that can benefit everyone. You deserve to enjoy it as a long-term relationship.

Usually, the guides show up by themselves, but occasionally, as in the following story, they split into several characters. Jim, the man you'll read about next, evidently needed a team to help him get over the mental hurdles his story potions had set up for him.

A Trio of Guides

Breaking up feels like prying your hold off the other person after rigor mortis has set into your fingers. It's hard for all of us when we still care but know it's over. Jim knew he needed to break up with his high school girlfriend. She was in college, a marine biology major, and she needed space to follow her dreams. But he felt lost and couldn't imagine life without her. She was the only girlfriend he'd ever had. Jim had strong "I'm not enough" and "I'll never make it on my own" story potions.

In hypnotherapy, I suggested he drift like a seahorse into the ocean depths. He found the water warm, and he could see through it, at least partially. Then he started getting frustrated because he wasn't getting the answers he wanted, and he couldn't see anything visually.

"What if you give yourself permission to enjoy some freedom from thinking?" I asked. "Imagine putting your inner critic outside a door of your consciousness."

> *That critic is like a two-tailed dog with no head that wants to guide me but can't.*

> *I'm noticing I feel tense all over. It's like my cells are a dried sponge.*

"Try soaking in the salt water of wisdom and let your hidden knowledge be awakened."

> *Love is everywhere—like saltwater.*

I asked Jim if he could imagine setting his girlfriend free. He pictured her sailing over the horizon to an adventure of her dreams. Tears rolled down his face, but he also seemed at peace. From that state of peace, he was able to imagine moving forward and was open to receiving help.

> *I'm turning toward the land now. I jump into a Land Rover. When I open the glove compartment, I find a treasure map inside. I drive to a way station for some gas. There's an old codger leaning against a post, smoking a cigarette. He offers to come with me, and I accept. This guy is full of advice and stories, and we are laughing like crazy.*

> *We make another stop for snacks and meet a nerdy guide who says he can help us find the way. I say okay, and he hops in the back seat. A pretty girl in a cheerleader outfit, who seems tender and sweet, wants to come along, too, and I say "sure."*

Somehow, these three guiding energies all blended into one internalized resource. Jim felt enlivened with the idea of having his own destiny and inner guidance to get there.

He found the courage to break up with his girlfriend, which allowed them to remain friends. Many adventures followed, including landing in a place he wouldn't have foreseen, where he enjoyed deep friendships and a new love. When breaking up, the necessary moves seem impossible, but the resources available through the fourth treatment, Going Beyond the Physical, are inexhaustible.

Bodhisattva

The next client had a different need. It didn't involve breaking up or finding a new direction. He was stuck in the present by outer circumstances coupled with his attitude about them.

Bo had taken off a few weeks from work due to chest pains that puzzled the doctors. He suspected he was suffocating with grief. Even though his symptoms were physical, and his pain was emotional, he was suffering from spiritual despair, which was underpinning the rest of the issues.

He worked with refugees. He described the legal and bureaucratic system as "defined by malevolence and purposely creating suffering." He felt like he was walking through hell. Bo was a highly empathic, spiritual man with a strong Buddhist practice. Raised in the Deep South, he had always felt out of step with some of the region's values and attitudes, especially toward those who were considered "others." His life work was being an advocate for "others," and he felt deeply connected to them and their struggles. Their suffering brought him great pain.

In hypnotherapy, Bo was led to a dark, dismal cave with many compartments, which he described like a scene from *Lord of the Rings*. His chest pain began to intensify. I prompted Bo to place his hand on his chest and tap, like he was knocking on the door of the pain, asking it to come out and reassuring the pain it was safe. As he did so, Bo began to cry and proceeded to share a few truly horrible stories of situations that had led clients of his to leave their countries in the hope of asylum, only to be met by more brutality and heartlessness in the US immigration court system.

Bo told me that a seasoned *bodhisattva* does not take on the suffering. Instead, they accompany people through the hell realms with compassion, not judgment. He felt called to be a *bodhisattva*—an enlightened being who returns to earth again and again to walk with humans and help set them free from suffering—but did not feel at all seasoned.

I asked Bo to imagine that a seasoned *bodhisattva* now came into the room to accompany him in his suffering. I suggested that this sacred presence could drain excess grief from his heart and infuse peace, faith, and joy. As he imagined that, the cavern changed to a warm, healing sanctuary with soft swirling light. Bathing in this light, Bo realized this was what he was called to do—radiate light rather than take on pain as he walked beside those who are suffering.

In a subsequent session, we returned to the light-filled space. This time, he said it felt like a womb in the earth. He felt a mother-like presence. I suggested to him that the great mother held him and saw his pure essence, his love-light.

If you've birthed a baby or even held a newborn, you know that perfection is all you can perceive in that little one. For many mothers, that sense that the child is just right and can do no wrong lasts for a very long time, despite many trials of patience. But, somewhere along the line, most people lose the ability to see the pure light of others, even our own children. And, consequently, most of us grow up believing we are somehow defective—to put it mildly. It's an insidious story potion that we should be something we never can be.

"But what if that's not true?" I asked Bo. "What if you are perfect and the Mother is cradling you now until you can feel it?"

I asked Bo to consider that seeing the perfection in others might be more useful than his outrage-fueled service work. Maybe this is the true work of the *bodhisattva*—walking beside a person without arguing about the circumstances, seeing only wholeness, holding their hand.

"What if you don't have to evolve over lifetimes to become a *bodhisattva*? What if you are born one and just have to settle into it?"

He felt into this question, and it resonated. He could feel light flowing through his body. The words of the Serenity Prayer came back to him but with new understanding.

> *God, grant me the serenity to accept the things I cannot change; the courage to change the things I can; and the wisdom to know the difference.*

He told me that gracious acceptance of life as it shows up is the field in which we can access both the wisdom and courage we need to act. We ended the session with an evident sense of deep contentment.

Bo continued his life work, and though he still had episodes of dismay and outrage, he generally was able to operate with serenity. What if you knew there was a bodhisattva walking beside you, allowing you to experience and evolve, but always keeping sight of your innate love-light? Imagine that's true. Maybe you will taste the deep peace Bo experienced.

Harriet Tubman—Break the Chains

The next helper from the Great Beyond is a well-known historical figure. Although Harriet's body finally gave out, her spirit is very much alive, and she's still operating the Underground Railroad in another realm.

The day Marcela came to see me, I had just finished reading a book by Spring Washam, *The Spirit of Harriet Tubman: Awakening from the Underground*. In the book, Washam talked about her ongoing relationship with Harriet, which started with channeled messages and then began showing up in her personal life experiences. Washam recognized Harriet as a *bodhisattva*. While she had helped to free many slaves in her renowned physical lifetime, Washam said that Harriet has now returned energetically to liberate people from emotional bonds as well. I always have a stack of books, but when I saw this one, I felt compelled to read it immediately. My book habit matters because Harriet was already in my energetic field when Marcela arrived. I believe she had come for Marcela.

I had worked with Marcela before. She grew up in Los Angeles, where she had lived until a few years before. She had complex issues with both her parents, her career and finances, and her health. The "something is wrong with me," "unworthy," and "I don't deserve" story potions were evident in all these areas. Marcela was a talented Chicana-rock singer, highly intuitive, outrageously smart, and desperately unhappy. She had been a rising musical star until a mugging at age twenty-eight left her with a traumatic brain injury. Now, at fifty, she was still floundering and so tired of the way her life had turned out.

Her father had been a wealthy businessman in Mexico who used his connections to immigrate with his wife to the US early in their marriage. Marcela's mother had a promising acting career in the making when she got pregnant with Marcela. She always blamed Marcela for ruining her shot at success and a meaningful life. She treated her daughter like a ball and chain and was verbally abusive. Marcela grew up feeling very unloved by her mother and pressured by her critical, hot-tempered father to stop being so dramatic and make something of herself. She said she was a disappointment to him because, despite a college education, she had never found a career that made sense to her after the brain injury. She felt like she missed her opportunity to make it big as a singer. She was too old for that now, even though she still had a beautiful voice. Any other job she tried ended with her being fired. These were usually positions that didn't interest her, taken out of financial desperation.

Marcela had been an unhealthy child with digestive issues that mystified her doctors. It was years before they identified her as having celiac disease. As she got older, Marcela developed various autoimmune conditions and increasingly destabilizing gut problems in addition to the celiac limitations.

Over the years, Marcela had tried many therapies to get free of her emotional baggage and physical issues. She had shifts, yet the core challenges remained. She had re-parented her inner child, done past-life regressions and soul retrievals, gone to psychics, and worked with *curanderos*. The one lasting impression she had from all that work was that she had incarnated to struggle and wander so she could develop compassion. Marcela had the struggle and wander part down. When it came to compassion, though she was kind and generous to others, she was busy arguing with God about her life conditions and had zero compassion for herself.

The first time Marcela came to see me, she wanted to heal her relationship with her father. She had moved to Portland, Oregon, where he had built a home after her mother died. He was now having health issues and was more mild-tempered, but he was still frustrated by her lack of financial success.

When we entered the inner world, the first impression Marcela received was that she'd been raped. She felt sensations of heat on her back, around her waist, and in her ovaries. She started thinking about her parents and her beloved younger sister who had died as a teen. I suggested she ask her sister, in her luminous form, to help her with the memory that was trying to emerge. Marcela did that and was surprised at the memory that came up.

> *It's my mom. She's trying to put her finger inside me. I'm five. I'm fighting. She's punishing me.*

Marcela began to sob. She told me that her mother had anger issues. Her father had shared that her mother had been molested by a friend of the family when she was a little girl. After we comforted Marcela's younger self, I encouraged Marcela to gather her mother's little girl self in her arms, too, and pour out love and healing to liberate her to walk a new path of love.

The surprising element of this session was that Marcela's intention had been to heal her relationship with her father, but the work had to deal with her mother. I think she may have been projecting some of the anger she held toward her mother onto him. Once she had freed her mother's little girl self, she had enough energetic space to get a new insight into her father.

> *He refused to see me as less. I've always focused on his criticism. Now I can see he believed in me and wouldn't stop.*

The second time Marcela made the trip to see me, her relationship with her father was somewhat better, but there was still tension because she continued to attract only lackluster job offers. She knew she had the ability to be a success but felt blocked professionally. She wanted to play on a bigger stage in life and that was her goal this time. Even though the door as a musical rock star was closed, she thought she might be successful as a professional speaker.

Entering the inner world, she came to a wooden door with metal hinges. When she opened it, she was on a cobbled path in an old monastery in Spain. The air was cool, and the energy of the place felt very spiritual.

> *I'm a friar. I'm wearing a robe with a rope belt and sandals. I'm a white male, smart, educated, wise, middle-aged, and stocky. I have a peaceful life.*

I asked Marcela to go to the spot where the friar served as a confessor and guide. She went to a confessional. (A confessional, in the Catholic tradition, is a dark booth where people meet behind screens with a priest who can hear and absolve their sins.)

The friar was meeting with his superior, the abbot. His superior was reminding him of the vows all friars take—poverty, chastity, and obedience. The obedience part includes being humble.

> *It's incumbent on us to be humble. I was being a political activist, speaking out against injustice on behalf of the downtrodden. To stand up for what is right is in my nature. The abbot doesn't approve of my behavior.*

The scene fast-forwarded, and Marcela cried out.

> *I'm being burned at the stake for being a heretic. Because I spoke up and I challenged authority. I've been nailed for that, multiple times, in this life, in work situations.*

Marcela now moved on to another past life, one she already knew about, where she was crossing a desert with her family. She was raped along the way and consequently disowned by her family. Without alternatives, she ended up working in a brothel as a prostitute and performer, and she died of tuberculosis. She felt betrayed by her family and never healed the wound in that lifetime.

Marcela told me that her essence hadn't been nurtured in her current life, either, and she'd been sexually shamed as a teenager. Singing as a star performer, for her, had been partly to prove her worth.

Singing in general was a source of joy for Marcela, but the specific musical thread that went through her life was singing in choirs. Her parents were devout Catholics, but she went to the Baptist church with her friend and started singing in that choir at age ten. Over the years she went to many churches, always joining the choirs, singing every kind of sacred music. Outside of the church environments, the Chicana rock genre helped her express her pain.

Marcela considered the most difficult years of her life to be the ones just before her accident, when she stopped singing in choirs to focus on recording her first CD with a group of L.A. rock musicians. Marcela realized now that the sacred music, sung with others, was an essential element for her soul. She couldn't just focus on her pain, singing Chicana rock. She needed the medicine of the sacred to elevate her. She realized that even though her days as a solo performer were over, she could still be singing in choirs.

Marcela had a tremendous sense of financial failure and shame because she hadn't made money with her music. She found an antidote to this perspective as she realized the sacred music moving through her had a healing vibration. It had the ability to heal the audience and heal her.

Marcela took that awareness back through time. She reimagined the friar. Instead of protesting and getting burned for it, she imagined him singing songs of hope to the downtrodden. She pictured the pioneer woman singing healing songs in the brothel. As she integrated the healing nature of the music into these lifetimes, Marcela owned her power in a new way. "I AM the healing song," Marcela proclaimed.

Seven years later, Marcela returned once more. She was singing in choirs again. She had solved her financial issues, having gotten a good-paying job that she loved with the Portland Center for the Performing Arts. The company valued her, and she was able to pay off all her debts. She had a much sweeter relationship with her father. He had thought for years that she had moved close because she wanted his money. Now that she'd paid off her debts, had a good job, and didn't need his financial help, he was surprised that she was still hanging around. He began to open to the idea that she loved him.

Their newfound closeness came about despite a surprising development. Her father had asked Marcela to get a DNA test. It revealed that she was not his biological daughter. He told her that confirmed his suspicions that her mother had been having an affair. He was pretty sure that she'd had many affairs over the years of their marriage. This was a shock to Marcela, but, in her mind and his, he remained her father. She also learned from her father that her mother had suffered severe postpartum depression, although at the time he hadn't understood what was going on with her.

With this new information fresh in her mind, Marcela was getting body-work when an image erupted from her subconscious. Her mother had tried to smother her as a baby. Marcela also discovered a card tucked away in an old book. It was in her mother's handwriting. It said, "Baby does not like to be held." It was dated three months after Marcela's birth, when her mother had gone back to work. A note for the babysitter, she presumed. It was clear to Marcela why her baby self would not have felt safe in the arms of someone who'd tried to kill her, and that her mother's note ensured she wouldn't get cuddled by anyone else.

Marcela's pain around this information was complicated by memories of her mom trying to be a good mother, and Marcela longing for her mother's love and acceptance. She knew it was time to forgive her mother. Which brings us back to Harriet Tubman.

To understand Harriet's role with Marcela, recall what Harriet did in her human lifetime. She not only escaped slavery herself but returned repeatedly to accompany slaves to freedom via the Underground Railroad. Harriet was tuned into a higher realm to find her way. She was courageous, compassionate, and fierce. Once a person agreed to come along, she would not permit them to turn back no matter how frightened they were or how dangerous the circumstances. Capture and death were always possibilities, but she guided seventy people to safety and never lost one.

Marcela was enslaved to her parents, particularly her mother, as they existed in her consciousness. They defined how she thought of herself. The "something is wrong with me," "unworthy," and "I don't deserve" story potions originated with their treatment of her and the beliefs she formed as a result. Until she escaped the hold they had on her, she could not be free. Metaphorically, they were the slave owners, and she had been in bondage her whole lifetime. She had tried, but failed, to get free on her own. Enter Harriet, who knew how to get a slave to freedom. We invoked the spirit of Harriet Tubman to lead the way.

As we entered the inner world, Harriet led Marcela to hide in a cave. Her parents soon passed by, looking for her.

> *My mother is angry. She looks like a demon. My father is floating behind her. He is pale. Ghostly. They're scaring me. They can't come into the cave. Maybe they can't see me there. But I want to get out of this cave. I have to get out of here. I can't keep being afraid of her.*

"Let them go," Harriet demands. "Stop chasing them."

"Have you been chasing them?" I asked.

Marcela was sobbing by now as she responded.

Yes. I've been holding onto my mother. She couldn't love me, but I wanted her to. I keep wondering what's wrong with me. I'm angry at my dad for not standing up to her for me.

"Break the chain that binds you to being a child," yells Harriet. "Break the chain."

Trembling, but with increasing volume, Marcela begins to shout at her parents.

Go away! Now.

Harriet hands Marcela a metal cutter. "Use this to cut the chain."

I suggested that Marcela imagine, as she cuts the chain, that it's caked with all the disease in her cells.

Marcela cuts the chain and watches her mother float away with the chain dragging behind her.

Dad isn't leaving. He has something he wants to tell me. He's apologizing for not protecting me from her. I'm afraid to respond to him. If I forgive him, there will be nothing holding him here. He's sick already and he's old. I'm afraid he will die. I realize that's why I've been hanging around here for so long. He thought I was just staying for his money, but I wasn't. He knows that now. I'm scared. If he dies, I'll be all alone.

"It's time," Harriet says, more gently but still firmly. "Cut the chain."

Marcela obeys.

I invited angels to patch up the holes in her energy field and clear out all remnants of illness. I asked Marcela to speak to the self who had just made this journey to freedom with Harriet.

I love you. I choose you. I will take care of you. You are free.

"These journeys take a toll," Harriet tells her. "Give yourself time for 'free' to settle into your bones, to know how to care for yourself."

Marcela rested in the stillness and then I brought her back to the room. She told me that after she cut the chain with her dad, she felt like singing "Break on through to the other side."

She said that in the past, she'd held onto her mother from neediness. The story potions had so much power because she had taken them personally. Yes, her parents had taken their fear and grief and anger out on her, but it wasn't about her. Any child would have received this treatment. Their demons were their own. In forgiving them, breaking the chains, she set herself free.

Marcela texted me after her session.

You won't believe the song lyrics on the radio as I was leaving. "Released from my chains, I'm a prisoner no more." The Universe has a sense of humor.

When I checked in with Marcela a couple of months later, she told me she was feeling peaceful. Her digestive symptoms had improved markedly, and she had found a highly respected naturopath who she believed would help her get to the bottom of her autoimmune issues as well as clear up most of the digestive problems.

She had also taken a leap of faith and booked a ticket for a trip to New York City. She was part of a choir that would soon be performing at Radio City Music Hall in Rockefeller Center. She was trusting that she would be well enough to go.

I believe that Harriet Tubman really showed up for Marcela on the energetic plane. But even if Harriet was only an archetype and this simply happened in Marcela's imagination, it was still powerful. If you are struggling to get free and have been stuck in a situation you feel powerless over, consider asking for energetic help from the higher dimensions. Ask who is available to lead you to freedom. Maybe Harriet will guide you. Maybe it will be someone else. Just know that freedom is available for you.

The final three stories in this section involve holy figures who exist outside of time and transmit unconditional love and acceptance to lost and traumatized people.

Nonna, Wild Woman and Savior

This first story pulls the divine feminine energy in, but in a very unconventional form, when a wild woman, full of contrast, shows up for a woman poisoned by criticism. Kay, who had been contemplating an affair in an earlier story, also had a lifelong history of shame and very little feeling of being loved when she was small. Her powerful encounter with this wild savior became a journey of loving acceptance.

Kay had always been riddled with self-criticism. As a child, she suffered abuse and relentless disparagement from her mother. There had been periods when Kay had a loving relationship with God, but she had also attracted abusive religious people who shamed her for not performing her duties to God or her religious practices correctly. As a result, her connection to the Christian God she believed in was never free of judgment. The "wrong" and "bad" story potions were very active in her consciousness.

One week, as Kay was drawing and writing, she encountered an inner wild woman who both frightened and intrigued her. The wild woman bragged about eating bugs and bees and bears. If this was her inner critic, she seemed like a force to be reckoned with. I asked Kay (an artist) to portray the wild woman, but when she came in the next week she was frustrated. She just couldn't pin down the image. It seemed to her like it kept changing.

The wild woman told her: *"I am many faces; you'll never know me."*

Kay had also drawn a tree in the center of a jumble of jigsaw puzzle pieces with words written on them. There were words like *secrets, buried, awaken, trap, snap, open, not, sought, silent, spoken, hidden in the cliffs.* Kay was fascinated by the mystery the wild woman represented. She had a sense that this woman was not only a sage but also someone who had no fear, who felt safe inside of herself and therefore was a good protector. She said that the wild woman was able to eat bugs, bees, and bears because there was nothing she was afraid of…she could eat (encompass) anything.

Kay related an extremely vivid dream she'd had the previous night about all the important people in her life, claiming that the abuse she experienced at the age of eight was somehow her fault. Another toxic story potion. She couldn't find anyone in the dream to defend the child's innocence.

We proceeded with hypnotherapy to connect with this wild woman and perhaps also work with the dream. What ensued was an astonishingly sacred experience that I felt honored to witness, a mystical experience where Kay discovered she was not just innocent but connected to the life force in her essence. The thought that came to me as I listened was, "Take off your shoes. You are on holy ground."

Here is Kay's journey as it unfolded. There were long moments of silence in between each phrase.

> *The wild-haired woman is reaching out to me. I feel warm. She has long arms, a gentle touch. She has long, long fingers. She pulls me toward her under the tree, to her body. She breathes. I can hear her heartbeat. She says, "You are loved, my child."*
>
> *She's happy I've come. She's full of light and darkness. How could she be both? She is many, many colors: roses, reds, yellows, purples, blues, and oranges. It's very beautiful. She wants to touch my heart.*

"Do you let the wild woman touch your heart?" I asked.

> *Yes. It bleeds but it does not hurt. Red, red rivers, red, red. I'm on a boat on this red river, like a sea that goes to the shore. There is a sunset in the distance. It's very quiet. I'm coming into the yellow, the yellow of the sunset. There are waterfalls on the horizon, like they're boiling. Lots and lots of turbulence. But I'm still very calm. The turbulence rises up, but it doesn't touch. I'm going back to the tree. The turbulence is surrounding my boat and it's getting darker.*
>
> *She asks me to trust her. I don't know her. She tells me I do know her. The place where I am is still very calm.*

"How can you recognize the wild woman as someone you know?"

The answer that followed was ancient, profound, and transcendent.

> *Turbulence is part of her. She's both calm and turbulent. She's both open and closed. Her name is Nonna. She lives inside me. She is every part of me—the giving and withholding, the loving and the turning away. How could she be all things? She's rough and smooth. She has many crevices and yet each crevice molds into the next one. How would you draw her? It's a façade. You can't draw her, can't see her.*

Is she a blessing or a curse? She's a blessing to some, good to some. She's some and she's all. She's many and she's none. She's very wise and she knows nothing. She doesn't make sense, yet she makes sense. She says, "It's what I believe that she is that she will be, for me." All those things—she has been all of them—the happy and the sad. So how can I know her?

We're on a beach now. The waves are coming in. Our toes are in the sand. It's both cold and warm. She's so large. She's everywhere and yet she's right by me. How can that be? Because she loves me. The essence of who she is. She says it's time to go. I don't want to leave.

This transmission of divine being, divine love, took place over a period of about forty-five minutes. Through it all, Kay was bathed in reverence. There was a hush in the room. I knew that Kay was experiencing an acceptance of the dark and light in her own self, such as she had never known. It was an experience of radical integration. While Nonna's portrayal of herself is totally consistent with religious teachings about the divine, Kay had never felt this love before with such "whole-i-ness."

Kay tapped into something ancient and cross-cultural as she encountered Nonna. In case you are not versed in the various religious descriptions of God, here is a short description to help you see the universality of the energy that Nonna represented. Even though Kay only knew the Judeo-Christian tradition, and the judgmental version of it at that, inside this medium of hypnotherapy, she was able to find something much bigger than what she had been taught.

Kali is a Hindu goddess, very complex in her attributes and powers. She is described as both the consort of Lord Shiva and the Supreme Entity. She is the Destroyer, Goddess of Death, but also the Creator of Worlds, along with Lord Shiva. She is seen as the dark sea from which ceaselessly bubble up the principal male deities of Brahma, Vishnu, and Shiva, leaving the Source, Kali, unchanged. All the opposites held within Nonna reminded me of Kali.

In Islam, by contrast, no images of Allah are permitted, perhaps acknowledging the impossibility of encompassing the immensity of the divine in any single picture. In Kay's words, *"How would you draw her? It's a façade. You can't draw her, can't see her."*

In the Judeo-Christian tradition, there is a great emphasis on the love of God for the individual and for the people. The Hebrew scriptures describe God as walking through the dark valleys with us and laying us down beside restful waters. Jesus describes God as a loving father. Kay says that Nonna tells her she is loved.

Because Kay was raised in the Judeo-Christian tradition with a strong emphasis on judgment and the need for salvation and forgiveness, it's worth noting that the Hebrew word that has been translated as salvation, *yasha*, means something very different. Something that Nonna embodies. It means to be wide, or roomy—a broad and spacious place. *Yasha* communicates the idea of freedom. It is liberation from confinement, constriction, and limitation. It is the love of Nonna.

Because the version of Christianity that emphasizes the need for salvation is so widespread, many people are affected by it. People's trauma is often magnified because of religious emphasis on sin. But what if we all got it wrong? What if Nonna is right? What if the salvation Jesus offered was *yasha*-style—acceptance without borders?

How would your world, our world, be different if instead of focusing on what and who was wrong, we celebrated the diversity of both our individual selves and the diversity of our culture? What if we collectively decided to make room for everyone? There are so many ramifications. I think this is the message Kay brought through for all of us from the energy she called Nonna.

Now that you've met Nonna, maybe you can cozy up to her and begin to accept all the contradictions, mysteries, and delights of the one you are. You are not a mistake. No matter what you've believed, experienced, or done, and no matter where you've come from or where you are now, you are perfect. A mystery in motion. Alive and evolving. Love everlasting. But don't take my word for it. Ask Nonna.

Jesus

This next story involves one of the best-known expressions of the sacred on the earthly plane: Jesus. He appears to Charlotte, the woman in Chapter 2 who was afraid to pitch her tent in the inner realm until her first session with her children and whom the wise woman helped feel safe.

By this time, the wise woman, along with a lion who represented strength and protection, had become a regular presence in Charlotte's sessions. But today Charlotte needed more. She had recently confirmed, through hypnotherapy, that she had been molested by her father when she was a little girl. She wanted release from the residue of this trauma, which felt evil and punishing, as if she had been targeted by demonic forces for the sin of losing her innocence. She wondered if the emotional alienation she experienced regularly and the pain from a botched surgical procedure were a legacy of that original abuse.

I guided Charlotte into the inner realm, with the wise woman on her left, the lion on her right, and a row of angels behind her. I asked for the highest healing power to appear for her benefit and cast out the demons that assaulted her so regularly. Immediately she began to speak in a whispered tone.

> *Jesus is there. His arms are all white light. He is stretching them out to me, inviting me to come to him. He takes my hands and they turn white. My arms are filled with light, too. I'm so honored to have him there. I feel like he understands me, understands my suffering. I haven't*

been able to cry about that surgery and the pain that has been constant ever since. He has so much compassion. I can feel it even though there are no words. It's like he's speaking to me telepathically.

I gave Charlotte five minutes of clock time, which always feels infinitely longer in the inner dimension, so that she could commune with Jesus and absorb his healing presence. When she could describe what had happened, she shared more of her experience with him.

He led me into a room that was filled with white light. God's light. I could sense him there more than see him. I felt prompted to offer him a cup of tea and he took it. We sat together, drinking tea. Then I asked him to heal my body and my mind. In response, he drew me into his arms and I felt all the pain draining away. He told me, "Your faith has healed you. Go now and be healed. Be healed."

Then I asked him about the ones who had hurt me. I couldn't let my anger at them go. I knew I had to talk to him about this because I suspected it was interfering with my healing. He told me I only have to be willing to forgive. He said that forgiveness is not saying someone's behavior is acceptable. It's bringing heaven to earth.

"Heaven is the white light," he told me. "Those who hurt you have lost their way. When you forgive, you help them find the way home to heaven, this energy of white light where we are all together, all healed, just existing as pure love. You start to transform the earthly experience as you dwell in the light of love and welcome everyone else to join you."

His words felt so deep and profound. They resonated deeply in me, as if a church bell was ringing inside my body. I felt peaceful and free.

Over the coming months, Charlotte began to notice changes. For example, she had pleasant interactions with multiple repairmen who came to do work in her house. Previously, she experienced great annoyance and anxiety whenever someone like that showed up. She also shared memories that had surfaced, including things she had never admitted to anyone, so she could release them. The results of the work she had done with Jesus on the inner plane, in that heaven of white light, were showing up more and more on the earth in her daily life. She continued to practice the fifth treatment, Steeping the Imagery, by communing with Jesus in her meditations.

If you are holding onto some secret shame or resentment, Jesus is a spiritual energy that is available to all. His special gift is forgiveness and unconditional love. You don't have to sign up for a religion. You can just invite him to come to you. You can picture that heavenly white light surrounding you and perhaps you will begin to sense the freedom that Charlotte discovered.

The Holy Man

The final story in this chapter takes place inside and outside of time. Safety and belonging are transmitted by a saint with the ability to offer *yasha*-like salvation who seems to have taken up permanent residence in the heavenly light.

Sometimes in hypnotherapy, we not only travel into a past that exists somewhere beyond a person's ability to remember—like the events of our infancy—but we cross into a spiritual dimension where there are experiences that affect the material plane but do not happen there. In this story, a holy man brings salvation to a baby on a busy street, and that saving grace ripples through time.

Nisha had been adopted as an infant from an orphanage in India. Now in her mid-twenties and pregnant with her second child, Nisha was hoping for relief from feelings of overwhelm that had plagued her all her life. She didn't understand these strong feelings and she longed for peace in her heart.

As we traveled inward, Nisha began to describe a scene that was partly sensory and partly emotional.

> *It's hot and loud. I'm a baby. I'm in India. I'm crying. I'm scared. I want my mama.*

The scene seemed to shift a little and now she was more of an observer.

> *I'm on the street in India. There are a lot of people. I'm alone. I'm wearing a white T-shirt. There are flies everywhere. I'm not crying. Nobody is paying attention to me. I seem content. I'm just lying on the sidewalk. So many people are walking around but nobody is noticing me. I have no family around.*

Then Nisha moved slightly backward in time.

> *I see a woman who sets me down. She seems happy. She's wearing a sari. She's tall. She sets me down and walks away. She is middle-aged.*

I admit I was horrified hearing that someone had left a baby on a sidewalk and walked away, but what happened next overrode my judgment and has stayed with me over the ten years since I initially met with Nisha.

> *There is an old man with a really big beard sitting beside me. He seems very happy, and he is just looking at me. I feel good. Safe.*

As Nisha said this, I saw the image of Sadhguru, a Hindu holy man who was teaching in the south of India at that time. When I later described what I'd seen, Nisha confirmed that this is exactly who she saw, though neither of us knew his name at that point. (We later looked online to find the picture that matched what we saw.)

I rarely see what a client is seeing, no matter how vivid the description. But the holy man was there with us, bridging time and space. I felt his presence and so did Nisha.

> *The holy man is telling me not to be afraid. I'm going to have a family that loves me. I won't always be alone. There is a soul reason why I needed to be born in India but not raised there. It's to give me a different perspective on life and so I don't take life for granted. He tells me I am a gift from the old world to the new.*

A couple of weeks later, Nisha reported that she had been feeling much better since that session.

Ten years later, Nisha and I reconnected online. She was now happily married with several children and living in Southern California. She said that while the holy man remained in the back of her mind if she needed him, what had stayed with her was the lightness. She said that right after the session, she felt like a different person. She told me that she'd called her mother and apologized for being such a difficult child to raise. Their once-troubled relationship had become much better, and they were now reasonably close.

Although what happened during that session falls into the realm of mystery, Nisha and I both believe she received a transmission that she was loved, that her life mattered, and she was safe. Her battle was over. She had found the remedy her soul needed.

While Nisha's journey was unusual, the truth that her life was significant is not unique to her. Each one of us matters. If you feel that your life has been a struggle, you may find that by reaching out, the forces of heaven reach back to you.

This sampling of experiences with healers illustrates the power of the spiritual dimension in healing. Human as we appear to be, we are so much more. We emerge from the field of divine possibility, unique in all the world. When we brush against the larger truth of who we are, there is a profound rearrangement of our psyches, beyond what mere words can convey. This is the full power of the first treatment, Embracing Yourself. In my experience, there is both a healing and a mystical element to every hypnotherapy session, but some are more deeply entangled in the mystery than others. As I said earlier, the devil is completely absent in hypnotherapy, but God, aka love, is present with full healing power and will show up in a form that makes sense to you.

Chapter 7

Dreams Can Come True

Here you go—the CliffsNotes of how much transformation can happen in eleven years using the treatments described in this book, told in the words of the person who made it happen. I first began working with Lisa in 2011, and for many years we met monthly. Lisa's sessions have always been very detailed and powerful. Together we addressed career, fertility, concern for her aging parents, reconnecting with spirituality and her tremendous healing power, childhood trauma, and finding and forgiving her birth parents, as well as issues around being adopted. It has been a rich relationship where her most important dreams ultimately came true.

When I told Lisa I was writing this book, she was excited to share her perspective of the work we did together. In the pages of this book, I have already shared a few stories about Lisa's in utero experiences, but I've left the bulk of her transformation for her to describe in her own words. To me, Lisa demonstrates the epitome of what a person who is committed to healing and growth can accomplish over time using hypnotherapy.

As you can imagine, eleven years of steady hypnotherapy could warrant a book of its own. I have chosen to focus on her fertility and adoption issues, and her path to becoming a healer.

Lisa's Story in Her Own Words:
My Impetus to Start Hypnotherapy

I am forty-three years old. It has been eleven years since I first started seeing Jane for hypnotherapy. Prior to working with Jane, I was filled with so much doubt, uncertainty, and fear. My parents were in poor health, and I was in my early thirties working as a food server and going to school to become a nurse. I had been a food server for at least nine years at this point and HATED it. There were only so many times I could say "Hi, welcome to blah dee blah blah…our specials tonight are duh duh duh…can I start you off with a glass of wine or a cocktail?"

While I was hustling tables for tips, I was also attending a junior college, finishing prerequisites toward a degree in nursing. School was fascinating and I was on the dean's list for the first time in my life. I had been diagnosed with ADHD and dyslexia in my early twenties. My primary years of education were dreadful: grades low, social skills high. It was an achievement for me to get on the dean's list, but one that put tremendous pressure on me. I was really getting to a place where I was suffering from anxiety, so I asked my MD for a list of therapists. I saw Jane's name and felt she was the one. I loved the idea of being hypnotized. I had tried a traditional therapist before, and it was a no-go for me.

Down the Rabbit Hole

I had my first appointment with Jane on April 11, 2011. 11-11. What great numerology! She had me lie on a couch, cover my eyes with an eye pillow, and relax to the sound of her calming voice. Jane asked me for a keyword to help get me into a relaxed state of mind. She used this word every time we would enter my wonderland (what I call my subconscious). That word is incredibly special to me, so I will keep it to myself.

For the first time, we entered what I called a rabbit hole. I imagined I was like Alice in Wonderland in the book *Through the Looking-Glass*. As Jane would count down from ten, I would float slowly toward the bottom of the rabbit hole. There were many times that I would see gemstones peeking out of the sides of the rabbit hole. When I heard zero, I landed on my feet gently and she would guide me to an opening, leading me into my wonderland. I would always see my feet first. Most times I would be wearing a floor-length dress and velvet Mary Janes on my feet. My dresses varied in style and color—often lace trim and velvet colors of white, green, and blue.

In this first session, as I walk through my dream world, what I see is clear but a bit fogged at the same time. It's like looking through an old window that needs a good cleaning but will never be clear again. The bright colors are muted shades. I don't really hear any sounds, but it's peaceful and safe. I am standing at what looks like the Temple of Asclepius. This temple for the god of healing dreams is in Rome, Italy. It is a beautiful, small old-world building made from quartz crystal—this is my vision.

> *I enter the front door, which is a heavy wood carved door. The carving is a continuous pattern of swirls. It feels so smooth when I touch the stained wood as I slowly walk into my healing dream.*

> *An exotic-looking woman welcomes me. She is older than I—in her fifties. I am in my thirties. She also looks familiar to me. I am surprised to realize she looks like me. Because I was adopted, I'm not used to seeing familial similarities. We both have long, dark hair, and we are both wearing long, floor-length cotton dresses and have bare feet. She is walking toward me. I feel like she wants to embrace me, hold me, and protect me. This is exactly what I want, to my surprise, and I relax in her loving embrace. This feels like motherly love, something pure and true. I feel supported, and I don't question anything about myself when I am in her arms.*

I was always questioning myself back then. I never felt completely confident in my body. However, in that very moment, in my subconscious, I felt a power of love, trust, and freedom. I left that session on cloud nine. I was amazed at how easy it was to tap into what my body, mind, and soul needed.

My Start in Life

In the last year of the seventies, I came into the world stressed, malnourished, and addicted to cocaine. My birth mom was sixteen years old at the time, as was my birth father. It was, from what I was told, a difficult delivery. There were medical issues that I was fighting. I ended up staying in the hospital, without a family, for two weeks until I was medically discharged to the foster family that took me in. My adoption was a closed one, meaning familial records were locked from me. When I was born, my birth mom wasn't allowed to hold or see me. None of my biological family members were.

Learning this broke my heart. I would imagine myself as a fighting newborn lying alone in a hospital crib with no one around loving me or holding me. I never was the new baby whom loads of family members came to see and hold. I was there alone…fighting for my strength, fighting to get healthy so I could get to my next destination. I must have had some incredible guardian angels watching over me. I ended up living in a loving home for four months with a large foster family.

After I was adopted by my mom and dad, plus an older brother, life was rather good for me. My mom had to take me to the pediatrician at least once a month to make sure I was hitting my marks on the baby growth charts. My muscles were floppy as a newborn, and one doctor wrote in my records that I had the signs of having upper motor neuron disease. I would have been destined to life in a wheelchair without all the care I received. I was also taken by my mom to a pediatric neurologist multiple times. I was pigeon-toed and had to wear special shoes that corrected my feet, for twenty-four hours a day, for about a year. Those shoes must have paid off, because I took dance classes from the ages of four to fifteen.

My mom has told me that for the first twelve months she played with me, took me to see doctors, and was so happy she had another baby to raise. My mom and brother almost died during his birth. She had an emergency C-section before the anesthetic took effect, and she felt the cut. This was also back when C-sections were cut vertically. My poor mom. After my brother was born, my parents tried to have more babies, but it wasn't happening. So they decided to start the adoption process. It took four years until I came along and that's also when they were cleared to adopt. It was meant to be.

My parents had immigrated to the United States in the sixties—my dad from Denmark and mom from Sweden. My family traveled quite a bit to both Sweden and Denmark. I remember on one of the trips, I had my first slap-in-the-face feeling about being adopted. My younger cousin and I were playing dress-up in our *mormor's* ("grandma's" in Swedish) clothes. I told her I was excited to see our aunt that night for dinner.

"She isn't really your aunt, because you were adopted," my cousin rudely replied.

I was stunned. I had never felt that sting of rejection before and I was only nine years old, my cousin seven. I froze while she kept on trying on clothes. I found my body again and ran to cry to my mom. I have never felt the same around my Swedish family. Even now, my heart still stings from that comment. I don't look Scandinavian, so it wasn't like I thought I blended in, but I didn't know that someone I looked at as my cousin could think that about me. Also, I realize now she learned that from an adult. I don't hold it against her, but it's a rejection that hurt my already wounded heart.

Here's my truth about being adopted. I was pulled away from the woman who created me. I knew her smell; I knew her voice; she was all I had known since my conception. Even though it wasn't a healthy environment, she was my creator. I was taken away from her when I needed that connection the most. I was left at the hospital, vulnerable, sick, and lonely. That pain is how I started this life. That pain is why I suffered years of promiscuity, drug use, bulimia, and a lack of self-confidence. My parents and brother loved me and never made me feel unwanted. But the cells in my body remember the pain, and Jane is the one who taught me that. Through hypnotherapy, cellular pain has lessened a lot. It may never fully go away, but I now know how to manage it with a healthy mind.

The Frog Dream

I am sitting on a large rock in a lake. The water is dark, and I can't see the bottom. This kind of water scares me. Sitting on this stone, I am not afraid. I am not in my human form either. I have become a slimy green frog. The moment I see I am a frog, panic begins rising inside of me, but it's a slow-moving panic. Within the hypnotic state, I can calm it down.

Once I am calm, I start to wonder what is happening and where I go from this big rock. Jane says, "Jump," so I jump into the dark water. I figure out how to swim in my new body. I swim to a shoreline where the ground is covered with fine pieces of rock mixed with sand. I can really feel the wet ground beneath me. I am on fire with pride and exhilaration. I just became a frog and swam in dark, scary water. I didn't drown; I swam.

I notice, in the distance, there are lots of people on dry land waiting for me—they are relatives of mine. As they get closer, their forms become silhouettes. They are spirits of both my adopted and biological family members who have passed on. The message I receive is "You are not alone; we are with you, loving you and guiding you when you need us to." This is absolute peace for me.

As I look down, I am once again my human self, no longer the frog that I had to become to get to this island of my people.

The frog helped me find something I was afraid to do myself. I was so scared of dark water. I once had a panic attack in Lake Tahoe standing on a stone like the one in this session. My subconscious brain knew I had to become this frog to heal from past trauma. The frog was not a suggestion by Jane. It was my own doing.

According to the website worldbirds.com, "The frog spirit will help you make the changes and transformations you need within yourself, and purify your body, mind and spirit."

The Shaman Mother

I started hypnotherapy because of anxiety. I was working to get into nursing school, but what if I didn't get accepted? What then? I was searching for what I was meant to do for a career. What was my purpose? That was the issue that propelled me into this fourth session, which is one of my favorites.

It is early morning sunrise. I am standing deep in a jungle. It's damp and warm. The trees and shrubs are varying colors of green. There is a beautiful older woman ahead of me, walking with a slight limp and holding a cane carved out of a eucalyptus tree. Her skin is tanned and leathery. It looks worn by the sun. She is glowing from within the way a pregnant woman does. She is not pregnant with a child, yet she is filled with bountiful love. She is wearing a linen tunic and a shawl draped around her shoulders. The lightweight scarves remind me of the silk ones my mormor used to wear. The color of the shawl is muted purple, blue, and white. Her aura is glowing with a vibrant light. What used to be black hair, but is now mostly gray, is pulled back into a bun at the base of her head. I also notice she has a satchel with colorful zigzag patterns, full of crystals. Her neck is covered in many layers of gold necklaces, cascading down her neck. Gold bangle bracelets are tight on both her wrists. As we come closer to each other, I see she has such beautiful light green eyes. I could get lost in them. They seem so wise. She has seen a tremendous amount of healing.

Her energy is warm and inviting. She has a sweet smile on her face, and she greets me by putting her hands on both of my cheeks and saying, "I've been waiting for you."

I am taken by surprise at her touch, yet it feels so comforting. She gives me an herbal potion to calm the fear I'm feeling in my chest.

While she is comforting, I am still unsure of her intentions. The fear of trusting her starts to override the calm. What if she is trying to persuade me to believe in something I don't want to?

These fears stem from being given up by my birth mom. I have deep cellular memories of the trauma I went through inside and outside the womb. At that point, I didn't know anything about my origin, but now that I do, I can confirm those feelings were true.

As the shaman mother continues to hold me, she holds me as a fetus in the womb as well. She is my true, deep mother. She is familiar to me on an energetic level. As she keeps holding me, I can sense the anxiety and fear I hold in my broken heart begin to ease. I sense heart healing for the newborn crying out for my mom, and heart healing for every stage of my life up till this moment.

I am thirty-two at the time of this session. As I come out of hypnotherapy and lift the eye mask, I feel like I am waking up from a deep sleep. The light is bright, and I have tears under my eyes.

The subconscious mind is so alive with feelings and emotions—more than the conscious mind, especially if you are an extremely sensitive person like me. When I leave to get in the car, I feel loved and supported in a way I have never felt before. My shaman mother is with me all the time now. We never got to the career part in this session, but that came the following week.

Past and Future Healer

The next session, we tap back into what area I should focus on for my career. We decide to try a past-life-regression. I should point out that, at the time of this session, I am studying for a huge test to get into nursing school. It's my second attempt after waiting a year to take it again. I know nursing is not the right path. I am years away from admitting to myself that I was trying to please my parents with this career path. I enter my subconscious mind with the intention of finding my purpose.

> *I see myself on a farm, my farm. It's the early 1900s. I'm in my late twenties. I have red hair in a long braid going down my back and I'm wearing a blue-plaid peasant dress with long sleeves. On my feet are brown leather boots, laced up to my mid-calf.*
>
> *I'm in my barn with my injured horse. She's lying on her side, crying out in pain. I'm calm, but worried about her. I know exactly what to do to help my horse. There is a large, deep cut on her leg. I'm cleaning it, wrapping it with clean fabric, and waiting for the vet to come. I look into her eyes and see sadness, which breaks my heart. I can feel I am giving this horse my energy, trying not to let the sadness affect me. I can do and think whatever is necessary, but I don't want to feel. I want to be numb to my emotions. I get so tired sometimes of being empathic.*

I tend to get drawn into other people's emotions. When my parents went through their various medical procedures, I would go to visit them and help them as much as I could, completely ignoring the emotional side of their healing. I would hold it all in until I flew back to my house and then process what I had just experienced while with my mom or dad. This wasn't great for me, because it would cause me to stress and worry about them—so much so that I would lose sleep and get sick. Jane and I realized this during this session as I visited another past life.

I am in a white nurse's uniform, working in an old warehouse converted into a hospital during WW2. The room is massive, the size of a football field, with tall cement walls. It's at least three stories high. The windows are long horizontal rectangles, placed high in the walls near the ceiling. It seems this warehouse was built to keep people from looking inside. The entire building was just this room with windows all around it. I could see the sky through these windows, which was helpful in restoring my energy.

I feel like we are all safe behind these walls, but the sounds inside this warehouse are not ones of safety. There are screams of pain, moans of agony, and cries of terror. The ratio of patients to medical personnel is vastly higher. I see blood, lots of blood on the floor, as well as vomit. The odor is nauseating. I do have a sense of calm once I tune out the noise and ignore the blood.

This is my battleground to fight along with the rest of my medical team. This feels good. Again, I am not feeling the depths of pain and the overwhelming despair that I could feel if I leaned into it. As sunlight cascades down on all of us through the high windows, I get a boost of peace and hope that some of these soldiers will live and go home to their families.

The shaman mother gives her advice. In the most dreadful places like war, I can still be hopeful and peaceful and find clarity. The ones who are supposed to live will. I just need to do my job and believe in something bigger than myself, beyond understanding, that is guiding me when disaster strikes. I need to believe in a god, however God looks to me. The light shining in through those rectangular windows is my god in that moment.

I start to understand what I need to do. The career will find me. It is already here inside of me. I need to stop fighting a relationship to God and trust that she is my guide. Just let go of all the negative conversations and conflicting ideas of what some people in my life think God should be.

I have had years of proselytizing by a family member, and it has really made me build a wall around myself from God. I am realizing with Jane's help that some people don't understand boundaries, no matter how many times I ask them to stop. Now I can let that wall start to break down and feel loved by a god I feel is right for me, just me, and no one else.

[Jane's note: Lisa did not get into nursing school, but by the time this happened, she had let go of the urgency around it and began thinking of what else she might do. She had previously been trained as a massage therapist, but that wasn't quite what she wanted. She came up with the idea of being an esthetician, focusing on facials, and that flowed with tremendous ease for her.

Between the sessions we did and the training she took, Lisa claimed her identity as a healer. She learned how to use her skills as an empath to her advantage rather than letting them drain her. She learned how to amplify her technical skills as an esthetician by radiating powerful energy and using crystals. Speaking of crystals, this seems like a good point at which to share another meeting Lisa had with the shaman mother.]

Elephant Energy

I had a huge need to be seen, and so I got a huge spirit animal to help me.

> *We are standing in the middle of the beautiful jungle. I am filled with joy and curiosity in the presence of my shaman mother. I can't see beyond her face. I want to know everything I can about her. Her energy is electrifying. Again, she is holding my cheeks and smiling at me. Then she lets go and grabs something from her satchel—a large garnet crystal. Once the crystal is in my two hands, I feel a surge of electricity run through me. It's awakening parts of me that have been hibernating since birth. Hibernating until I woke them up by discovering my truth and my higher power. I had to work on myself first. I had to stumble and struggle to find the strength inside me. The true gift of this jewel was belief in myself that I had never truly felt before. My shaman mother had been waiting for me to see the beauty in myself.*

> *I am standing in a white cotton summer dress in front of my shaman mother holding the most beautiful crystal I have ever seen. I feel like I could fly. I feel like I can do anything I imagine. I am filled with so much hope, desire, and what feels like liquid excitement running through my veins. She whispers to me, "Believe in the elephant energy that you carry. She is always with you."*

That was a point of transformation for me; I needed to feel that people noticed me and got me. I wasn't easy to understand for many of my family members. Honestly, I didn't get who I was either.

With that interaction with my shaman mother, I felt high on joy and possibility for the first time in my adult life. That elephant energy she spoke of made sense to me. In the beginning of my therapy with Jane, I felt an elephant sitting on my chest and knew she was a spirit guide for me. The spirit of my elephant is that of the solar plexus chakra, perseverance, strong drive, daring, and power. When this chakra is working properly, you can reach high achievement.

Becoming Mother: Father Time and Lady of Guadalupe

[Jane's note: Lisa had difficulties getting pregnant, but it was her dream to be a mother. She first needed to heal her issues with her birth mother and the negative story potions she had consumed that prevented her from believing she was worthy of being a mother. She had many journeys dealing with aspects of this dream.]

I never suspected how complicated my childbearing journey would be. When Alan and I decided to start trying for a family, I got pregnant within a couple of months after getting an IUD taken out. I remember taking the test and being shocked that it was positive. I was thirty-two years old, Alan thirty-seven. I got extremely excited when I learned I was six weeks pregnant. I decided to go on a run and started a new painting. I was feeling high on life, like I could do anything I wanted, because I was going to be a mom.

The next day, that excitement was replaced with fear and sadness. I was having a miscarriage. It was so surreal to go from such a high to deep sadness. It was a day I will never forget. Days later, I had a nightmare that I still remember vividly.

> *There is a thin woman who kind of looks like me but is sickly and has dark energy inside of her. I can feel her darkness surrounding me. She looks dreadful. Her hair is black, greasy, and matted—the perfect home for a spider's web. I can't look away from her. I am standing right in front of her. She is naked and is scrubbing her vagina with a loofah. Ouch! While she is scrubbing, she is also screaming to me, "You will never conceive a baby to full term. No matter how much you*

scrub your vagina, you will never be clean enough." I scream back at her, "No!"

Then I wake up.

The session I had with Jane after the miscarriage was so healing for me.

I am swimming to a healing center. I arrive to meet with Father Time. He has long silvery-blue hair and pale white skin and is very tall. He resembles Gandalf from The Lord of the Rings. *He has a very warm energy, and I like him instantly. He is wearing a floor-length robe with a white hood. He is carrying a beautiful lacquered wooden wand with a crystal ball at the top. There is an electric purple current buzzing through the crystal ball.*

I am walking toward him and know that I must pray to him. Prayer is not a normal thought in my conscious mind. I kneel in front of him, asking him for relief from all the pain, agony, and stress in my heart, and to be able to endure stress with grace, patience, and a calm mind. I can feel and see my heart strings being stretched and pulled by a silver chain on top of my heart, connected to a metal ball at the bottom of my heart. It's heavy and painful. With a turn of his magical wand, pointing at my chest, he dissolves the chain.

I feel light and free from the burden of dark sadness. My heart is glowing red with a bright light shining within it. There is still the fear I need to face—the woman from my nightmare. Her name is Blue. She looks like me, but with dark energy inside of her and she is very gaunt. I must push her away, knock her down to the ground, and tell her to stop haunting me.

Blue lifts her hair out of her face to reveal blue-green eyes and soft porcelain skin. She seems gentle. She is reaching out to me and letting me know she's there to protect me, not scare me. She looks beautiful now, unlike the way she appeared in my nightmare. I believe she looks

this way so as not to terrify me. Possibly this is her true form. I feel
compassion for her.

After all, fear is unlike beauty, its opposite. Fear is ugly and painful.
Beauty is magnetic and joyful. We are uplifted by beauty. I now understand the nightmare version of Blue was there to help me push through
my fear of never conceiving a healthy baby.

Now I call in a top healer to help me with Blue. I am being lifted
and protected. The healer is strong, demanding, and forceful, but also
comforting, trustworthy, and gentle. She is wearing a ruby-red velvet
cloak, protecting me from my fear to restore my uterus. My entire body
starts to shake with her healing light. I am crying and she is holding
me and comforting me. I feel so safe in her arms. I sense a baby is close
by. I look up from her arms and see an empty pink blanket lying on
the ground. It belongs to the baby I lost. Just beyond the blanket, I can
feel a baby presence. I am not sure of the gender, but I feel like there
are two of them.

I was getting the message again that I need to be more open and believe
in some higher power. It's okay to believe and ask for guidance. I have
always had something in me telling me it's not okay to ask. But that is
an old thought. I need to ask now more than ever.

I had also needed to know the bird of the month that this baby would
have been born. I found out it was a ruby-throated hummingbird.
Now every time I see a ruby-throated hummingbird, I know the healer
in the ruby-red cloak is telling me that I will have a baby and to believe
in a higher power.

It's possible that the miscarriage was a painful prompt for me to connect to God. The top healer I asked to come help me with Blue turned
out to be Our Lady of Guadalupe. This was the first time she entered
my hypnotherapy, but not the last. She is always with me. She is the

love and light of the higher power, and I now believe in and ask for guidance from her.

[Jane's note: Not having been raised religious, Lisa was unfamiliar with Our Lady of Guadalupe. When she described the healer, I showed her a picture and she said that was exactly whom she'd seen. Lisa didn't yet know about her birth parents, but her father and his family were indigenous Mexican Americans, and Our Lady of Guadalupe is the patron saint of Mexico.]

A couple of weeks after this session, I had started seeing a fertility specialist plus an acupuncturist to help me get pregnant. I was taking about nine different herbs a day, plus getting treatments. My husband was seeing the same acupuncturist. It was a team effort. Jane suggested that I start to speak to our future child and let the baby know we were ready for it.

I loved this idea. I would talk to this baby of ours in the car, in the shower, while making dinner, anytime I was alone. Over time, I started to feel joy instead of sadness. I could feel I was letting go of the anger and blame I had for the miscarriage.

I started to see the spirit of the baby we lost as our guardian angel. She was a creation of my husband and me, and she would always be with us. The miscarriage was meant to happen. Her soul was not meant for Earth. This traumatic time for my husband and me changed us. Together we had created and lost this baby. This was the first time we'd experienced loss as a couple. I had comforted him with loss, but I had never felt it inside of me like this. Through grieving together, it opened a higher feeling of love for each other, a new sense of adoration for each other. This was very healing for us. We knew this was not the end of starting a family, but the beginning of learning that we will keep dreaming and hoping for children.

Fertility Armor

About six months after the hypnotherapy session with Lady Guadalupe and Blue, we focused on me becoming open to new life and
being fertile. Within minutes of our session starting, Jane's sweet dog
Ringo jumped on my lap. After the surprise of him joining me, I felt
comforted.

*We are in Wonderland now. I am walking in a lush garden filled with
wildflowers three feet tall. Butterflies, dragonflies, hummingbirds, and
even tiny ladybugs greet me as I wander through the fertile garden. The
colors of the flowers are so vibrant, it's a living rainbow. The petals are so
soft on my fingertips that they feel like satin. I see that if I look closely at
the ground there is a trail of ladybugs. They are telling me to follow them
down a dirt path in the middle of the wildflowers. I follow them.*

*I am heading toward a gray castle with a turret, surrounded by water
and trees. The flowers continue and the other insects I saw in the beginning are there as well. I cross a creaky wooden bridge. Underneath, the
water is flowing. I see fish swimming in the moving water. There is so
much life all around me. I get to the large doors to the castle and know
I must knock three times to get the doors to open. Inside, all I see are
plants. There are hanging vines from windows, potted plants, and moss
growing on rocks. Growth is happening right before me.*

*I am guided to follow a spiral path, surrounded by more sweet-smelling
flowers and plants. As I walk on the path, the colors get brighter, and
the flowers get bigger. There are peonies that look like they could float
away like hot air balloons. Sunflowers are the size of dinner plates,
their petals paper thin, smooth, and bright yellow in color. I feel like
Alice in Wonderland walking through the flowers.*

*As I reach the center of the swirl, I find a huge, shiny purple and white
rock, about three feet tall. It's a dream amethyst. It's so magnificent I*

must touch it. Its surface is cool, and I sit on it. Slowly the stone starts to soften and becomes pliable. I am not scared. I am curiously excited to see what is going to happen.

As I sit, the dream amethyst starts to move up my body. It's warm and feels like a gentle massage. As it migrates up my back, the crystal transforms into a lightweight crystalline corset that covers my chest to hips perfectly. I am wearing fertility armor. Oh, this is a beautiful corset. It's shiny and it sparkles where the purple and white blend. It's snug on my body, fitting perfectly. This armor makes me feel powerful, like the goddess Aphrodite. Within this surge of power come joy, peace, and trust in myself and in the future. Love washes over me. I look back and the spiral path is no longer visible, overgrown with flowers.

What I am learning is that fear is always going to be with me, but the fear doesn't get to control me. I can let it go, and I'll be okay. The energy of this image of the dream amethyst being wrapped around my feminine body stayed with me until I gave birth to a beautiful baby boy.

Do I Deserve to Be a Mother?

In this next session, I came in with feelings that I don't fit in or deserve to be a mom. In my past, I've had an impression of suffocating in the womb, a cellular memory of being uncomfortable and unloved. I also have a nagging sense of guilt that I don't understand. These feelings followed me until I started to see Jane on a regular basis.

I am four or five years old, playing in our family room. I can see my mom in the kitchen. She's multitasking, talking on the red landline telephone, while doing things in the kitchen. I want her to play with me instead of what she is doing. I have an older brother, ten years older than me, so I always wanted someone to play with who was closer to my age. I have a sense of loneliness. I am wondering where this is coming from. I know my parents and brother played with me a lot.

My stomach starts to warm up, so I let Jane know. This can happen to me occasionally during hypnotherapy: A part of my body will tingle or change to alert me to focus on it. Jane redirects me to think of what this could be telling me.

> *I start thinking of my birth mom while she was pregnant with me. The energy of being unwanted washes over me. I see my birth mom when she finds out she is pregnant with me.*

Remember, I am her second child, and she is only fifteen when she learns she is pregnant again. She kept my older half-brother, who is sixteen months ahead of me. Interesting, it was in January of the year I was born that she finally saw an OB to confirm the pregnancy. It's January now, too.

> *I can feel how angry and upset she is to learn that she is carrying another baby. I see her hitting her stomach. She is disgusted that she has me in her uterus. She's running herself into a chair trying to get rid of me.*
>
> *I can feel inside her family home that her parents and older sibling just wish I wasn't real, that she wasn't pregnant. How could she do this again? They are all just getting used to having an almost one-year-old to help her take care of and now she is growing me inside of her. I feel so sad for my mother. I feel heaviness and darkness surrounding me while I fight to survive.*

She had so much anger and shame and that was extended to me. I wasn't fed well, either. When I was born, I was malnourished and stressed. I know she snorted cocaine, smoked marijuana, and drank alcohol when she was pregnant with me. I felt that I shouldn't have been born. I also felt that maybe I shouldn't be a mother because I didn't deserve to be one. I felt that I caused so much pain to my birth mother's heart and so much shame to her family that I wouldn't be able to have my own baby. I also feared that if I became a mother that I might bring some of that negativity I had felt in the womb to my child or children.

> *I am now seeing an image of my teenage birth dad signing the adoption papers in the hospital on my birthday. I know he doesn't want to be giving up his parental rights. I was his first child. That heaviness is still the energy I am feeling as I see this image. Seeing what my birth dad was like then, I realize he had a lot of love for me, unlike my birth mom. I like the energy I feel around him. He and his family didn't condone me being put up for adoption. They believed I belonged with them.*

> *I see clips of me at three weeks old living with my loving foster family. This makes me so happy.*

I know from my parents that the foster parents were wonderful to me for the first four months of my life. I was told that my birth mom asked for a picture of me around my three-week mark. She still has it.

> *I now see a large cardboard box with a lid and a red bow on it. It is on the floor of a room with an ugly seventies-style carpeted floor. I go and open the box, untying the bow first. I find a letter. The writing is in black ink and it's from my birth mother. I am shocked and extremely excited.*

At the time of this session, I had not yet connected with anyone in my biological family.

> *She is writing to me to apologize for the way she treated me in her womb, apologizing to me for all I had felt. She is letting me know that it wasn't my fault. This letter means the world to me. I know I must move on from this pain I have been holding for thirty-three years.*

I let forgiveness and compassion in for her, to heal and enrich my story. As I lie there and feel this love pour through me, I see an eye looking at me. It's a peaceful eye, hers maybe? This eye has come to me in dreams before, once when I was pregnant in 2011. It's an eye that has power and spirit in it. I believe it's a window into my future. I can finally see it because I am letting go of so much heartache and abandonment.

This session really helped me see that the guilt I thought I was feeling was a cellular memory of my birth mom's that I picked up from being in her womb. This was not her fault. I know that she was a kid herself. She did right for me the only way she knew how. I was strong inside of her. I knew my soul had a purpose. I have a deep love for her. She was my carrier, and I am a part of her and my birth dad. I love who I am. I am grateful to them for my life. I was meant to be created by their love for each other. They gave birth to me so I could be raised by my adopted parents. I am forever grateful to both my biological parents and my adopted parents for their individual love for me.

It is amazing to feel the change from hypnotherapy. The hopelessness I had been feeling is melting away, and my confidence growing in its place. Alan and I did a burning ritual about our future baby. We wrote down on individual pieces of paper positive words about us being parents and words to the baby. We added sage to the fire to clear the energy and then with love set each word into the fire. We held our individual cocktails into the air and clinked glasses with eye contact and said, "Skol" (Scandinavian word for "Cheers").

Field of Babies

In the last hypnotherapy session about being able to have a baby, I travel to an underground cave.

The walls and ground have round cobblestones. It's wet down here. I am curled up on the ground. I look the same as I do now. I feel afraid. I do see a small light coming in from overhead. I am not alone. I see a girl and I ask her, "What is the matter?"

Her face is burned. She doesn't speak, just cries. I understand that she hates herself and believes this is where she belongs. She is shocked that I even bothered to talk to her.

In my peripheral vision, I see a green frog with a gold crown on its head. The frog is as small as a kitten. I get a good feeling from this frog, warm energy. I also see, just beyond this royal amphibian, a white light coming from a large window. Outside this cave is a beautiful, enchanted forest. Maybe this is where the frog lives.

I feel I am here to save this girl. I start to stroke her face lovingly. I can feel a lot of pain being released from her. She has lived down in this cave for many years. She doesn't know how to speak, but I don't need her to. I am intuitively reading her energy as she communicates with me without using words. She is grabbing onto my wrists with her frail hands. Her nails are jagged and dirty. She lets me know she is so happy I am finally here. I've seen her before in a dream. She confirms that she's been calling out to me. She is connected to my womb.

She tells me that I wasn't energetically ready to have the baby last year. I needed to do more work on myself. Now she is asking me if I will accept help from her to have a baby.

"Yes," I tell her.

She reassures me that everything I am doing is right. She then asks me to kiss her, which takes me by surprise. I kiss her, just a peck on her lips. Her lips are surprisingly smooth. After the kiss, there is purple, yellow, and orange energy all around us. We let go of each other's hands and start to laugh. Her form begins to change. She is turning into a bright, beautiful woman. Her face is no longer burned. Her hair is clean and blond. That kiss was a connecting point from her energy body to mine. (Modern-day fairy tale.) The sweet little frog hops into her hand. He is her friend and protector.

I suddenly notice fluttering in my womb. It takes me by surprise. I understand this woman is here to save me from my fear and doubt. I must let go of it and hold onto hope instead. I feel relieved. I've been carrying this fear, and it's been heavy. My body feels lighter now that it's leaving. She is now leaving the cave with her royal friend, the frog. She thanks me and is telling me, "You've found peace. Hold onto this peace and let go of fear."

Alone now in the cave, I notice carvings in the cobblestones that I hadn't seen before. They are hearts and they are carved in all the stones, on the walls and on the ground. I feel joy bubbling inside of me. I start to notice moss growing inside the large window. I sit down and soak in the energy that surrounds me. I close my eyes for a moment and when I open them up, I see gems and crystals on the ground. Wow! They are so rich with assorted colors. I see deep red ones—garnets, dark blue ones—sapphires, and bright green ones—emeralds. I notice a single quartz crystal lying loose on the ground. It's there for me to have. I pick it up. It is soft and smooth. I start to rub my left thumb on its smooth surface.

Still inside the cave, I am shown two paths. One leads to a forest, and another path leads to a labyrinth, a walking spiral path. I choose the labyrinth. I see that the spiral path has gemstones on it. It's so magical. The gems sparkle from the sunlight's reflection. I still have the quartz crystal in my hand, rubbing it with my thumb. I am leaving the cave through a room with a skylight and tall stone doors, which are very heavy to open. There are beautiful polished wooden door handles. Once I step outside, the door slams shut behind me, picking up wind as it shuts. My time is done in the cave.

I find the gems in the labyrinth so beautiful. I want to gather them all up in front of me and make a rainbow. Most of them are embedded into the dirt, and a few are loose. I grab a loose garnet and impulsively put it in my mouth and swallow it. The garnet turns into liquid once I put it in my mouth.

I believe I swallowed the garnet because I knew it would amp up the energy inside of me, to help me continue the path my subconscious and Jane were taking me on.

The labyrinth leads me to a field of babies. So many babies. They are all wrapped up in soft cotton swaddle blankets. Their faces are so beautiful. Their sweet, soft cries are like a song to me. I can feel the soul of my future baby in this field in front of me. This is unbelievable. I am so happy.

I am not able to stop just yet; there is some more footwork I need to do. I can still feel the energy of my sweet baby. This energy propels me to keep searching. Now I come to a fork in the trail. The yellow path to the left is the one I need to take. Without hesitation, I turn left and go. It's a long walk and I keep seeing sweet babies, but none are mine. I keep going left. I know this is the way to go. I am thankful I have a quartz crystal in my hand to calm me, and I can still feel the soothing energy of the garnet I drank.

I feel him stronger now as I continue walking on the yellow path. I look to the left and again turn left. It's interesting how the left side is where I am guided to. There he is! I see a crying baby boy. It's my son! The connection I feel with him is unlike anything I have ever felt. The love I feel for him makes me cry with joy as I pick him up and hold him tight to my heart. Oh, he smells so sweet and pure. I could breathe this in forever. I can't see his face, but I don't care, I don't need to see his face. All I need is to hold him, smell him, and love him. I feel my husband, Alan, with me. I know he is our creation. This little one is waiting for us to be ready for him. When we are, then he will come into our lives.

That was a wild session. It started out so scary but ended so beautifully. In the beginning, I loved that I was helping release the pain from the face of the girl in the cave, since I work as an esthetician. I find that facial massage can release stress from clients' bodies. The way I could feel her energy and sense just what she was telling me without words being exchanged is something I am still working on in my treatment room. The calm I felt as I was helping her is what I feel when working on a client's skin. The cobblestone in the cave recalled trips I've taken to my parents' countries of Sweden and Denmark. The frog in this session was a flashback to the frog I became in my very first hypnotherapy session with Jane, reminding me I am on the right path. I used to carry so much fear inside of me. The fear took up so much space that I didn't have room for my intuition to grow. The colorful gems brought in so much light and hope to soften my fears. They were little earthly delights to warm my soul and re-emphasize that it's safe to push the fear away.

I found my inner strength time after time with hypnotherapy. Little by little I chipped away at the enormous walls I'd built around myself for protection. I still carry a quartz crystal in my purse. They are my favorite crystals. I rub the crystal when I need to calm myself. I also have a lot of them in my treatment room. I have found that programming them can help clear my space from unwanted energy.

I found out I was pregnant with Hudson in September, just five months after this hypnotherapy session. He is almost nine years old. I remember the day I gave birth. I held him, inhaled his sweet baby smell, and loved him with all of me. Just as I did in the session.

It's All for the Best

Over the many years of hypnotherapy, I have faced ugly beliefs hidden inside of me, from the traumatic experiences in my life. What I appreciate the most about getting to see them is that they are not as ugly as I thought they were. They're also not true. They are just misunderstood fears I carried to protect me, until I faced them with Jane in a safe environment.

Finding the right therapist and the right therapy is the key to unlocking the door to our subconscious mind. On the other side of this door, we get to explore our own answers to the many questions we ask ourselves when struggling in a place of pain or frustration.

In 2022, I met my birth dad's mom, my Nana. I look like her. She has met my mom, husband, and my two sons. I have spoken to both my birth parents on the phone, along with a few other biological family members. The impressions I had about my time in utero were correct. I now know that what my birth parents went through was traumatic for them, and they did what they felt was right for me and them. Although there was a lot of heartache felt by all three of us, I wasn't meant to be raised in their homes.

I believe in the power of fate and that my fate was to be raised by two people who longed for more children yet couldn't have any more. I healed from the pain of what I thought was abandonment but was actually the greatest gift of love and constancy when my parents adopted me into their family. My adopted parents provided me with the stability I needed as a struggling infant with health issues, along with the necessary resources to support me, and the wisdom and confidence of being adults. Now that I am an adult and a mom, I see just how much my parents did for me, and I am so proud to have been adopted by them.

Hypnotherapy also helped me see all the beautiful gems I hid from myself and, in turn, from the world. I became the mom I had always dreamed of being to two amazing souls. I have found my gift and natural ability of being a healer and trusting my intuition, and that has led to a very successful business for me, where I get to pass on the healing goodness I have received to others. I will always be grateful for the time I spent in hypnotherapy.

CONCLUSION

Closing Thoughts

In the end, as in the beginning, it's all about you. Wondrous you. I hope this book has convinced you that, despite whatever happened to you or how you've been limited by the assessments of others, you are magnificent and streaming with possibilities. Story potions do not define you. Unlimited creative power, beyond sensory awareness, is vibrating in every cell of your being. I hope I've shown you that healing is possible for you by applying these five deep medicine treatments.

Although trauma is widespread and can attach to us from many sources, it is not as powerful as we are when we remember who we are and the medicine we have access to. Our worlds are formed by the stories we tell. We are the storytellers. As we tell a better story, one infused with love and compassion, we transform our experience of reality. When we tell those stories inside the hypnotherapy container, the impact can be lasting. In this process, our essential selves come back out to play.

Despite plentiful trauma, our world is also filled with dreamers—people like you and me who long for a world where everyone is safe and cherished, and we get to develop our talents and make our contributions. Each one of us can play a part in that creation, and we must. Healing trauma is not just so we feel better, but so the world evolves through the benefit of our brilliance.

By examining our own histories, particularly our trauma, we can discover hidden story potions. By activating the powers of love and imagination and drawing on unseen powers, we can find lasting antidotes for the story potions. This leaves us free to respond to life rather than react from a need to protect ourselves.

In doing our own work, we gain compassion for others who have suffered from traumas, and we grow in our ability to extend acceptance and grace. In becoming freed agents of life, we can focus on creation and love instead of damage control.

Hypnotherapy is just one path. It's a mystical and powerful path. I hope you will give yourself the gift of trying it and discovering how much more there is to you and for you.

As you reflect on the stories you have read in this book, may you challenge the limitations you've accepted as your lot in life and be inspired to step more fully into the field of infinite possibilities. You are more powerful and precious than you may have been led to believe. You are a cosmic spark of life, love, and brilliance. You are here to shine brightly and be a blessing. Our world needs you in your fullness. You have what it takes, so please give us your whole, wholly light.

Acknowledgments

Because of You

A book comes to life because an author has a vision and the commitment needed to complete it, but no book is birthed without an assortment of midwives. Mine is no exception. I want to acknowledge the people who were essential to the birth of this book.

I am filled with gratitude for the sacred voice that has guided me through the years, and for all those brave individuals who entrusted me with their healing and growth as clients. Without you, I wouldn't have learned to be a hypnotherapist or have any stories to share. Your trust in me, your vulnerability and courage to face your trauma, and your openness to the mystery within you have inspired me from the very beginning. You're the reason I can't imagine retiring from hypnotherapy and the reason I had to write this book. Whether you find your story in the pages of this book or you're one of the many whose story remains untold, please know you are one of the brave ones I so appreciate.

I give special thanks to Lisa Nunes. Not only has she been an amazing client, always ready for the deep dives, but she poured her heart out in the final chapter of this book, sharing the hypnotherapy experience from her perspective.

My huge appreciation goes out to my writing group. Carol Fox and I started the group back in January 2020. Eight of us met weekly for dinner at her home and shared our writing. When the pandemic hit, some of us kept meeting by moving the venue to Zoom. Over the years, group members have come and gone and sometimes returned, but Carol has been there for the whole ride. Nate Hitchcock has been there for most of it as well. This group has provided me with valuable feedback that has shaped my writing. They have ensured my progress. If you have a book in you, the best writing advice I can offer is to find a group of folks who need to write and meet with them every week. It's impossible to show up repeatedly with only excuses about why you didn't write. My current group consists of Carol, Nate, Sarah Hood, and Charlotte Oakes and they have really helped me with the manuscript and cheered me over the finish line. We are all writing books and can't wait to read each other's, so we won't allow quitting. Thank you to all the others along the way: Kevin Kubota, Naomi Steele, Chelsea Callicott, Cherie Swenson, Jody Kemple, Steven Koski, William Gregory, and Tobin Blake.

Thank you to Melissa McGlenn, an early collaborator and inspiration to me, who has a few stories tucked secretly inside these pages. Appreciation to LaLee Faro, Sarah Root, Tamera Schmidt, and Carol Rossio, early readers who gave me invaluable feedback. Thank you to my sister-in-heart, Loma Smith-Weber. She read my draft—just like she read the draft of my first book—and gave me much encouragement.

Of course, I must give a big cheer of appreciation to my editor, Linden Gross. She did all the things a good editor does and did them brilliantly. But her biggest contribution was helping me to frame this book as being about healing trauma. After reading my first draft, she asked me who this book was for—people with trauma or the general public? Of course, I thought everyone would want to read my book. She replied that, in that case, I needed more stories that didn't involve trauma. As she said that, I pictured the work of digging through all my untouched files looking for the "boring" stories. When I caught that thought, I knew I wanted to write specifically about healing trauma. That gave my book focus, depth, and passion. Linden didn't stop there, though. She persisted in pushing me to bring my best to every page. If you could see all the drafts and edits, you'd know how much of her genius is in this book.

And thank you to Cory Jubitz who went through the last version of the manuscript, catching punctuation errors and the like. To me, this is like I imagine picking nits would be and I have no patience for it, so I am so grateful to her for helping in this way.

Thank you to Kelly Notaris and Reid Tracy at Hay House, who offered so much helpful coaching that inspired me to refine my book further. Their writers' community program was invaluable.

Thank you to Keri-Rae Barnum, my publishing consultant, whom my editor Linden connected me to. Keri and Linden make a great team for publishing. Keri was magical in the way she helped me conceptualize the cover. What she delivered was so helpful that I also got a potential cover for my next book just from her initial ideas. And thank you to all the folks on social media who weighed in on the choice for cover designs. That was a fun experience of generous feedback and hive mind.

Thank you to my husband, Jeff Hiatt. You encouraged me but, more importantly, you were independent enough to allow me all the space I needed to write, even on our vacations, without a word of complaint. Instead, you kept affirming that my dedicated work was an essential ingredient to guarantee success. That was a precious gift to me. I happily steep in the pride you have in me.

Finally, thank you to all my readers. Even though I didn't know in advance who you would be, I knew you'd be out there. I've been writing to you from the start. You gave me the courage and faith to keep going. Special thanks if you're still reading. When I read a book that I love, I don't want to stop when I get to the end. If the acknowledgments tell a story instead of just listing names, I get to live inside the book just a little bit longer and so I read every word. That's what I tried for here. Just like I knew you'd be reading, I know this book is already making a difference for you. I can see your brilliant love-light shining from here. Shine on!

About the Author

Jane Hiatt is a transformational healer, hypnotherapist, and spiritual teacher whose work bridges the subconscious mind with soul-deep restoration. For over thirty years, she has guided people through the hidden layers of trauma—developmental, ancestral, even past-life—helping them rewrite limiting narratives and remember their true essence.

A practicing hypnotherapist since 1992 and ordained Unity minister since 2015, Jane draws on the sacred tools of love, imagination, and storytelling to reach places traditional methods often can't. Her sessions go beyond symptom relief, diving into the subconscious to uncover and heal what she calls story potions—the inherited beliefs that shape our lives until we consciously transform them.

Her purpose is to remove the landmines of trauma from the collective field and plant wildflowers of joy in their place. Deep Medicine for Trauma is her boldest and most intimate work to date: part guidebook, part spiritual transmission, and a powerful invitation to healing that meets you exactly where you are.

Jane is also the author of Love Letters from the Mother (2017) and Magic Child (1998), originally published under the name Jane Meyers.